PN
1442.2
.453
2007

CAÑADA COLLEGE LIBRARY

3 9366 06364960 2

D0745887

Television in American Society

Primary Sources

Television in American Society

Primary Sources

Laurie Collier Hillstrom

Allison McNeill Gudenau, Project Editor

U·X·L
An imprint of Thomson Gale,
a part of The Thomson Corporation

THOMSON

GALE

Detroit • New York • San Francisco • New Haven, Conn. • Waterville, Maine • London

LIBRARY - CAÑADA COLLEGE

THOMSON

GALE

Television in American Society: Primary Sources

Laurie Collier Hillstrom

Project Editor
Allison McNeill Gudenau

Rights and Acquisitions
Shalice Shah-Caldwell,
Emma Hull

Imaging and Multimedia
Leitha Etheridge-Sims, Lezlie Light,
Dan Newell

Product Design
Kate Scheible, Deborah van Rooyen

Composition
Evi Seoud

Manufacturing
Rita Wimberley

©2007 Thomson Gale, a part of
The Thomson Corporation.

Thomson and Star Logo are trademarks and Gale is a registered trade-
mark used herein under license.

For more information, contact
Thomson Gale
27500 Drake Rd.
Farmington Hills, MI 48331-3535
Or you can visit our Internet site at
http://www.gale.com

ALL RIGHTS RESERVED
No part of this work covered by the
copyright hereon may be reproduced
or used in any form or by any means---
graphic, electronic, or mechanical, including photocopying, recording, taping, Web distribution, or information
storage retrieval systems---without the
written permission of the publisher.

For permission to use material from
this product, submit your request via
Web at http://www.gale-edit.com/per-
missions, or you may download our
Permissions Request form and submit
your request by fax or mail to:

Permissions Department
Thomson Gale
27500 Drake Rd.
Farmington Hills, MI 48331-3535
Permissions Hotline:
248-699-8006 or 800-877-4253, ext. 8006
Fax: 248-699-8074 or 800-762-4058

Cover photographs reproduced by
permission of © Steve Marcus/Reuters/
Corbis (TiVo screen shot), © Bettmann/
Corbis (Edward R. Murrow), and AP
Images (Al Gore).

Since this page cannot legibly accommodate all copyright notices, the

acknowledgements constitute an
extension of the copyright notice.

While every effort has been made to
ensure the reliability of the information presented in this publication,
Thomson Gale does not guarantee the
accuracy of the data contained herein.
Thomson Gale accepts no payment for
listing; and inclusion in the publication
of any organization, agency, institution, publication, service, or individual
does not imply endorsement by the
editors or publisher. Errors brought to
the attention of the publisher and
verified to the satisfaction of the
publisher will be corrected in future
editions.

LIBRARY OF CONGRESS CATALOGING-IN-PUBLICATION DATA

Hillstrom, Laurie Collier, 1965–
   Television in American society. Primary sources / Laurie Collier Hillstrom; Allison McNeill,
project editor.
       p. cm. -- (Television in American society reference library)
   Includes bibliographical references and index.
   ISBN-13: 978-1-4144-0224-6 (hardcover : alk. paper) -- ISBN-13: 978-1-4144-0221-5
(set : alk. paper)
       ISBN-10: 1-4144-0224-4 (hardcover : alk. paper) -- ISBN-10: 1-4144-0221-X (set : alk. paper)
   1. Television broadcasting -- Social aspects -- United States -- Sources -- Juvenile literature.
I. Title. -- II. Series.
   PN1992.6.H534 2006
   302.23' 450973--dc22
                                                                        2006011891

This title is also available as an e-book.
ISBN-13: 978-1-4144-1075-3, ISBN-10: 1-4144-1075-1
Contact your Thomson Gale sales representative for ordering information.

Printed in the United States of America
10 9 8 7 6 5 4 3 2

Contents

Reader's Guide

Television in American Society: Primary Sources presents fifteen full or excerpted documents relating to the development and impact of television. These documents range from notable speeches that mark important points in TV history to critical analyses of television's influence on American culture. The documents are arranged chronologically, beginning with longtime RCA chairman David Sarnoff's 1936 remarks to the press at his company's first demonstration of television technology, and ending with former vice president Al Gore's 2005 speech about the effects of television on democracy.

Included are excerpts from legendary broadcast journalist Edward R. Murrow's famous 1958 speech to the Radio and Television News Directors Association, in which he criticizes network executives for emphasizing entertainment rather than information in TV news; former FCC chairman Newton N. Minow's historic 1961 speech to the National Association of Broadcasters, in which he describes television programming as a "vast wasteland"; President Lyndon B. Johnson's remarks upon signing the Public Broadcasting Act of 1967, which led to the creation of PBS; the 1999 "Appeal to Hollywood," which complains about the level of violence and inappropriate content in television programs; and Ted Turner's 2004 article "My Beef with Big Media," which outlines the potential drawbacks of the consolidation that took place in American broadcasting during the 1990s and 2000s.

Features

Each document included in *Television in American Society: Primary Sources* features the following additional text:

- **Introductory material** places the document and its author in historical context.

- **Things to remember while reading** offers readers important background information and directs them to central ideas in the text.

- **Excerpt/full document** presents the document in its original spelling and format.

- **What happened next . . .** discusses the impact of the document and provides an account of subsequent historical events.

- **Did you know . . .** provides interesting facts about the document and its author.

- **Consider the following . . .** offers suggestions for study questions, group projects, and oral presentations.

- **For More Information** provides resources for further study of the document and its author, as well as sources used by the author in writing the material.

Television in American Society: Primary Sources includes informative sidebars highlighting interesting, related information. Approximately thirty black-and-white photographs illustrate the text. Each chapter has a glossary that runs alongside the reprinted document to identify unfamiliar terms and ideas contained within the material. *Television in American Society: Primary Sources* also includes a timeline of important events and a section defining important words to know. The volume concludes with a bibliography of sources for further reading, and a subject index.

Television in American Society Reference Library

Television in American Society: Primary Sources is only one component of a three-volume Television in American Society Reference Library. The other two titles in this multivolume set are:

- *Television in American Society: Almanac* presents a comprehensive overview of the development of television technology, the growth of the broadcast and cable industries, the evolution of television programming, and the impact of television on American society and culture. The volume's eleven chapters cover all aspects of television in the United States, from the invention of the technology in the 1920s to programming trends in the 2000s. The main emphasis of the volume concerns the many ways in which television has both reflected and influenced American life throughout its history.

- *Television in American Society: Biographies* presents profiles of twenty-six men and women who influenced the development of television in a significant way. The volume covers such key figures as inventors Philo T. Farnsworth and Vladimir Zworykin; industry leaders David Sarnoff and William S. Paley; cable TV pioneers Ted Turner and Robert L. Johnson; program producers Joan Ganz Cooney and Norman Lear; TV news journalists Walter Cronkite and Barbara Walters; and television personalities Lucille Ball, Bill Cosby, and Oprah Winfrey.
- A cumulative index of all three titles in Television in American Society Reference Library is also available.

Comments and Suggestions

We welcome your comments on *Television in American Society: Primary Sources* and suggestions for other topics in history to consider. Please write: Editors, *Television in American Society: Primary Sources,* U*X*L, 27500 Drake Road, Farmington Hills, MI 48331-3535; call toll-free 800-877-4253; fax to 248-699-8097; or send e-mail via http://www. gale.com.

Timeline

1835 Samuel Morse invents the telegraph.

1876 Alexander Graham Bell invents the telephone.

1880 *Scientific American* magazine runs an article about the possibility of distance vision (television).

1884 German scientist Paul Nipkow invents the optical scanning disk used in mechanical television systems.

1887 Heinrich Rudolph Hertz discovers radio waves.

1895 Guglielmo Marconi develops a wireless or radio telegraph.

1897 German scientist Karl Ferdinand Braun develops the first cathode ray tube.

1900 Russian scientist Constantin Perskyi coins the term "television" at the Paris World's Fair.

1900 David Sarnoff immigrates to the United States from Russia.

1901 Guglielmo Marconi sends and receives radio signals across the Atlantic Ocean.

1907 Russian physicist Boris Rosing designs an electronic television receiver with a cathode ray tube.

1911 Boris Rosing and his assistant, Vladimir Zworykin, achieve the first successful transmission of crude television images, using a mechanical transmitter and an electronic receiver.

1912 The Radio Act of 1912 allows the U.S. government to issue licenses to people who wish to broadcast signals over radio waves.

1912 David Sarnoff, working as a telegraph operator, claims to have received distress signals from the sinking luxury oceanliner *Titanic.*

1919 The Radio Corporation of America (RCA) is formed.

1921 American inventor Philo T. Farnsworth, age 14, has a vision of an all-electronic television system.

1921 Commercial radio broadcasting begins in the United States.

1922 Philo T. Farnsworth explains his television system to his high school science teacher.

1923 Vladimir Zworykin applies for a patent on an all-electronic television system.

1925 Vladimir Zworykin demonstrates a TV system for his bosses at Westinghouse, but they decide against funding further TV research.

1926 Philo T. Farnsworth gathers investors and opens a television research laboratory in San Francisco, California.

1926 The National Broadcasting Company (NBC) is formed as a radio network.

1926 American Charles Francis Jenkins and Scotsman John Logie Baird independently invent working mechanical television systems.

1927 Philo T. Farnsworth builds his all-electronic TV system and successfully transmits an image.

1927 The Columbia Broadcasting System (CBS) is founded as a radio network.

1927 Secretary of Commerce Herbert Hoover appears in the first long-distance transmission of television signals, between Washington, D.C., and New York City.

1927 The Radio Act of 1927 first mentions broadcasters' duty to serve the public interest.

1928 The U.S. government issues the first permits for experimental TV stations.

1928 Philo T. Farnsworth demonstrates his TV system for the press.

1929 Vladimir Zworykin goes to work for RCA and begins developing his Kinescope electronic television receiver.

1929 The Great Depression begins in the United States.

1930 David Sarnoff becomes president of RCA.

1930 Philo T. Farnsworth receives a patent for his Image Dissector television camera.

1931 CBS begins experimental TV broadcasting.

1932 NBC begins experimental TV broadcasting.

1934 The Communications Act of 1934 established the Federal Communications Commission (FCC).

1935 Philo T. Farnsworth wins the patent battle against Vladimir Zworykin, preventing RCA from gaining total control over electronic television technology.

1935 David Sarnoff announces RCA's million-dollar television research and testing program.

1936 RCA demonstrates an all-electronic television system.

1936 Philo T. Farnsworth begins experimental TV broadcasts from his Philco laboratory in Philadelphia, Pennsylvania.

1936 The Olympic Games in Berlin, Germany, are televised using both RCA and Farnsworth equipment.

1936 About 200 television sets are in use worldwide.

1937 The Paramount Eyes and Ears of the World Newsreel series presents a *Popular Science* feature on Philo T. Farnsworth and his early television system.

1938 Vladimir Zworykin and RCA introduce an improved Iconoscope television camera that is ten times more sensitive to light than the original version.

April 20, 1939 David Sarnoff introduces television to the public at the New York World's Fair.

April 30, 1939 Franklin D. Roosevelt becomes the first U.S. president to be televised.

May 1, 1939 RCA begins selling television sets to the public, followed by DuMont, General Electric, and Philco.

October 2, 1939 RCA pays a licensing fee to Philo T. Farnsworth for use of his television patents.

1940 Peter Goldmark of CBS develops the first working color television system, which uses both mechanical and electronic elements.

March 1941 The FCC's National Television Standards Committee (NTSC) announces a technical standard for monochrome (black-and-white) television sets.

July 1, 1941 NBC makes the first commercial television broadcast in the United States.

December 7, 1941 Japanese fighter planes attack the U.S. naval base in Pearl Harbor, Hawaii, drawing the United States into World War II.

1942–45 Most television broadcasting and manufacturing stops for the duration of the war.

1942–45 About 10,000 television sets had been sold, and 23 TV stations exist in the United States.

1943 The American Broadcasting Company (ABC) is formed when NBC is forced to sell its Blue radio network.

1946 Postwar production of television sets begins.

1946 CBS demonstrates its color television system for the FCC.

1947 When sales of television sets are slow to take off after the war, Robert Berenson of Grey Advertising defends the technology against criticism that it is a failure.

1948 The first cable TV systems (known as Community Antenna Television or CATV) are installed to improve reception in rural areas of the United States.

1948 The FCC places a temporary freeze on new broadcast licenses in order to study interference between stations and develop an orderly system for assigning licenses.

1948 There are 107 television stations operating in 63 markets.

1949 Philo T. Farnsworth sells his company, Farnsworth Radio and Television, to ITT and leaves the television industry.

1949 The Academy of Television Arts and Sciences creates the Emmy Awards to honor excellence in TV performance and production.

1950 The FCC approves the CBS mechanical-electronic color television system.

June 1951 CBS begins broadcasting TV programs in color; only a few hundred TV sets can receive the broadcasts.

June 1951 RCA demonstrates its all-electronic color television system.

October 1951 Color TV production stops during the Korean War (1950–53).

December 1951 The National Association of Broadcasters (NAB) adopts its Code of Practices for Television Broadcasters.

1952 The FCC ends its freeze on new broadcast licenses and approves broadcasting on UHF channels.

1952 The first political campaign advertisements appear on television.

1953 The FCC reverses its 1950 decision and approves the RCA color television system.

1953 NBC begins broadcasting in color.

1954 Broadcast journalist Edward R. Murrow exposes Joseph McCarthy (1908–1957), a U.S. Senator from Wisconsin who had ruined the careers of many American politicians and entertainers by falsely accusing them of being Communists, on his news program *See It Now.*

1954 Engineer Vladimir Zworykin retires after twenty-five years of television development at RCA.

1956 Ampex Corporation demonstrates videotape recorder (VTR) technology, which makes it possible to record television programs for immediate viewing.

1958 Edward R. Murrow criticizes the quality of TV news in a famous speech before the Radio and Television News Directors Association (RTNDA).

1959 Senator John F. Kennedy evaluates the impact of television on politics in an article for *TV Guide.*

1959 The U.S. Congress uncovers the quiz show scandal, in which producers and sponsors provided answers to some game show contestants in advance.

1959 Congress adds the Fairness Doctrine, written by the FCC in 1949, as an amendment to the Communications Act of 1934.

1960 John F. Kennedy and Richard M. Nixon take part in the first televised presidential debates.

1960 Approximately 87 percent of American homes contain at least one television set.

1961 Newton N. Minow becomes chairman of the FCC under President John F. Kennedy.

1961 In a famous speech before the National Association of Broadcasters, Newton N. Minow criticizes the state of television programming as a "vast wasteland."

1962 The Telstar communications satellite is launched into orbit, allowing for the first international transmission of television images.

1962 The All-Channel Receiver Act requires all new television sets to be equipped to receive both UHF and VHF broadcasts.

1962 The FCC decides that it has the authority to regulate cable television.

1963 President John F. Kennedy is assassinated; television news provides around-the-clock coverage of the story for four days.

1967 ABC Sports introduces slow-motion and stop-action features to sports telecasts.

1967 Most television broadcasts are now in color.

1967 The Public Broadcasting Act of 1967 creates the framework for public radio and television in the United States.

1969 A worldwide television audience estimated at 600 million watches American astronaut Neil Armstrong become the first human being to set foot on the Moon.

1970 The Public Broadcasting Service (PBS) is established.

1970 The invention of fiberoptic cable increases the amount of information that can be transmitted through wires.

1972 The FCC issues its open-skies decision, allowing commercial use of satellites.

1972 The U.S. government releases the results of a large-scale study which shows that viewing violent programs on television tends to increase children's aggressive behavior.

1975 The pay-cable channel Home Box Office (HBO) broadcasts a heavyweight championship fight between Muhammad Ali and Joe Frazier live via satellite from Manila, in the Philippines.

1976 The first videocassette recorders (VCRs) are introduced for home use.

1976 Ted Turner turns his Atlanta-based independent TV station into the national cable network Superstation TBS by arranging to deliver his signal to cable systems across the country via satellite.

1978 PBS becomes the first network to deliver all of its programming via satellite.

1979 The Entertainment and Sports Programming Network (ESPN) becomes the first sports network on cable TV.

1980 Ted Turner launches the Cable News Network (CNN), television's first twenty-four hour news channel.

1981 Electronic News Gathering (ENG) technology gives a boost to local television newscasts.

1981 Mark S. Fowler becomes chairman of the FCC under President Ronald Reagan.

August 1, 1981 Cable channel MTV (Music Television) makes its debut.

1982 The FCC authorizes Direct Broadcast Satellite (DBS) services.

1984 The FCC deregulates broadcasting under President Ronald Reagan, eliminating rules about the number of commercials allowed per hour of programming and increasing the limits on ownership of TV stations.

1984 The FCC authorizes stereo TV broadcasting, and sales of stereo TV sets begin.

1984 The U.S. Supreme Court rules in favor of Sony in the *Betamax* case, making VCR technology legal for home use.

1987 Fox becomes the fourth broadcast TV network operating in the United States.

1989 The FCC eliminates the Fairness Doctrine.

1990 General Instrument (GI) develops the world's first all-digital TV broadcasting system.

1990 The U.S. Congress passes the Children's Television Act (CTA), which requires all television networks to broadcast at least three hours of educational/informational (E/I) programming per week and limits the amount of advertising allowed during children's programs.

1992 The broadcast networks adopt a ratings system, modeled after that used for theatrical films, to inform parents about program content that might be inappropriate for younger viewers.

1994 The FCC establishes technical standards for high-definition television (HDTV) in the United States.

1995 The first television program is delivered over the Internet.

1995 Broadcast networks WB (the Warner Brothers Network) and UPN (the United Paramount Network) are formed.

1996 The Telecommunications Act of 1996 reduces limits on TV station ownership and removes barriers between different areas of the communication industry, leading to increased media consolidation.

1996 Approximately one billion television sets are in use worldwide.

1997 The FCC establishes a schedule for the transition to digital television broadcasting.

1999 TV talk show pioneer Steve Allen and a group of sixty other prominent Americans release "An Appeal to Hollywood," which asks the entertainment industry to reduce the level of violence on television and in the movies.

2000 All new television sets sold in the United States are required to contain a V-chip to allow parents to block programs electronically based on their content ratings.

2000 Television news comes under criticism for its coverage of the 2000 presidential election, after several broadcast and cable networks report results before they have enough information to do so accurately.

2004 During the presidential campaign, Democratic Senator John Kerry and Republican President George W. Bush, combined, spend more than $600 million on television and radio advertising.

2006 The ABC network charges advertisers $2.5 million for each 30-second commercial that airs during Super Bowl XL; these ads reach more than 100 million people in the United States and hundreds of millions more around the world.

2006 The WB and UPN networks merge, forming a new network, The CW.

Words to Know

affiliate: A local television station that is connected or grouped together with a major network. Local affiliate stations are required to carry the network's programs according to a regular schedule.

airwaves: Naturally occurring waves of electromagnetic energy that travel through the air and can be used to carry information, such as television signals. In the United States, the airwaves belong to the American people, and the FCC grants individuals and companies the right to use the public airwaves by issuing broadcast licenses.

American Broadcasting Company (ABC): One of the major U.S. broadcast television networks, formed in 1943.

analog: A naturally occurring form of electromagnetic energy that is composed of waves and can be used to carry information, such as television signals.

anchor: The main host or presenter on a television news program.

animated: A type of television program that features cartoon characters rather than live actors.

bandwidth: A measurement of the amount of space on the airwaves needed to carry a television signal, based on the frequency and wavelength characteristics of that signal.

Big Three: The major networks (ABC, CBS, and NBC) that controlled television broadcasting in the United States from the 1940s until the 1980s.

broadcast: The act of sending communication signals, such as radio or television programs, over a large area to be received by many people. The term is also used to distinguish television networks that deliver their signals over the airwaves from those that deliver their signals by cable or satellite.

broadcast license: A permit granted by the FCC that gives an individual or company the right to operate a radio or television station that sends communications signals over the public airwaves.

cable television: A type of service that delivers television signals to customers through cables, or long wires buried underground or strung along electrical poles, rather than through the airwaves.

cathode ray tube: The part of a television set that makes it possible to see an image on the screen. Invented in 1897, it works by shooting a beam of electrons (tiny, negatively charged particles) toward the inside of the TV screen, which is coated with a substance that glows when struck by the beam of radiation. Also known as a picture tube.

coaxial cable: A type of line or wire used to transmit electronic communication signals, consisting of a copper wire surrounded by insulation, with an aluminum coating.

Columbia Broadcasting System (CBS): One of the major U.S. broadcast television networks, formed in 1927 as a radio network.

commercial television broadcasting: A type of service, approved by the FCC in 1941, in which television networks sell commercial time to advertisers. The networks use advertising money to create and distribute programs according to a regular schedule. Before 1941, television broadcasting was experimental, and it was paid for by the television networks and TV set manufacturers.

Communications Act of 1934: The first major U.S. law that covered television. It created the Federal Communications Commission to oversee and regulate all forms of electronic communication, including radio, television, telephone, and telegraph.

consolidation: The combination or merger of several different companies that each operate in one part of the media industry to form a large communications firm that controls many types of media outlets.

content: The topics or subject matter included in a television program.

content ratings: A labeling system for television programs that provides viewers with information about the types of subject matter they contain. The system in effect in 2006 included warnings about violence (V), strong language (L), and sexuality (S).

deregulation: The process of reducing or eliminating government rules and regulations affecting a business or industry.

digital: A method of storing and transmitting electronic information as a binary code consisting of long strings of the digits zero and one. The main advantage of digital television signals is that they can be understood, changed, and enhanced by computers.

digital video recorder (DVR): A device that saves television programs onto a computer hard drive, making it easy for users to record shows for later viewing.

Direct Broadcast Satellite (DBS): A technology that allows television signals to be sent from satellites orbiting Earth directly to small, individual dish antennas on the roofs of houses and buildings.

electronic television: The type of television system used in the United States, which has no moving parts and works using the properties of electricity.

Emmy Awards: Annual honors presented by the Academy of Television Arts and Sciences for excellence in television programming. There are separate Emmy Awards for prime time and daytime programs.

experimental television broadcasting: A type of service provided by early television networks and manufacturers in order to test their facilities and equipment and try out different kinds of programming. It was used in the United States until 1941, when the

FCC approved commercial (advertiser-supported) television broadcasting.

Fairness Doctrine: An FCC rule, in effect from 1949 to 1989, that required broadcasters to present opposing viewpoints on controversial issues of public importance.

Federal Communications Commission (FCC): The U.S. government agency, created in 1934, charged with regulating all forms of electronic communication, including television, radio, telephone, and walkie-talkie.

fiberoptic cable: A type of line or wire consisting of clear rods of glass or plastic, which transmits electronic communication signals as rapid pulses of light.

Fox: The fourth major U.S. broadcast television network, formed in 1987 by Australian businessman Rupert Murdoch.

frequency: A characteristic of radio waves that refers to how often the wave pattern repeats itself. The entire range of frequencies is called the radio spectrum. The FCC assigns every television station a specific operating frequency within the radio spectrum to broadcast its signal.

game show: A type of television program in which contestants answer questions, solve puzzles, or complete physical challenges in an effort to win money or prizes.

genre: A general type or format of television program, such as a drama, situation comedy, talk show, or soap opera.

high-definition (HD): A technology that scans and transmits a visual image at a higher resolution, or number of horizontal lines per screen, than the original U.S. technical standard of 525 lines. The U.S. standard for high-definition television established in 1994 divides a TV screen into 1,080 lines, creating a picture twice as sharp as the old system.

interactive: A technology that allows two-way communication between the sender and receiver of TV signals. It gives viewers more control over programming by enabling them to select, respond to, and change the content of shows.

Internet Protocol Television (IPTV): The process of delivering television signals over the vast computer network known as the Internet.

market: A geographic area that is served by a distinct group of television stations.

mechanical television: An early type of television system that used a spinning disk with holes punched in it to measure the light reflected off a moving image and turn it into an electrical impulse. It required extremely bright lights to create a decent image, and it was replaced by electronic television in the 1940s.

media: Plural of medium; often used to refer to all sources of news and information, or all types of mass communication.

media outlets: Specific modes or systems of mass communication, such as radio and TV stations, cable TV systems, newspapers, and magazines.

medium: A mode or system of communication, information, or entertainment.

miniseries: A type of television program in which the story continues over several episodes, but then ends rather than extending for a full season.

National Association of Broadcasters (NAB): An industry organization made up of representatives of U.S. radio and television networks and local stations.

National Broadcasting Company (NBC): One of the major U.S. broadcast television networks, formed by the Radio Corporation of America (RCA) in 1926 as a radio network.

network: A business organization that creates programs and distributes them to a group of affiliated or linked local stations.

news magazine: A type of television program that features several different segments, like the articles in a print magazine, ranging from investigative news reports to celebrity interviews.

on the air: Short for "on the airwaves," referring to the airwaves that carry television and radio signals. Slang term for the broadcast of a program.

patent: A form of legal protection that gives an inventor the exclusive right to use or make money from an invention for a period of seventeen years.

pilot: An initial test episode of a television program, which is used to determine whether the program will attract enough viewers to become a continuing series.

prime time: The evening hours, roughly between 8 P.M. and 11 P.M., when television programs generally reach the largest number of viewers.

Public Broadcasting Service (PBS): A national nonprofit organization, consisting of more than 350 member stations, designed to air TV programs that serve the public interest. Instead of selling commercial time to make money, PBS stations receive funding from individual viewers, businesses, charities, and the federal government.

public interest: A phrase that was included in the Communications Act of 1934, which said that people who received licenses to use the public airwaves had a duty to serve the public interest. Although never fully defined by the U.S. government, the phrase was generally taken to mean that the broadcast industry had a responsibility to benefit American society by providing informative and educational programming.

Radio Corporation of America (RCA): A company that was formed in 1919 and became the nation's leading producer of televisions, operator of TV stations, and broadcaster of TV programs (through its ownership of the NBC network) in the 1940s and 1950s.

radio spectrum: The entire range of frequencies, or repeating patterns, in which radio waves exist. Television signals are broadcast over a small part of the radio spectrum.

radio wave: A form of electromagnetic energy that travels through the air and can be used to carry communication signals.

ratings: Measurements of the percentage of all television viewers who watched a particular program. A program's ratings determine how much money the network can charge advertisers to place commercials on that program. Ratings also influence whether programs are renewed for another season or canceled.

reality TV: A type of program that features regular people, rather than actors, who compete against one another or experience unusual situations together, while television cameras film their interactions. Reality shows are also known as unscripted programs, because the participants use their own words instead of reading lines from a script.

regulate: To establish rules or guidelines to control the operation of a business or industry.

rerun: A repeat showing of a television program that has already been broadcast.

satellite: A man-made object that orbits around Earth and can be used to relay television signals.

signal: A set of instructions that tells a television set how to display an image. A TV set can receive video signals from a broadcast network, a cable box, a satellite dish, or a VCR/DVD player. A complete video signal consists of three parts: picture, color, and synchronization (which forces the TV set to lock onto the signal in order to reproduce the image correctly).

situation comedy (sitcom): A type of television program that draws humor from continuing characters and their environment.

soap opera: A type of television program, also known as serial drama or daytime drama, that involves continuing characters and a complex story line.

spin-off: A television series that centers around a character who first appeared on another TV series.

sponsor: An individual or business that provides the money to create or broadcast a television program. Sponsors want their products and services to be associated with a television program for advertising purposes.

standard: A basic rule or guideline established by the U.S. government that applies to an entire industry.

syndication: The process of selling the legal rights to a television program to customers other than the major broadcast networks, such as independent TV stations and cable channels. First-run syndication describes programs that are created especially for independent distribution, or are syndicated when they appear on television for the first time. Off-network syndication occurs when programs that originally ran as network series are sold for a second time in syndication.

talk show: A type of television program that features a host, whose name often appears in the title, and includes some discussion of current events in the fields of news and entertainment.

transmit: To send or broadcast.

Ultra-High Frequency (UHF): A portion of the radio spectrum used to broadcast television signals. When most TV signals were sent over the airwaves, rather than by cable or satellite, UHF channels were generally considered technically inferior to VHF channels because they sent a weaker signal over a smaller area.

variety show: A type of television program that features a wide range of entertainment, such as music, comedy, and skits.

Very-High Frequency (VHF): A portion of the radio spectrum used to broadcast television signals. When most TV signals were sent over the airwaves, rather than by cable or satellite, VHF channels were generally considered technically superior to UHF channels because they sent a stronger signal over a wider area.

videocassette recorder (VCR): A device that saves television programs on videotape enclosed in a plastic cassette, allowing users to record shows at home for later viewing. By the 2000s it was being replaced by digital video recorder (DVR) technology.

wavelength: A characteristic of radio waves that refers to the time or distance between waves.

Television in American Society

Primary Sources

David Sarnoff

Television Statement to Press
Delivered November 6, 1936
Text reprinted from the Restelli Collection at History TV Net, *available at*
http://framemaster.tripod.com/index5.html

"Ten years ago the National Broadcasting Company began a national service of sound broadcasting. Now it enters upon its second decade of service by contributing its facilities and experience to the new art of television."

The earliest television technology grew out of the work of numerous inventors, scientists, and engineers at the beginning of the twentieth century. The first public demonstration of the new technology took place in 1927, when U.S. secretary of commerce Herbert Hoover (who later became president of the United States) made a speech in Washington, D.C., that was broadcast live to a group of journalists located two hundred miles away in New York City. The *New York Times* reported that seeing Hoover's moving image on a television screen was as amazing "as if a photograph had suddenly come to life and begun to talk."

One of the leading companies in the development of television technology in the United States was the Radio Corporation of America (RCA). RCA was formed in 1919 and soon became a top manufacturer of radios, operator of radio stations, and broadcaster of radio programs. It got involved in television research under the visionary leadership of David Sarnoff.

Sarnoff was born in Russia in 1891 and came to the United States in 1900. He went to work selling newspapers at an early age to help support his family. During his teen years he became a telegraph operator. Always good at attracting publicity, Sarnoff became famous in 1912 by claiming

Under the guidance and vision of its president David Sarnoff, pictured, RCA became the leader in television technology. AP IMAGES.

to be the sole telegraph operator to receive distress calls from the luxury ocean liner *Titanic* after it hit an iceberg in the northern Atlantic Ocean. In reality, a number of wireless operators had received the messages and informed authorities about the sinking ship.

Sarnoff joined RCA shortly after its formation in 1919 and quickly began rising through the ranks of the company. In 1926, he played an important role in creating RCA's broadcasting division, called the National Broadcasting Company (NBC), and increasing the company's involvement in commercial radio broadcasting. The following year Sarnoff was elected to RCA's board of directors, and in 1930—at the age of thirty-nine—he became president of the company.

Sarnoff had been interested in television from the first time he had heard descriptions of the technology. By the time he became the head of RCA, he was convinced that television would be the future of mass communications. Determined to make RCA the leader in television technology, Sarnoff held a meeting with an engineer named **Vladimir Zworykin** (1889–1982; see Chapter 9). Several years earlier, Zworykin had applied for patents (a form of legal protection for an invention) on a television camera he called the Iconoscope and a television display screen he called the Kinescope. Following their meeting, Sarnoff hired Zworykin to develop an electronic television system for RCA. Over the next few years, Sarnoff also bought the patents for TV-related technologies from several other inventors.

In 1936, RCA launched a million-dollar research program aimed at producing affordable electronic television systems for American homes. Sarnoff came up with a three-part plan for RCA to follow in order to increase demand for TV technology. This plan involved mass-producing TV sets to make them more affordable for consumers, expanding entertainment programming on NBC to make TV ownership more appealing, and organizing public demonstrations of television to expose more people to the possibilities of the exciting new technology.

On November 6, 1936, Sarnoff gave one of these demonstrations at a press conference. In his statement to reporters, which is excerpted below, he provides current information on RCA's progress in developing television broadcasting systems. Sarnoff explains that his researchers have managed to transmit TV programs from the top of the Empire State Building in New York City to receiver sets located forty-five miles away. In the process, he says that they have learned a great deal about the behavior of television signals and confirmed that they were working on a promising technical system. Sarnoff also notes that RCA is using its experience in radio broadcasting to develop new types of television programming. Finally, he says that one of his goals for the future is establishing a network of television broadcasting facilities across the country.

Things to remember while reading David Sarnoff's "Television Statement to Press":

- Television signals, like other forms of wireless electronic communication, are carried by radio waves. Radio waves are a form of electromagnetic energy that travels through the air. The waves exist in a range of frequencies called the radio spectrum. In 1936, when David Sarnoff made his speech, RCA and other companies were testing the capacity of different frequencies to carry television broadcasts. Sarnoff mentions experiments involving ultra-short waves and micro-waves, which are types of electromagnetic signals that have very short wavelengths.

- In his speech, Sarnoff mentions the need to establish basic rules or guidelines for television transmission. He wants the Federal Communications Commission (the government agency responsible for regulating television) to set industry-wide standards for television broadcasting. A number of different companies were working to develop TV technology around this time, and each one came up with different kinds of equipment for sending and receiving television signals. While many companies in the industry supported the idea of government standards, they all wanted the standards to favor their own technology. As a result, many competitors fought against the adoption of RCA technology as an industry standard. Disagreements between various companies eventually led the Radio Manufacturers Association to set up a technical committee to recommend industry-wide standards to the FCC. The FCC finally adopted technical standards for television transmission in 1941. These rules said that all television sets produced in the United States would divide images into 525 horizontal lines, each of which would be scanned by the TV camera and reproduced on the TV screen 30 times per second.

- Several other countries—most notably Great Britain and Germany—developed television technology around the same time as the United States. In his speech, Sarnoff claims that American technology is superior to that being developed in other parts of the world. He says this is because the U.S. government allowed private companies to develop TV as a profit-making business enterprise. Under the British system of broadcasting, in contrast, the government owned all television and radio stations and financed their operations through taxes. RCA stood to make a great deal of money from television, so Sarnoff had a strong interest in preserving the American system of broadcasting.

- Sarnoff also mentions that his goal is to establish a "television service to the public which will supplement and not supplant the present service of broadcasting." RCA was already a leader in radio broadcasting, and he does not want to lose this advantage. So he emphasizes the idea that television broadcasting should merely add to, rather than replace, existing facilities and services.

• • •

"Television Statement to Press"

In view of the public interest in the promise of sight as well as sound through the air, we have invited you here today to witness an experimental television test so that the progress in this new and promising art may be reflected to the public factually rather than through the haze of **conjecture** or **speculation**.

You will recall that our **field tests** in television began only on June 29 of this year. That date marked the beginning in this country of organized television experiments between a regular transmitting station and a number of homes. Since then we have advanced and are continuing to advance simultaneously along the three broad fronts of television development—research which must point the road to effective **transmission** and **reception**; technical progress which must translate into practical sets for the home the achievements of our laboratories; and field tests to determine the needs and possibilities of a public service that will ultimately enable us to see as well as to hear programs through the air. On all these fronts our work has made definite progress and has brought us nearer the desired goal.

First and as of immediate interest, let me tell you the progress of our field tests. As you know, we have been transmitting from our television station on top of the Empire State Building in New York City which is controlled from the NBC television studios in the RCA Building. We have observed and measured these transmissions through a number of experimental receivers located in the **metropolitan area** and **adjacent** suburbs. The results thus far have been encouraging, and instructive. As we anticipated, many needs that must be met by a **commercial** service have been made clear by these tests.

We have successfully transmitted through the air, motion pictures as well as **talent** before the **televisor**. The distance over which these television programs have been received has exceeded our immediate expectations. In one favorable location due to extreme height of our transmitter, we have consistently received transmissions as far as 45 miles from the Empire State Building.

The tests have been very instructive in that we have learned a great deal more about the behavior of **ultra short waves** and how to handle them. We know more about **interferences**, most of which are man made and susceptible

Conjecture: Guessing.

Speculation: Making assumptions or predictions.

Field tests: Experiments that take place outside a laboratory, in the place where a technology will actually be used.

Transmission: Sending or broadcasting of television signals.

Reception: Receiving of television signals.

Metropolitan area: A large city.

Adjacent: Nearby or surrounding.

Commercial: Engaged in business activities for the purpose of earning profits.

Talent: Performers or entertainers.

Televisor: Television camera or transmitting device.

Ultra short waves: Electromagnetic signals with an extremely short wavelength.

Interferences: A problem that occurs when radio waves of similar frequencies interact with each other.

Surmounted: Overcome.

Apparatus: Equipment or devices.

Observation points: Places where the quality of television reception is monitored.

Standards: Basic levels.

Definition: The sharpness of a televised image, based on the number of lines scanned by the camera and reproduced on the receiver screen per second.

Synchronized: Working together in unison.

Prematurely: Too early.

Obsolescence: Becoming out of date; useless.

Micro waves: Electromagnetic signals with a somewhat short wavelength.

Potentialities: Possibilities.

Domain: Area of activity.

Ether: Part of Earth's atmosphere that transmits radio waves.

Program technique: Process of creating television shows.

Network syndication: Development of a large number of local broadcast facilities that can be linked together.

Multiplicity: Large number.

of elimination. We have **surmounted** the difficulties of making **apparatus** function outside of the laboratory. We have confirmed the soundness of the technical fundamentals of our system, and the experience gained through these tests enables us to chart the needs of a practical television service.

We shall now proceed to expand our field test in a number of ways. First, we shall increase the number of **observation points** in the service area. Next we will raise the **standards** of transmission.

In our present field tests we are using a 343 line **definition**. Radio Corporation of America and the radio industry have, through the Radio Manufacturers Association, recommended to the Federal Communications Commission the adoption of 441 line definition as a standard for commercial operation. Our New York transmitter will be rearranged to conform to the recommended standards. That also means building **synchronized** receivers to conform to the new standards of the transmitter. Synchronization of transmitting and receiving equipment is a requirement of television that imposes responsibilities upon those who would furnish a satisfactory product and render a useful service to the public. On the one hand, standards cannot be frozen **prematurely** or progress would be prevented, while on the other hand, frequently changing standards means rapid **obsolescence** of television equipment.

Basic research is a continuing process in our laboratories not only that the problems of television may be solved but also to develop other uses of the ultra short and **micro waves** which possess such vast **potentialities** in this new **domain** of the **ether**.

While we have thus proceeded on the technical front of television, the construction and operation of television studios have enabled us to coordinate our technical advance with the **program technique** that a service to the home will ultimately require. Today, you are the guests of RCA's broadcasting unit—the National Broadcasting Company. Under the direction of its president, Mr. Lenox Lohr, the NBC has instituted a series of television program tests in which we have sought to ascertain initial requirements.

Ten years ago the National Broadcasting Company began a national service of sound broadcasting. Now it enters upon its second decade of service by contributing its facilities and experience to the new art of television.

One of the major problems in television is that of **network syndication**. Our present facilities for distribution of sound broadcasting cover the vast area of the United States and serve its 128,000,000 people. Similar coverage for television programs, in the present state of the television art, would require a **multiplicity** of transmitters and network interconnection by wire or radio facilities still to be developed.

Our program is three fold: first we must develop suitable commercial equipment for television and reception; second, we must develop a program

David Sarnoff delivering his speech, "The Birth of an Industry," at the 1939 World's Fair. Days later, RCA began offering television services to the public for the first time. © BETTMANN/CORBIS.

service suitable for network syndication; third, we must also develop a sound economic base to support a television service.

From the standpoint of research, laboratory development, and technical demonstration, television progress in the United States continues to give us an unquestioned position of leadership in the development of the art. In whatever form such progress may be evident in other countries, we lead in the research which is daily extending the **radio horizon**, and in technical developments that have made possible a transmitting and receiving system that meets the highest standards thus far obtainable in field demonstration.

We are now engaged in the development of studio and program techniques that will touch upon every possibility within the growing progress of the art. The distinction between television in this country and **abroad** is the distinction between experimental public services undertaken under government **subsidy** in countries of vastly smaller **extent**, and the progressive stages of commercial development undertaken by the free **initiative**, **enterprise** and **capital** of those who have pioneered the art in the United States.

Radio horizon: Reach of radio technology.

Abroad: Overseas; in other countries.

Subsidy: Financial support.

Extent: Geographic area.

Initiative: Energy and ideas needed to start a project.

Enterprise: Willingness to engage in business activity.

Capital: Money.

Supplement: Add to.

Supplant: Replace.

While the problems of television are formidable, I firmly believe they will be solved. With the establishment of a television service to the public which will **supplement** and not **supplant** the present service of broadcasting, a new industry and new opportunities will have been created.

• • •

What happened next . . .

Following several more years of development and testing, RCA officially began offering television services to the public in 1939. Sarnoff marked this historic occasion with a speech called "The Birth of an Industry." He gave the speech on April 20, 1939, at the opening of the RCA pavilion (a large exhibit) at the New York World's Fair. World's Fairs were major events during the late 1800s and early 1900s. Held in large cities around the world, the fairs gave people an opportunity to see and experience new technologies as they developed.

Sarnoff's speech was captured on television cameras at the fair and transmitted to the RCA Building eight miles away, where reporters watched it on television screens. He announced that "now we add radio sight to sound. It is with a feeling of humbleness that I come to this moment of announcing the birth in this country of a new art so important in its implications that it is bound to affect all of society." Ten days later, RCA launched its first regular television broadcast with an address by President Franklin D. Roosevelt (1882–1945; served 1933–45). The president's speech was sent from a mobile TV van at the World's Fair to the NBC transmitter at the top of the Empire State Building. From there, it was broadcast across the city and surrounding area.

Although only about two hundred people owned television sets that could receive the broadcasts, the new technology still created a sensation. RCA set up dozens of sets inside its pavilion at the fair, and huge crowds of people lined up to get their first glimpse of television. Each day of the fair, NBC broadcast different types of programs to appeal to a wide audience, including cartoons, puppet shows, a circus, sporting events, cooking demonstrations, fashion shows, and musical acts. Visitors to the RCA pavilion could even step in front of a television camera and see themselves on a nearby TV set. Afterward, they received cards that said "I was televised," as souvenirs of the experience.

RCA offered four types of TV receiver sets for sale to the public in 1939. The price of the sets ranged from $200 to $600, or the equivalent of about two months' salary for an average worker. Partly due to the high cost, only about 10,000 TV sets were sold over the next two years. Television development and most broadcasting came to a halt when the United States entered World War II in 1941. During the war, Sarnoff joined the military with the rank of brigadier general and served as a communications consultant to General Dwight Eisenhower (1890–1969). Commercial television broadcasting began after the war ended in 1945, and RCA emerged as the industry leader. Sarnoff was named chairman of the company's board of directors in 1947 and remained in that position until his death in 1971.

Did you know...

- At the historic 1929 meeting between RCA head David Sarnoff and television engineer Vladimir Zworykin, Sarnoff asked the inventor what it would take to develop a marketable TV system. Zworykin replied that he would need "$100,000 and a year and a half." But his prediction turned out to be overly optimistic. It ended up taking RCA ten years and $50 million to introduce television broadcasting at the 1939 World's Fair. Of course, the technology eventually proved so profitable for the company that Sarnoff never complained.

- In 1936, the year that Sarnoff held his press conference, television equipment manufactured by RCA was used to broadcast the Olympic Games in Berlin, Germany. Very few German citizens owned TV sets, so the German government set up 25 large screens around the city so that residents could watch the athletic events.

- In his 1936 statement to the press, Sarnoff boasted that RCA engineers were able to broadcast television signals over a distance of forty-five miles. By the time he died in 1971, satellite technology made it possible for television viewers to see live footage of events taking place around the world—or even in outer space.

Consider the following...

- Imagine if television technology had never been perfected, and the American people still received their news and entertainment from radio broadcasts, newspapers, magazines, and telegraph messages. How would the world be different today?

- Visitors to the RCA pavilion at the 1939 World's Fair were amazed to see moving images reproduced on television. But their reaction seems amazing now, when television is an ordinary part of daily life. Can you think of a technology that you found amazing when it was first introduced, but that now seems commonplace or even outdated? Can you think of one that has maintained your original level of interest over time? What do your responses tell you about the evolution of technology?

For More Information

BOOKS

Bilby, Kenneth. *The General: David Sarnoff and the Rise of the Communications Industry.* New York: Harper and Row, 1986.

Lewis, Thomas S. W. *Empire of the Air: The Men Who Made Radio.* New York: Edward Burlingame Books, 1991.

PERIODICALS

Baird, Iain. "Television in the World of Tomorrow." *Echoes,* Winter 1997.

"David Sarnoff of RCA Is Dead: Visionary Broadcast Pioneer." *New York Times,* December 13, 1971.

WEB SITES

"The Birth of an Industry." *Museum of Television.* http://www.mztv.com/birth.html (accessed on July 26, 2006).

"The Birth of Live Entertainment and Music on Television." *The Restelli Collection at History TV Net,* http://framemaster.tripod.com/index5.html (accessed on July 26, 2006).

"David Sarnoff." *Museum of Broadcast Communications.* http://www.museum.tv/archives/etv/S/htmlS/sarnoffdavi/sarnoffdavi.htm (accessed on July 26, 2006).

Podrazik, Walter J. "TV's Debut at the 1939 World's Fair." *1939 World's Fair.* http://home.flash.net/∼podrazik/WorldsFair.htm (accessed on July 26, 2006).

"Television in the World of Tomorrow." *Museum of Television.* http://www.mztv.com/worldhome.html (accessed on July 26, 2006).

"A World's Fair for the Information Age." *The Internet 1996 World Exposition.* http://park.org/Pavilions/WorldExpositions/new_york2.html (accessed on July 26, 2006).

Paramount "Popular Science" Newsreel

From the Paramount Eyes and Ears of the World *Newsreel Series, 1937*
Available online at Farnovision, *http://www.farnovision.com/media/newsreel.html*

"The most fanciful dream of mankind is today a startling reality, destined to become the world's most popular science."

Although a number of prominent scientists, engineers, and inventors contributed to the development of television technology, some of the most significant contributions came from an unlikely source: an Idaho farm boy named Philo T. Farnsworth. Farnsworth was born in 1906 in Utah, and his family moved to Idaho when he was eleven years old. Despite the fact that his family's farm did not have electricity, Farnsworth became interested in the concept at an early age. He learned about developments in the field by reading library books and issues of *Popular Science* magazine that he found in the attic of his house.

In 1920, at the age of fourteen, Farnsworth showed his high school science teacher an original drawing of an electronic television system—something that had not been invented yet. He later claimed that the idea had come to him while he was plowing his family's potato field. As he drove his horse-drawn plow back and forth in straight rows, he envisioned a television camera scanning a moving image in that same pattern, line by line.

By this time, scientists had been dreaming about the possibility of transmitting live, moving pictures across a distance for many years. But most researchers working on the problem had developed mechanical television systems. These systems used spinning metal disks with holes in them to continuously measure the amount of light reflected off a moving image. The holes sent electrical signals, which varied in strength depending on the amount of light hitting them, across a wire to a similar device at the other end. The second device reversed the process and turned the electrical signals back into light, creating a crude representation of the moving image at the other end of the wire.

Farnsworth's electronic television system, in contrast, did not have any moving parts. Instead, the early television camera he called an Image Dissector captured the light reflected off a moving image with a glass lens. The lens focused the light onto a special plate that was coated with the element cesium, which responded to the light by giving off electrons (tiny, negatively charged particles). Farnsworth used an electrical circuit inside the camera to detect the electrons. He then amplified (increased the power of) the electronic signal and transmitted it to a television receiver set, which would display the image.

Farnsworth's TV receiver used a picture tube he invented called a Cathode Oscillite Tube. A cathode is a filament inside a sealed glass tube, similar in nature to those found in lightbulbs. When the filament is heated, it forms a vacuum, or an empty space that does not contain any matter. A cathode ray is a stream of electrons that pour off the cathode into the vacuum. Farnsworth's system used electrical circuits to focus these electrons into a beam and shoot them toward a flat screen at one end of the tube. The inside of the screen was coated in phosphor, a substance that emits light, or glows, when struck by a beam of radiation. The beam reproduced moving images by "painting" them onto the screen, line by line.

At the age of nineteen, Farnsworth started raising money to build his television system. He convinced enough people to invest in his ideas to enable him to open his own research laboratory in San Francisco. In 1927, he successfully transmitted the first all-electronic television picture. Farnsworth also applied to the U.S. government for patents (a form of legal protection that gives an inventor the exclusive right to use or make money from an invention for a period of seventeen years) on his television camera and receiver. In 1928, Farnsworth demonstrated his television system to the public for the first time. He received a great deal of media attention, including a feature article in the *San Francisco Chronicle*. Newspapers across the country picked up the story of the "boy genius" who had solved the problem of electronic television.

Going to battle against RCA

One of the people who read about Farnsworth's inventions was **David Sarnoff** (1891–1971; see Chapter 1), an ambitious businessman who had recently become acting president of the Radio Corporation of America (RCA). RCA was the leading producer of radios in the United States.

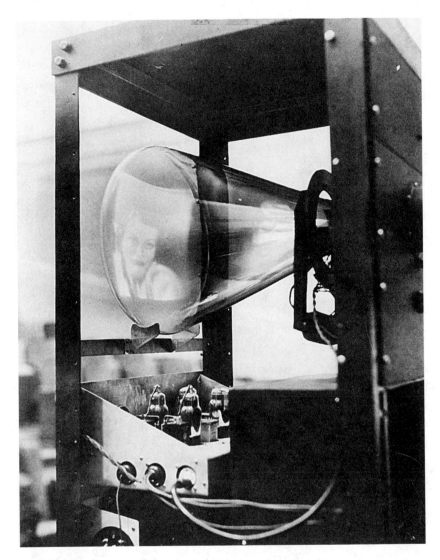

A 1934 TV demonstration using Philo T. Farnsworth's cathode tube. © BETTMANN/ CORBIS.

It also held a strong position in radio broadcasting through its ownership of the National Broadcasting Company (NBC). Sarnoff had been interested in television since the earliest mention of the potential new technology. As the head of RCA, he was also concerned the development of television might cause people to stop buying radios. Once it appeared that TV would become a reality, Sarnoff became determined to make RCA a leader in the television industry as well.

In 1929, Sarnoff held a meeting with an engineer named **Vladimir Zworykin** (1889–1982; see Chapter 9). Several years earlier, Zworykin had applied for patents on a television camera he called the Iconoscope and a television display screen he called the Kinescope. The basic idea of Zworykin's TV system was similar to Farnsworth's. Unlike Farnsworth, however, Zworykin had been unable to turn his idea into a working model. Still, Sarnoff was impressed with Zworykin's work and hired the engineer to develop an electronic television system for RCA.

In 1930, Farnsworth's application for a U.S. patent on his electronic TV system was approved. A short time later, Sarnoff sent Zworykin to San Francisco to visit Farnsworth's laboratory and check out his inventions. Farnsworth gladly gave the prominent engineer a tour and let Zworykin examine a model of the Image Dissector camera. According to Evan I. Schwartz in *The Last Lone Inventor,* Zworykin said, "This is a beautiful instrument. I wish I had invented it myself." In 1931, Sarnoff himself visited Farnsworth's laboratory in San Francisco. Before he left, he offered to give Farnsworth a job at RCA and pay $100,000 for Farnsworth's television patents and all of his working models. But the young inventor and his business partners felt that the offer was much too low and rejected it.

At this point, RCA filed a legal challenge against Farnsworth's patents. The giant company claimed that Zworykin had invented his electronic television system first. They asked the court to throw out Farnsworth's TV patents and award the rights to the invention to Zworykin instead. The patent battles between Farnsworth and RCA continued throughout the 1930s. "They slowed the development of television, delayed its introduction to the public, squandered [wasted] Farnsworth's already thin resources, drove him to drink, and contributed to his development of a bleeding ulcer [a painful stomach problem that is often related to stress]," Schwartz wrote.

In 1931, shortly after the legal battle started, Farnsworth accepted a job with Philco—one of RCA's competitors in the manufacture of radios and electronic equipment—and moved to Philadelphia. In 1936, the U.S. Patent Office issued its first ruling in his favor. After hearing testimony from Farnsworth's high school science teacher and seeing his early television drawings, the patent inspectors concluded that Farnsworth had indeed invented electronic television before Zworykin. But RCA appealed the decision and continued working to develop its own TV system. Sarnoff also bought the patents for TV-related technologies from several other inventors during this time.

Following the 1936 ruling, Farnsworth built a television studio at his Philco laboratory. He and his team of engineers created a special TV transmitter and constructed a hundred-foot-tall tower that could send experimental television signals across Philadelphia. They also designed and built the world's first electronic video switcher in the studio, which allowed them to cut back and forth between the views provided by two TV cameras while a program was being broadcast. In 1937, Farnsworth received a broadcast license from the Federal Communications Commission (FCC), the U.S. government agency responsible for regulating television, and began making regular television broadcasts.

Sharing the excitement of TV technology

Shortly after Farnsworth launched his experimental TV broadcasts, the Paramount Eyes and Ears of the World newsreel series sent a camera crew to his studio to cover the latest developments in television technology. Newsreels were an important source of news and information for Americans in the 1930s. These short news films were commonly shown at movie theaters before the feature presentation. They covered the latest developments in such areas as world events, politics, sports, fashion, and science. Several major film companies produced newsreels. Each reel typically lasted about five minutes and included four or five stories. Theaters usually changed newsreels a couple of times each week so that movie audiences could receive the most up-to-date information.

As television developed during the 1930s, the new technology created a great deal of excitement. The Paramount newsreel series recognized the public interest in television and decided to do a feature story on Farnsworth's broadcasts for its "Popular Science" segment. The Paramount crew visited Farnsworth's laboratory and TV studio in Philadelphia and filmed the inventor at work. A transcript of the newsreel, which is excerpted below, describes the basic scientific concepts behind television technology and also demonstrates the level of excitement surrounding the first TV broadcasts.

Things to remember while reading the excerpt of the Paramount "Popular Science" Newsreel:

- Television sets were not available to the public in 1937, so very few people could actually receive Farnsworth's experimental broadcasts. In fact, there were only around fifty TV sets within the range of his signal. Most of these sets belonged to people who dabbled in electronics as a hobby, or to engineers and executives of manufacturers like Philco and RCA.

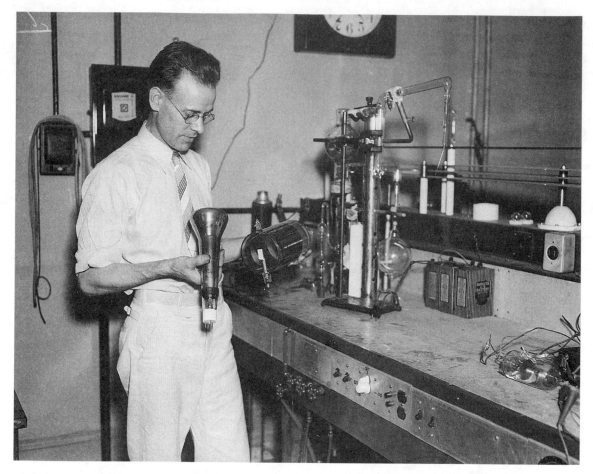

Inventor Philo T. Farnsworth holding components for an early television circa 1935. In his left hand is his own invention, the Image Dissector. © BETTMANN/CORBIS.

- The Paramount "Popular Science" newsreel feature marked the high point in publicity for Farnsworth and his TV system. Two years later, David Sarnoff and RCA grabbed the headlines by holding a historic public demonstration of television broadcasting at the 1939 World's Fair in New York City. Although RCA's TV system used many parts invented by Farnsworth, Sarnoff made no mention of the independent inventor and instead gave the credit to RCA's engineers.

- Ironically, the increasing popularity of television as a source of news and information led to the end of newsreels in the 1950s.

• • •

Excerpt of the Paramount "Popular Science" Newsreel

[*Voice of announcer.*] Popular Science: A backstage look at television, the newest miracle of modern engineering.

[*Images of television production in a laboratory setting.*] Technicians in the Farnsworth-Philco laboratories have helped to make television—the dazzling dream of a decade—a practical reality today. Mr. Philo T. Farnsworth, shown at the right, is working on the **Image Dissector Tube**—a **photoelectric** camera tube of his own invention that distinguishes his system of television from others. It is said to be responsible for the most clearly defined television pictures.

[*Images of the assembly of a television receiver set.*] Placed in the **circuit** of this receiving system is a funnel-shaped **cathode tube**. The round, flat surface of its bulb becomes the picture screen in **studio monitor sets**, as well as in home receiving sets. The Image Dissector Tube and the **Cathode Oscillite Tube** are the heart and brain of the Farnsworth system.

[*Images of equipment in a television broadcasting studio.*] Television engineers are now adjusting studio equipment to demonstrate the technical routine of broadcasting a television program. . . .

In this camera is an Image Dissector Tube. [*Images of a woman dancing.*] The camera lens picks up the artist as an image of light, causing **electrodes** within the Dissector Tube to emit **electrons**. Passing through [TV] station equipment, the electrons become radio **impulses** to be broadcast and picked up by receiving sets, where the routine is reversed—the radio impulses becoming points of light that appear on the screen as pictures. Thirty pictures are completed every second. These pictures are composed of 200,000 light points that strike the screen one at a time at the rate of 6 million points per second. Music and sound accompany the performer's action, both visual and **audible** elements going on the air in perfect **synchronization**.

[*Images of studio engineers adjusting equipment.*] As the action is photographed from various angles, engineers at **control boards** select long shots and close-ups, editing the show as it passes instantly through the station's facility. [*Images of viewers watching television at home.*] Traveling with the speed of light through a maze of tubes and equipment, the show leaves the station's **sending towers**, to be viewed by the television public, an audience as yet small and comparatively ignorant of the enormous research and experiment that makes it possible for us to see and hear people many miles away. . . .

Image Dissector Tube: A television camera patented by Philo Farnsworth in 1930 that reproduced moving images by turning light into electrons (tiny, negatively charged particles).

Photoelectric: A technology involving the interaction of light and physical material.

Circuit: The path of an electric current.

Cathode tube: The vacuum tube inside a TV set that creates the picture.

Studio monitor sets: Screens in a television studio that producers use to select the scenes viewers see at home.

Cathode Oscillite Tube: A type of cathode tube invented by Farnsworth.

Electrodes: Pieces that conduct electricity within a circuit.

Electrons: Tiny, negatively charged particles.

Impulses: Electromagnetic signals.

Audible: Able to be heard.

Synchronization: Occurring at the same time.

Control boards: Banks of technical equipment.

Sending towers: Antennas for transmitting TV signals.

Pervade: Spread throughout.

Maneuvers: Troop movements.

[Images of a magician performing his act.] Silent, invisible, instantly—human speech, music, and appearance **pervade** the airwaves together, to be received in magic boxes for distant reproduction. *[Images of viewers watching television at home.]* It may not be long before our news events and current world happenings will be witnessed in thousands of homes. Television may picture for those at home the work of far-off explorers, or it may reveal to military officials the details of distant **maneuvers**. The most fanciful dream of mankind is today a startling reality, destined to become the world's most popular science.

• • •

What happened next...

After losing the final appeal in its long legal challenge, RCA was forced to pay Farnsworth one million dollars for a license to use his television patents in 1939. This marked the first time in the history of RCA—a company known for its pioneering research and development—that it had paid for the right to use technology created by an independent inventor. But licensing his patents to RCA was only a small victory for Farnsworth. The legal battle cost him a great deal of money and took a serious toll on his health. And in the end, David Sarnoff and RCA received most of the credit for inventing television.

World War II (1939–45) temporarily halted the development of TV technology, especially after the United States entered the conflict in 1941. By the time commercial television broadcasting got started after the war, Farnsworth was no longer involved in the industry. His TV patents expired in 1947, just before the number of TV sets sold nationwide exploded from a few thousand to several million. RCA produced around 80 percent of the units sold.

When Farnsworth died in 1971, few people remembered his contributions to the development of television. But his importance increasingly has been recognized in the years since then. In 1984, for instance, he was inducted into the National Inventors Hall of Fame. In 1990, following a successful campaign by Utah schoolchildren, a statue of Farnsworth—with the words "Father of Television" at its base—was placed in the National Statuary Hall at the U.S. Capitol. In 2003, the Academy of Television Arts and Sciences named an Emmy Award in his honor: the Philo T. Farnsworth Award for Technical Achievement. A number of books published in the 1990s and early 2000s have also tried to set the record straight about the invention of television.

Did you know...

- When Philo Farnsworth and his associates started making experimental television broadcasts from the Philco-Farnsworth studios in 1937, they discovered that the Image Dissector camera was extremely sensitive to infrared light. This caused the color red, which normally appears dark in black-and-white pictures, to televise as white. In order to make the performers in his early TV broadcasts appear normal, Farnsworth turned to makeup artists from the Max Factor Company. Based on their experience in doing makeup for actors in early color movies, the Max Factor artists applied blue makeup on the TV performers' lips and eyes. This made them look normal on a TV screen. In person, however, they appeared to be wearing scary makeup for Halloween.

- Farnsworth received over 150 U.S. patents during his lifetime. Besides some of the first electronic television systems, his inventions included an air traffic control system, an incubator for premature babies, and an early electron microscope.

- When Farnsworth died in 1971, the average television set sold in the United States still included about 100 parts originally patented by him.

- By the time of his death, Farnsworth was deeply disappointed with the programming available on commercial television. In fact, he would not allow his children to watch TV. "I suppose you could say that he felt he had created kind of a monster, a way for people to waste a lot of their lives," his son Kent told *Time*.

- The creators of the modern animated TV series *Futurama* named a character Professor Farnsworth after the inventor of television.

Consider the following...

- It seems hard to believe that an Idaho farm boy who did not even have electricity at home invented the first working electronic television system. Can you think of any modern examples of young people who came up with brilliant ideas (hint: think about the world of computers and the Internet)? What kinds of things do these young inventors have in common with Philo Farnsworth?

- The U.S. government issues patents to provide a form of legal protection for inventions. A patent gives an inventor the exclusive right to use, sell, and profit from an invention for a period of seventeen years. Did the U.S. patent system work for Philo Farnsworth?

How did RCA use the system in its favor? What kinds of changes could be made to the system to ensure that it protects independent inventors?

- The 1937 Paramount newsreel says that television "is destined to become the world's most popular science." Do you think this statement came true? Is it still true in the twenty-first century, or have new technologies emerged to take its place?

For More Information

BOOKS

Fisher, David E., and Marshall J. Fisher. *Tube: The Invention of Television.* Washington, DC: Counterpoint, 1996.

Godfrey, Donald G., and Christopher H. Sterling. *Philo T. Farnsworth: The Father of Television.* Provo: University of Utah Press, 2001.

McPherson, Stephanie S. *TV's Forgotten Hero: The Story of Philo Farnsworth.* New York: Carolrhoda Books, 1996.

Schwartz, Evan I. *The Last Lone Inventor: A Tale of Genius, Deceit, and the Birth of Television.* New York: HarperCollins, 2002.

Stashower, Daniel. *The Boy Genius and the Mogul: The Untold Story of Television.* New York: Broadway Books, 2002.

PERIODICALS

Postman, Neil. "100 Most Important Scientists and Thinkers of the Century: Philo Farnsworth." *Time,* March 29, 1999.

Schwartz, Evan I. "Televisionary." *Wired,* April 2002.

WEB SITES

Arrington, Leonard J. "Philo T. Farnsworth." *Museum of Broadcast Communications.* http://www.museum.tv/archives/etv/F/htmlF/farnsworthp/farnsworthp.htm (accessed on July 26, 2006).

"Elma Farnsworth Passes at 98: Widow of TV Pioneer." *Academy of Television Arts and Sciences,* April 28, 2006. http://www.emmys.org/news/2006/april/farnsworth.php (accessed on July 26, 2006).

"Farnsworth's Image Dissector" and "Electronic Television." *IEEE Virtual Museum.* http://www.ieee-virtual-museum.org/collection/tech.php?taid=&id=2345850&lid=1 (accessed on July 26, 2006).

Schatzkin, Paul. "The Farnsworth Chronicles." *Farnovision.* http://www.farnovision.com/chronicles (accessed on July 26, 2006).

Robert Berenson

Excerpt of "Will 1947 Tell Tele's Tale?"
Originally published in Grey Advertising's Grey Matter *series, June 1947*
Excerpted from Mediaweek, *May 5, 1997*

"Today, the public wants 'movies' in the home! Television is capable of granting that desire."

Television broadcasting took a while to develop. The first public demonstrations of TV systems took place during the 1920s. Yet by the time the United States entered World War II in 1941, only twenty-three television stations existed nationwide, and only a few thousand TV sets had been sold. These early sets were very expensive and did not work very well. In addition, the people who bought them soon discovered that there were very few programs to watch. After hearing about the exciting potential of television technology for so long, some Americans were disappointed with the reality.

During World War II (1939–45), both the production of television sets and most TV broadcasting came to a halt. The U.S. government needed a large supply of electronic parts and communications equipment for the war effort, so many television and radio assembly plants were converted in order to produce materials for national defense. Many of the scientists and engineers who had been working to perfect television technology began developing defense systems such as radar instead. The government also prohibited the construction of new radio and TV stations during the war years due to fears that spies might use such facilities to transmit information to the enemy. For the duration of the conflict, millions of Americans forgot about television and relied on their radio sets to hear the latest news from the front lines of battle.

Commercial television broadcasting got started in the United States as soon as the war ended in 1945. But it took some time for television manufacturers to convert their factories back to producing consumer electronics, so few TV sets were available in stores at first. The broadcast networks also struggled to figure out what kinds of programs would have broad appeal for television viewers. Many analysts had predicted that television sales and programming would take off after the war. When this failed to happen immediately, some critics began complaining that television was a flop.

Advertisers express doubts about television

Some of the most vocal criticism of television in the mid-1940s came from the American advertising industry. Many advertising executives had been waiting anxiously for television to develop into a powerful new medium of mass communication. They looked forward to using television to expand the reach and impact of their commercial messages. By 1947, though, many people in the advertising industry were expressing doubts as to whether television would ever live up to its potential.

In June 1947, Robert L. Berenson, the president of Grey Advertising, published a strong defense of television in his company's influential *Grey Matter* newsletter. Founded in 1917, Grey Advertising started out publishing direct-mail catalogs displaying the products of New York City's fur and clothing manufacturers. The agency grew rapidly and placed its first national advertisement in *Ladies' Home Journal* magazine in 1926. By the 1940s, Grey Advertising had branched out beyond the fashion industry to create advertising for producers of packaged goods (food, cleaning products, and other household goods). These sorts of companies were among the first to use television as an advertising medium.

In his historic article "Will 1947 Tell Tele's Tale?," which is excerpted below, Berenson acknowledges critics' feelings of frustration about the slow development of commercial television broadcasting. But he argues that it is not reasonable to expect TV to be an instant success. Berenson points out that other new technologies, such as automobiles and radio broadcasting, took a while to catch on with the public. He also mentions that a number of big advertisers had already committed to television, despite the fact that the medium was struggling to get going after the war.

Berenson also discusses the fact that most early buyers of TV sets were very wealthy. When television sets first became available to American consumers, the technology was too expensive for ordinary people to afford. Berenson claims that the tastes and interests of the

The eventual success of television allowed advertisers to reach the largest audiences possible for their products. Pictured here is a 1950s TV ad for Contac cold medicine. TED RUSSELL/TIME LIFE PICTURES/GETTY IMAGES.

richest Americans are very different from those of average Americans. Therefore, he is not surprised that the first wave of TV owners expressed unhappiness with the type of entertainment programs being broadcast. Berenson concludes by encouraging advertisers to be patient and give television a few years to prove itself as a mass communications medium.

Things to remember while reading the excerpt of "Will 1947 Tell Tele's Tale?":

- In his article, Berenson mentions that "television was held up, until just a few months ago, by the uncertainty of the FCC ruling on color video." The Federal Communications Commission (FCC) is the U.S. government agency responsible for regulating television. In the mid-1940s, the FCC examined several different proposed color TV systems to decide whether any of them worked well enough to serve as a standard (basic rule or guideline) for the industry. Some consumers held off on buying a black-and-white television set because they suspected that the FCC would approve a color TV system and thus make all existing TV sets out of date. In early 1947, however, the FCC announced that it was postponing its decision on color TV because the technology was not ready yet.

- Berenson also points out that the high cost of early TV sets made television a "class medium," or a form of communication that appeals only to a certain social class or income group. He claims that television will only succeed when it becomes a "mass medium," or a form of communication that is available to the larger society. From an advertising perspective, mass media offer the greatest value to advertisers because they allow commercial messages to reach the largest possible audience.

• • •

Excerpt of "Will 1947 Tell Tele's Tale?"

Video's skeptics have settled down comfortably, determined to wait out the year 1947. At its end they expect to be able to say: "See—we told you so. Television is a **flop**!"

Flop: Failure.

Precisely what television must accomplish in its first **peacetime year** to earn its right to existence isn't quite clear. If any goals have been fixed, we have yet to hear about them. Must 500,000 sets be sold in 1947? Must 12 or 20 or 30 new video [television] stations be opened? Must so-and-so many sponsors be snared with budgets totaling so-and-so many dollars? Must surveys show a certain minimum number of listeners per program, or a **stipulated** minimum dollar of return per video advertising dollar?

Peacetime year: Full year after the end of World War II.

Stipulated: Agreed upon.

By what standards of accomplishment will television rise or fall in 1947? We don't know the answer to that question. Do you?

Why A One-Year Test?

We believe it pertinent to ask: Why must television prove itself (assuming a sane and sensible **standard** of required performance could be established) in its first peacetime year?

Standard: Base or guideline.

Phonograph: Record player.

Did the **phonograph** prove itself in its first full year? Did the automobile? Did the telephone? How many years were required before newspapers could prove their right to existence as an advertising medium? **Ditto** with regard to magazines, and to outdoor advertising.

And what about radio? Yes—what about radio? That's an interesting question.

Suppose radio had had to pass certain tests (fixed by magazines and newspapers of that era) in its first full year after **KDKA** began to broadcast? Where would radio be today?

Historically, radio didn't even **cut its first tooth** at the end of its first full year of existence! One of our staff members, who was then in the editorial department of *Printers' Ink* [an advertising industry trade journal], can recall visiting, among others, the offices of **WEAF** in those early days, and his recollection is that that particular **infant** looked as if it would never graduate from the **incubator** stage.

Why, then, this one-year test for television?

Television To Date

At the present time, television has a small handful of sponsors who are committed to video budgets in 1947 of at least $200,000 each.

That's rather interesting. Significant, in fact. Have you any idea how many advertisers in 1924 had total advertising budgets, in all national media, of $200,000 and over? We would say not much more than 300. And, so far as we can find out, there wasn't a single advertiser who spent anything like $200,000 in radio's first full year. But television, at this very moment, has at least a half dozen advertisers committed to video budgets of $200,000 and over, and at least a dozen committed to video budgets of $100,000 and over.

That's pretty good progress—especially when you bear in mind that a considerable percentage of our largest national advertisers are holding back on their best **Sunday advertising punch** because they're still behind on deliveries [of TV sets ordered by consumers].

And that's pretty good progress when you bear in mind that the number of television sets in operation is still pitifully small. . . .

And that's pretty good progress when you bear in mind that television has scarcely begun its first full peacetime year because production of both sets and station equipment is still **retarded** by factory difficulties.

And that's pretty good progress when you bear in mind that television was held up, until just a few months ago, by the uncertainty of the **FCC** ruling on color video.

And that's pretty good progress when you bear in mind that radio advertising has shown a decided tendency to drop from its wartime peak and that radio sets are our current Number One **distribution headache**. . . .

Ditto: The same thing.

KDKA: Call letters of the Pittsburgh radio station that made the first commercial broadcast in 1920.

Cut its first tooth: Grow beyond the infant stage.

WEAF: A New York City radio station that became the flagship of the NBC national network in 1926.

Infant: Refers to radio in its early "infant" days.

Incubator: A device that maintains controlled conditions favorable to babies, for their care and protection.

Sunday advertising punch: Powerful commercials intended to reach the largest possible audiences.

Retarded: Slowed down.

FCC: Federal Communications Commission, the U.S. government agency responsible for regulating television.

Distribution headache: Product that was difficult to get into the hands of consumers.

Catering: Serving
or meeting.

Profitably: In a way that
earns money.

400: Individuals listed on the
Forbes magazine annual list
of the 400 richest Americans.

Detractors: Critics.

Fare: Programs.

Top income groups:
Wealthiest people.

**Metropolitan's Diamond
Horseshoe patrons:**
Extremely wealthy people
who occupied the premium
seats at New York City's
Metropolitan Opera House.

Nickelodeon: An early
movie theater.

Pierced the ether: Sent a
signal into the part of the
atmosphere that carries
radio waves.

Verdict: Judgment
or review.

Flickers: Movies.

Symphonic: Orchestra
performances.

Hooper ratings:
Measurements of the
popularity of radio programs
provided by the Hooper
Company.

Crooners: Popular singers.

Class medium: A form of
communication that appeals
only to a certain social class
or income group.

Economic cataclysm: Major
period of decline or hardship
in American business and
economy.

Today, the public wants "movies" in the home! Television is capable of granting that desire.

That is a simple, inescapable fact. We are willing to gamble on the certainty that where there is a strong public demand for something—someone, somehow, will find a method for **catering profitably** to that demand.

We doubt that television will prove to be an exception.

The "400" Of Yesterday And Today

Television's **detractors** are making much of the fact that the 1946–47 buyers of video sets aren't well pleased with the entertainment **fare**, other than sports events, spread before them. That leads us to a few questions.

What do you think the **top income groups** of the very early 1900s thought of the movies? Do you suppose the **Metropolitan's Diamond Horseshoe patrons** got a wallop out of the **nickelodeon**, or did they look down their noses at it?

What do you think the top income groups thought of the entertainment provided by radio in its first several years? Do you suppose the "400" were inclined to applaud the entertainment KDKA provided when it first **pierced the ether**? And even now, what **verdict** do you think you'd get from today's "400" on radio's entertainment fare? Those same members of the upper income groups, who constitute the majority of the purchasers of video sets at the moment, probably think as poorly of contemporary radio programs as they admittedly do with respect to current television programs. Does that mean that radio is a flop as an advertising medium?

Does that mean that television will be a flop as an advertising medium?

And, looking back at the early days of the "**flickers**," does that mean the movies were destined to be a flop as a medium of entertainment?

Since when did the tastes, desires and interests of our top income groups in any manner, shape or form resemble the tastes, desires and interests of our masses of people? Why is it that the finest **symphonic** programs receive the lowest **Hooper ratings**? Why is it that our **crooners**, comedians and dance orchestras receive the highest Hooper ratings?

If television, as it will eventually emerge, were to be hugely applauded by its present-day audience of top income groups that would be sorry news indeed. It would mean that television is destined to be a **class medium**, whereas it can only succeed when and if it becomes a mass medium.

Give Television Five Years

We say: Give television five years. Within that time, and assuming the absence of any **economic cataclysm**, television should prove whether or not

Television ownership expanded from 9 percent of American homes in 1950 to 67 percent in 1955, and 87 percent by 1960.
DOUGLAS MILLER/KEYSTONE/GETTY IMAGES.

it has the answers to all the problems hurled at it by all the doubters and skeptics today.

We think it has those answers.

•   •   •

What happened next...

Just as Berenson predicted, the medium of television began growing rapidly. According to the *TV History* Web site, annual sales of television sets—which stood at a disappointing 178,000 units in 1947—increased to 975,000 units in 1948. Sales continued rising over the next few years to reach 3 million units in 1949 and 7.4 million units in 1950. Television ownership expanded from 9 percent of American homes in 1950 to 23 percent the following year, 67 percent in 1955, and 87 percent by 1960. In addition, the number of commercial television stations on the air increased from 9 immediately after the war ended in 1945 to 48 in 1948. By 1960, there were over 500 television stations broadcasting across the United States.

Advertising on television increased rapidly during the postwar years as well. In 1948, the year after Grey Advertising published its defense of TV, 933 advertisers placed commercials on television—an increase of 515 percent from the year before. Many companies saw their sales increase dramatically after they began advertising on television. The growth of TV broadcasting also produced a number of cultural changes in the United States. For instance, attendance at movie theaters, sporting events, and nightclubs declined in cities that had television stations, as more people stayed home and watched TV.

Did you know . . .

- The first television commercial appeared on an experimental NBC broadcast in New York City in 1941. The Bulova Watch Company paid nine dollars for the spot, which only reached a few hundred people since TV sets were not widely available at that time.
- The ABC network charged advertisers $2.5 million for each 30-second commercial that aired during Super Bowl XL in 2006. These ads reached over 100 million people in the United States and hundreds of millions more around the world.
- Grey Advertising grew along with television. It eventually became one of the largest advertising agencies in the world, with offices in 83 countries. In 2000, the company was reorganized under the name Grey Global Group Inc.

Consider the following . . .

- Make a list of the various factors that may have played a role in slowing down the public acceptance of television in the mid-1940s. Do these factors explain the slow early growth of television, or did TV simply develop along the same timetable as all new technologies?
- Research the early stages of development of a modern communications medium, such as the Internet, cellular telephones, or satellite radio. How long did it take to achieve widespread use in

American society? Was there a point at which people doubted whether the technology would ever live up to its potential?

- How has television advertising changed over time? How do you think it will change in the future?

For More Information

BOOKS

Samuel, Lawrence R. *Brought to You By: Postwar TV Advertising and the American Dream.* El Paso: University of Texas Press, 2002.

PERIODICALS

Baughman, James L. "Show Business in the Living Room: Management Expectations for American Television, 1947–56." *Business and Economic History,* Winter 1997.

Berenson, Robert. "Will 1947 Tell Tele's Tale?" *Mediaweek,* May 5, 1997.

WEB SITES

"The History of Film and Television." *High-Tech Productions.* http://www.high-techproductions.com/historyoftelevision.htm (accessed on July 26, 2006).

"History of Television: The First 75 Years." *TV History.* http://www.tvhistory.tv/facts-stats.htm (accessed on July 26, 2006).

Mashon, Michael. "Sponsor." *Museum of Broadcast Communications.* http://www.museum.tv/archives/etv/S/htmlS/sponsor/sponsor.htm (accessed on July 26, 2006).

Rutherford, Paul. "Advertising." *Museum of Broadcast Communications.* http://www.museum.tv/archives/etv/A/htmlA/advertising/advertising.htm (accessed on July 26, 2006).

Federal Communications Commission

Excerpt of "The Fairness Doctrine"

Officially known as the Report on Editorializing by Broadcast Licensees (13 FCC 1246)
Released by the Federal Communications Commission in April 1949
Excerpted from the FCC Web site, http://www.fcc.gov/ftp/Bureaus/Mass_Media/Databases/
documents_collection/490608.pdf

> "We have recognized . . . the paramount right of the public in a free society to be informed and to have presented to it for acceptance or rejection the different attitudes and viewpoints concerning these vital and often controversial issues."

The U.S. government's first effort to regulate electronic communications came with the Radio Act of 1912. This act allowed the secretary of commerce to issue licenses to people who wished to broadcast signals over the airwaves. Telegraph operators were the only ones using the airwaves at this time, though, so the number of usable frequencies was large enough to accommodate everyone who applied for a broadcasting license.

By the 1920s, however, the new mass communication medium of radio was quickly gaining popularity. Recognizing the trend, thousands of people began applying for broadcast licenses in hopes of operating radio stations. The airwaves quickly became overcrowded, causing interference between stations broadcasting in the same geographic area. The U.S. Congress responded to this situation by passing the Radio Act of 1927. This act created the Federal Radio Commission (FRC) to regulate the issuance of broadcast licenses.

The act said that the FRC should consider the "public interest, convenience, and necessity" when allocating frequencies to broadcasters. In those days, large, powerful corporations had established monopoly control over a number of industries. The U.S. government wanted to prevent anyone from gaining similar control over the airwaves. In effect, the act granted ownership of the airwaves to the American people and gave broadcasters the right to use this public property through a system of licenses.

With the invention of television, Congress passed the Communications Act of 1934. The main purpose of this act was to update the Radio Act of 1927 to cover television and other new technologies. It created the Federal Communications Commission (FCC) and gave it responsibility for overseeing all forms of electronic communication—including telephone, telegraph, radio, and television.

Under the Communications Act of 1934, the FCC continued to regulate radio and television in order to ensure that broadcasters served the public interest. For instance, the FCC required radio stations to give all qualified candidates for political office equal access to the airwaves. Since this rule did not apply to news programs, interviews, or documentaries, however, it did not affect broadcasters' programming decisions. Instead, it merely ensured that radio stations sold advertising time equally to all political candidates.

The Fairness Doctrine

In its early years of existence, the FCC prohibited broadcasters from editorializing (expressing their own opinions on the air about various issues). The agency gradually softened this position during the 1940s, until the rules had changed so much that a new policy was needed. In 1948, the FCC held a series of hearings in Washington, D.C. It heard testimony from seventy witnesses representing the broadcasting industry, other interested organizations, and the public. The hearings had two purposes: to determine whether broadcasters should be allowed to express editorial opinions; and to determine how editorializing would affect efforts to provide the public with fair and balanced information about controversial issues.

In April 1949, the FCC issued a report that outlined the commissioners' findings from the hearings. This report, officially known as "Report on Editorializing by Broadcast Licensees (13 FCC 1246)" and more commonly known as the Fairness Doctrine, is excerpted below. It explains the FCC's policies about editorializing and the presentation of controversial issues by broadcasters. It was intended to clear up any confusion regarding previous FCC statements and policies.

The Fairness Doctrine was based on the idea that broadcast licensees used the public airwaves, so they had a duty to operate in ways that served the public interest. In the case of news and informational programs, the FCC defined "serving the public interest" to mean presenting both sides of controversial issues fairly and accurately. The commissioners wanted to make sure that one point of view did not dominate the airwaves simply because its supporters held more financial or political power than the other side. They saw an important role for the FCC in making sure that less powerful groups, and less popular opinions, were able to gain access to the public airwaves. The Fairness Doctrine required broadcasters to devote a reasonable amount of time to covering controversial issues of public importance, and it also required licensees to make an effort to present different, opposing views on those issues. The FCC had the power to revoke the broadcasting license of any radio or television station that did not follow these rules.

The FCC report also considers the question of whether and how broadcast licensees should express their own opinions about controversial issues. The commissioners acknowledge that station owners make decisions about how much attention to give various issues and what types of information to present. They note, however, that this should not give broadcasters unlimited freedom to use the airwaves in their own interest, rather than in the public interest. Instead, they declare that the public's right to be informed is vital to the American systems of government and broadcasting. Therefore, the FCC says that broadcasters have a responsibility to allow for the presentation of opposing viewpoints on controversial issues. The FCC report stops short of telling broadcasters exactly how to ensure fairness and balance. It gives broadcasters room to use their own judgment in dealing with specific issues and programming decisions.

The Fairness Doctrine also addresses the question of editorializing by broadcast licensees. The FCC acknowledges that broadcasters have a unique opportunity to weight news and commentary to serve their own interests and promote their own views. But the agency also says that editorials that are clearly identified as the licensee's own opinion do not necessarily go against the public interest. The new policy allows broadcasters to present their own views on controversial issues, as long as they also provide access to others who wish to present different views. The FCC also warns licensees not to broadcast false or misleading information.

Finally, the report considers the question of whether requiring broadcasters to present opposing views on controversial issues amounts to government control of program content and thus violates licensees' right to free speech. The commissioners say that this is not the case. They cite a U.S. Supreme Court ruling that said the government must protect the right to free speech for all citizens, not only those who are lucky enough to own radio or television stations.

Things to remember while reading the excerpt of "The Fairness Doctrine":

- Since commercial television was just getting started in 1949, the FCC report talks mostly about radio broadcasting. As television grew to become the dominant form of electronic communication, however, all of the commissioners' statements were applied to TV as well.

- The report mentions the fact that, under the Communications Act of 1934, radio and television broadcasters were not considered "common carriers." This term refers to businesses such as airlines, railroads, power companies, and telephone companies that use a combination of their own and publicly owned facilities to provide services. Most businesses that are classified as common carriers operate in industries where the necessary facilities are very expensive to build, and therefore must be shared among competitors, such as airports, railroad tracks, and power lines. Common carriers are usually subject to different laws and regulations than private businesses. In general, the government maintains stricter control over their operations in order to protect the public's interests. Even though television and radio broadcasters use the public airwaves, Congress did not classify them as common carriers because the lawmakers wanted to give licensees greater choice in program selection.

- The Fairness Doctrine was always somewhat controversial. The radio and television networks argued that the government should not intrude into programming decisions. Broadcasters also claimed that they should be allowed to say what they wanted on their stations without the government forcing them to give equal time to opposing viewpoints. On the other hand, supporters of the Fairness Doctrine said that the law actually promoted freedom of speech for members of the larger community who held opinions different from those of station owners.

• • •

Excerpt of "The Fairness Doctrine"

Because of the importance of the issues considered in the hearing, and because of the possible confusion which may have existed in the past concerning the policies applicable to the matters which were the subject of the hearing, we have deemed it advisable to set forth in detail and at some length our conclusions as to the basic considerations relevant to the expression of editorial opinion by **broadcast licensees** and the relationship of any such expression to the general obligations of broadcast licensees with respect to the presentation of programs involving controversial issues.

3. In approaching the issues upon which this proceeding has been held, we believe that the **paramount** and controlling consideration is the relationship between the American system of broadcasting carried on through a large number of private licensees upon whom **devolves** the responsibility for the selection and presentation of program material, and the congressional **mandate** that this licensee responsibility is to be exercised in the interests of, and as a **trustee** for the public at large which retains ultimate control over the channels of radio and television communications. One important aspect of this relationship, we believe, results from the fact that the needs and interests of the general public with respect to programs devoted to news commentary and opinion can only be satisfied by making available to them for their consideration and acceptance or rejection, of varying and conflicting views held by responsible elements of the community. And it is in the light of these basic concepts that the problems of insuring fairness in the presentation of news and opinion and the place in such a picture of any expression of the views of the station licensee as such must be considered.

4. It is apparent that our system of broadcasting, under which private persons and organizations are licensed to provide broadcasting service to the various communities and regions, imposes responsibility in the selection and presentation of radio program material upon such licensees. Congress has recognized that the requests for radio time may exceed the amount of time reasonably available for distribution by broadcasters. It provided, therefore, in Section 3 (h) of the Communications Act [of 1934] that a person engaged in radio broadcasting shall not be deemed a **common carrier.** It is the licensee, therefore, who must determine what percentage of the limited broadcast day should appropriately be devoted to news and discussion or consideration of public issues, rather than to the other legitimate services

Broadcast licensees: Holders of permits from the government to operate television or radio stations.

Paramount: Most important.

Devolves: Settles; is handed down.

Mandate: Official command or instruction.

Trustee: Caretaker.

Common carrier: Public utility.

of radio broadcasting, and who must select or be responsible for the selection of the particular news items to be reported or the particular local, state, national, or international issues or questions of public interest to be considered, as well as the person or persons to comment or analyze the news or to discuss or debate the issues chosen as topics for radio consideration, "The life of each community involves a multitude of interests, some dominant and all-pervasive, such as interest in public affairs, education, and similar matters, and some highly specialized and limited to few. The practical day-to-day problem with which every licensee is faced is one of striking a balance between these various interests to reflect them in a program service which is useful to the community, and which will in some way fulfill the needs and interests of the many." . . .

Inevitability: Certainty.

Claimants: People who make a claim or request.

Amended: Updated or changed.

Interstate: Taking place between two or more states.

Commerce: Business activities.

Impairment: Damage.

Express: Clear or specific.

Legislative: Legal; having to do with the process of making laws.

Predecessor: Something that preceded or came before.

Caprices: Sudden changes or impulses.

Upheld: Agreed with; allowed to stand.

Axiomatic: Widely accepted as true; taken for granted.

Democracy: System of government controlled by the people, usually through elected representatives.

5. But the **inevitability** that there must be some choosing between various **claimants** for access to a licensee's microphone, does not mean that the licensee is free to utilize his facilities as he sees fit or in his own particular interests as contrasted with the interests of the general public. The Communications Act of 1934, as **amended**, makes clear that licenses are to be issued only where the public interest, convenience, or necessity would be served thereby. And we think it is equally clear that one of the basic elements of any such operation is the maintenance of radio and television as a medium of freedom of speech and freedom of expression for the people of the Nation as a whole. Section 301 of the Communications Act provides that it is the purpose of the act to maintain the control of the United States over all channels of **interstate** or foreign **commerce**. Section 326 of the act provides that this control of the United States shall not result in any **impairment** of the right of free speech by means of such radio communications. It would be inconsistent with these **express** provisions of the act to assert that, while it is the purpose of the act to maintain the control of the United States over radio channels, but free from any regulation or condition which interferes with the right of free speech, nevertheless persons who are granted limited rights to be licensees of radio stations, upon a finding under Sections 307 (a) and 309 of the act that the public interest, convenience, or necessity would be served thereby, may themselves make radio unavailable as a medium of free speech. The **legislative** history of the Communications Act and its **predecessor**, the Radio Act of 1927 shows, on the contrary, that Congress intended that radio stations should not be used for the private interest, whims, or **caprices** of the particular persons who have been granted licenses, but in a manner which will serve the community generally and the various groups which make up the community. And the courts have consistently **upheld** action giving recognition to and fulfilling that intent of Congress. . . .

6. It is **axiomatic** that one of the most vital questions of mass communication in a **democracy** is the development of an informed public opinion

through the public **dissemination** of news and ideas concerning the vital public issues of the day. Basically, it is in recognition of the great contribution which radio can make in the advancement of this purpose that portions of the radio **spectrum** are allocated to that form of radio communications known as radio broadcasting. Unquestionably, then, the standard of public interest, convenience, and necessity as applied to radio broadcasting must be interpreted in the light of this basic purpose. The [Federal Communications] Commission has consequently recognized the necessity for licensees to devote a reasonable percentage of their broadcast time to the presentation of news and programs devoted to the consideration and discussion of public issues of interest in the community served by the particular station. And we have recognized, with respect to such programs, the paramount right of the public in a free society to be informed and to have presented to it for acceptance or rejection the different attitudes and viewpoints concerning these vital and often controversial issues which are held by the various groups which make up the community. It is this right of the public to be informed, rather than any right on the part of the Government, any broadcast licensee, or any individual member of the public to broadcast his own particular views on any matter, which is the foundation stone of the American system of broadcasting.

7. This **affirmative** responsibility on the part of broadcast licensees to provide a reasonable amount of time for the presentation over their facilities of programs devoted to the discussion and consideration of public issues has been reaffirmed by this Commission in a long series of decisions. The *United Broadcasting Co. (WHKC)* case, 10 FCC 675, emphasized that this duty includes the making of reasonable provision for the discussion of controversial issues of public importance in the community served, and to make sufficient time available for full discussion thereof. The *Scott* case, 3 Pike and Fischer, radio regulation 259, stated our conclusions that this duty extends to all subjects of substantial importance to the community coming within the scope of free discussion under the first amendment [to the U.S. Constitution] without regard to personal views and opinions of the licensees on the matter, or any determination by the licensee as to the possible unpopularity of the views to be expressed on the subject matter to be discussed among particular elements of the station's listening audience. . . . And the Commission has made clear that in such presentation of news and comment the public interest requires that the licensee must operate on a basis of overall fairness, making his facilities available for the expression of the contrasting views of all responsible elements in the community on the various issues which arise. Only where the licensee's **discretion** in the choice of the particular programs to be broadcast over his facilities is exercised so as to afford a reasonable

Dissemination: Distribution; passing around.

Spectrum: Range of broadcast frequencies.

Affirmative: Positive.

Discretion: Good judgment.

opportunity for the presentation of all responsible positions on matters of sufficient importance to be afforded radio time can radio be maintained as a medium of freedom of speech for the people as a whole. These concepts, of course, do restrict the licensee's freedom to utilize his station in whatever manner he chooses but they do so in order to make possible the maintenance of radio as a medium of freedom of speech for the general public. . . .

9. We do not believe, however, that the licensee's obligations to serve the public interest can be met merely through the adoption of a general policy of not refusing to broadcast opposing views where a demand is made of the station for broadcast time. If, as we believe to be the case, the public interest is best served in a democracy through the ability of the people to hear **expositions** of the various positions taken by responsible groups and individuals on particular topics and to choose between them, it is evident that broadcast licensees have an affirmative duty generally to encourage and implement the broadcast of all sides of controversial public issues over their facilities, over and beyond their obligation to make available on demand opportunities for the expression of opposing views. It is clear that any approximation of fairness in the presentation of any controversy will be difficult if not impossible of achievement unless the licensee plays a conscious and positive role in bringing about balanced presentation of the opposing viewpoints. . . .

11. It is against this background that we must approach the question of "editorialization"—the use of radio facilities by the licensees thereof for the expression of the opinions and ideas of the licensee on the various controversial and significant issues of interest to the members of the general public afforded radio (or television) service by the particular station. In considering this problem it must be kept in mind that such editorial expression may take many forms, ranging from the **overt** statement of position by the licensee in person or by his acknowledged spokesmen, to the selection and presentation of news editors and commentators sharing the licensee's general opinions or the making available of the licensee's facilities, either free of charge or for a fee, to persons or organizations reflecting the licensee's viewpoint either generally or with regard to specific issues. It should also be clearly indicated that the question of the relationship of broadcast editorialization, as defined above, to operation in the public interest, is not identical with the broader problem of assuring "fairness" in the presentation of news, comment, or opinion, but is rather one specific **facet** of this larger problem.

12. It is clear that the licensee's authority to determine the specific programs to be broadcast over his station gives him an opportunity, not available to other persons, to insure that his personal viewpoint on any particular

Expositions: Presentations or explanations.

Overt: Clear and straightforward.

Facet: One of several parts of something.

issue is presented in his station's broadcasts, whether or not these views are expressly identified with the licensee. And, in the absence of governmental restraint, he would, if he so chose, be able to utilize his position as a broadcast licensee to weight the scales in line with his personal views, or even directly or indirectly to **propagandize** in behalf of his particular philosophy or views on the various public issues to the exclusion of any contrary opinions. Such action can be effective and persuasive whether or not it is accompanied by any editorialization in the narrow sense of overt statement of particular opinions and views identified as those of the licensee.

Propagandize: Spread information or ideas that support one's own position or damage another's position.

13. The narrower question of whether any overt editorialization or **advocacy** by broadcast licensees, identified as such, is **consonant** with the operation of their stations in the public interest, resolves itself, primarily into the issue of whether such identification of comment or opinion broadcast over a radio or television station with the licensee, as such, would inevitably or even probably result in such overemphasis on the side of any particular controversy which the licensee chooses to **espouse** as to make impossible any reasonably balanced presentation of all sides of such issues or to render ineffective the available safeguards of that overall fairness which is the essential element of operation in the public interest. We do not believe that any such **consequence** is either inevitable or probable, and we have therefore come to the conclusion that overt licensee editorialization, within reasonable limits and subject to the general requirements of fairness detailed above, is not contrary to the public interest. . . .

Advocacy: Active support of a idea or position.

Consonant: In agreement.

Espouse: Promote or support.

Consequence: Result.

17. It must be recognized, however, that the licensee's opportunity to express his own views as part of a general presentation of varying opinions on particular controversial issues, does not justify or empower any licensee to exercise his authority over the selection of program material to distort or **suppress** the basic factual information upon which any truly fair and free discussion of public issues must necessarily depend. The basis for any fair consideration of public issues, and particularly those of a controversial nature, is the presentation of news and information concerning the basic facts of the controversy in as complete and **impartial** a manner as possible. A licensee would be abusing his position as the public trustee of these important means of mass communication were he to withhold from expression over his facilities relevant news or facts concerning a controversy or to slant or distort the presentation of such news. No discussion of the issues involved in any controversy can be fair or in the public interest where such discussion must take place in a climate of false or misleading information concerning the basic facts of the controversy. . . .

Suppress: Hide; prevent from becoming public knowledge.

Impartial: Objective; without bias.

19. There remains for consideration the **allegation** made by a few of the witnesses in the hearing that any action by the Commission in this field enforcing a basic standard of fairness upon broadcast licensees

Allegation: Charge or claim.

Abridgement: Reduction in scope.

Franchises: Rights as license holders.

Monopoly: A situation where one company controls an entire industry or line of business.

Antagonistic: Opposing.

Impede: Restrict.

Refuge: Place of safety.

Subordinated: Ranked lower in importance.

Exploit: Take advantage of.

Precedence: The highest level of importance.

Inherent: Basic.

Chaotic: Messy and confusing.

Enlightenment: Knowledge; learning.

necessarily constitutes an "**abridgement** of the right of free speech" in violation of the first amendment of the United States Constitution. We can see no sound basis for any such conclusion. The freedom of speech protected against governmental abridgement by the first amendment does not extend any privilege to government licensees of means of public communication to exclude the expression of opinions and ideas with which they are in disagreement. We believe, on the contrary, that a requirement that broadcast licensees utilize their **franchises** in a manner in which the listening public may be assured of hearing varying opinions on the paramount issues facing the American people is within both the spirit and letter of the first amendment. As the Supreme Court of the United States has pointed out in the *Associated Press* **monopoly** case:

> It would be strange indeed, however, if the grave concern for freedom of the press which prompted adoption of the first amendment should be read as a command that the Government was without the power to protect that freedom. . . . That amendment rests on the assumption that the widest possible dissemination of information from diverse and **antagonistic** sources is essential to the welfare of the public, that a free press is a condition of a free society. Surely a command that the Government itself shall not **impede** the free flow of ideas does not afford nongovernmental combinations a **refuge** if they impose restraints upon that constitutionally guaranteed freedom. Freedom to publish is guaranteed by the Constitution but freedom to combine to keep others from publishing is not. (*Associated Press v. United States,* 326 U.S. 1 at p. 20.)

20. We fully recognize that freedom of the radio is included among the freedoms protected against governmental abridgement by the first amendment. . . . But this does not mean that the freedom of the people as a whole to enjoy the maximum possible utilization of this medium of mass communication may be **subordinated** to the freedom of any single person to **exploit** the medium for his own private interest. Indeed, it seems indisputable that full effect can only be given to the concept of freedom of speech on the radio by giving **precedence** to the right of the American public to be informed on all sides of public questions over any such individual exploitation for private purposes. Any regulation of radio, especially a system of limited licensees, is in a real sense an abridgement of the **inherent** freedom of persons to express themselves by means of radio communications. It is, however, a necessary and constitutional abridgement in order to prevent **chaotic** interference from destroying the great potential of this medium for public **enlightenment** and entertainment. . . . Nothing in the Communications Act or its history supports any conclusion that the people of the Nation, acting through Congress, have intended to surrender or diminish their paramount rights in the air waves, including access to radio broadcasting

facilities to a limited number of private licensees to be used as such licensees see fit, without regard to the paramount interests of the people. The most significant meaning of freedom of the radio is the right of the American people to listen to this great medium of communications free from any government **dictation** as to what they can or cannot hear and free alike from similar restraints by private licensees.

Dictation: Rules.

21. To **recapitulate**, the Commission believes that under the American system of broadcasting the individual licensees of radio stations have the responsibility for determining the specific program material to be broadcast over their stations. This choice, however, must be exercised in a manner consistent with the basic policy of the Congress that radio be maintained as a medium of free speech for the general public as a whole rather than as an outlet for the purely personal or private interests of the licensee. This requires that licensees devote a reasonable percentage of their broadcasting time to the discussion of public issues of interest in the community served by their stations and that such programs be designed so that the public has a reasonable opportunity to hear different opposing positions on the public issues of interest and importance in the community. The particular format best suited for the presentation of such programs in a manner consistent with the public interest must be determined by the licensee in the light of the facts of each individual situation. Such presentation may include the identified expression of the licensee's personal viewpoint as part of the more general presentation of views or comments on the various issues, but the opportunity of licensees to present such views as they may have on matters of controversy may not be utilized to achieve a **partisan** or one-sided presentation of issues. Licensee editorialization is but one aspect of freedom of expression by means of radio. Only insofar as it is exercised in **conformity** with the paramount right of the public to hear a reasonably balanced presentation of all responsible viewpoints on particular issues can such editorialization be considered to be consistent with the licensee's duty to operate in the public interest. For the licensee is a trustee impressed with the duty of preserving for the public generally radio as a medium of free expression and fair presentation.

Recapitulate: Repeat the main points; summarize.

Partisan: Firm support of one political party or view.

Conformity: Agreement.

• • •

What happened next . . .

Although the Fairness Doctrine was unpopular in the broadcasting industry, the policy was gradually expanded and given the force of law over the next thirty years. In 1959, Congress added an amendment to the Communications Act of 1934 that spelled out broadcasters' obligation "to operate in the public interest," and specifically "to afford reasonable opportunity for the discussion of conflicting views on issues of public importance." In 1967, the FCC introduced new regulations concerning personal attacks and political editorials. The rules said that if a licensee aired an editorial supporting one political candidate, it must allow the opponent time to present his or her case to the listening audience. Similarly, if a station aired a personal attack against an individual's character, the rules required it to give that person a chance to respond.

In 1969, the "personal attack" rule became the subject of a high-profile court challenge. The case concerned a television station group called Red Lion Broadcasting Company. In 1964, it had aired a program called *Christian Crusade,* in which the Reverend Billy James Hargis launched a personal attack against author Fred J. Cook. Cook contacted Red Lion and requested air time to respond to the attack. When the station group refused to grant the request, the FCC penalized Red Lion for failing to follow federal regulations. Red Lion appealed the FCC's decision, and the case made it all the way to the U.S. Supreme Court. The Court's ruling in *Red Lion Broadcasting Company v. FCC* provided legal support for the Fairness Doctrine. The justices said that broadcast licensees did not have a constitutional right to control the airwaves at the expense of fellow citizens. They rejected the idea that the Fairness Doctrine violated broadcasters' right to free speech, and they agreed that the FCC could regulate use of the airwaves in order to serve the public interest.

Deregulation ends the Fairness Doctrine

The Fairness Doctrine was always somewhat controversial, and broadcasters fought against it from the beginning. Broadcast licensees said that the FCC policy held radio and television to a different standard than newspapers and magazines, which were allowed to publish editorials and opinions without restriction under the constitutional guarantee of freedom of the press. The policy also disturbed many journalists, who considered it a violation of their right to free speech under the First Amendment to the U.S. Constitution. They argued that they should be allowed to make their own decisions about how to report and achieve balance in news stories.

Some critics claimed that broadcasters simply stopped covering controversial issues in order to avoid the FCC requirement to provide opposing viewpoints. According to the *Weekly Standard,* respected television news anchor Dan Rather told the FCC that, in his experience, journalists "were very much aware of this government presence looking over their shoulders. I can recall newsroom conversations about what the FCC implications of broadcasting a particular report would be. Once a newsperson has to stop and consider what a government agency will think of something he or she wants to put on the air, an invaluable element of freedom has been lost." This "chilling effect" on the coverage of controversial issues was the opposite of what the FCC had intended to happen under the Fairness Doctrine.

The broadcast industry saw significant deregulation (reduction in rules) during the 1980s under President Ronald Reagan (1911–2004; served 1981–89). Reagan strongly believed in limiting the government's role in business. He felt that free competition between companies would provide consumers with more choices at a lower cost. Reagan appointed Mark Fowler as chairman of the FCC in 1981. Fowler was a former lawyer for the broadcast industry and a vocal critic of the Fairness Doctrine. Immediately after taking office, Fowler began dismantling the system of regulations that the FCC had long used to guide the television industry. For instance, the FCC lowered the qualifications for people to receive broadcast licenses. The agency also eliminated requirements for TV stations to provide educational children's programming.

The main target of Fowler's deregulation efforts, however, was the Fairness Doctrine. He and other critics of the FCC policy argued that the broadcast industry had changed dramatically since the 1940s. They pointed out that the rise of cable television systems had made many more TV channels available to viewers across the country. They claimed that these channels provided plenty of opportunities for minority views to be expressed, so the airwaves no longer needed government regulation to protect the interests of the public.

In 1985, the FCC issued its "Fairness Report," which said that the Fairness Doctrine no longer served its intended purpose of providing the American people with multiple perspectives on controversial issues. The commissioners wrote: "We no longer believe that the Fairness Doctrine, as a matter of policy, serves the public interests. In making this determination, we do not question the interest of the listening and viewing public in obtaining access to diverse and antagonistic [opposing] sources of information. Rather, we conclude that the Fairness Doctrine is no longer a necessary or appropriate means by which to effectuate [serve] this interest. We believe that the interest of the public in viewpoint diversity is fully served by the multiplicity of voices in the marketplace today and that the intrusion by government into the content of programming occasioned by the enforcement of the doctrine unnecessarily restricts the journalistic freedom of broadcasters."

The FCC's decision to stop enforcing the Fairness Doctrine alarmed many people. Supporters of the policy worried that eliminating it would allow wealthy and politically powerful people to slant the news and information broadcast on television and radio. In 1987, the U.S. Congress decided to turn the Fairness Doctrine into a law, rather than merely an FCC policy. Although the legislation passed both houses of Congress easily, President Reagan vetoed it. (Bills passed by Congress must be signed by the president to become law. If the president does not like a bill, he has the power to veto it and prevent it from becoming law. In this case, two-thirds of the members of Congress must vote to pass a bill again for it to become law without the president's signature.) Congress did not have enough votes to override Reagan's veto, and the FCC formally dropped the Fairness Doctrine in August 1987. Congress made another effort to reinstate the Fairness Doctrine in 1991, but the bill failed when President George H. W. Bush (1924–; served 1989–93) threatened to veto it. The FCC rules allowing responses to personal attacks and political editorials remained in effect until 2000, when they were dropped as well.

Ongoing debates about fairness

The debate over the Fairness Doctrine continued into the twenty-first century. As of 2006, the U.S. government did not require the broadcast industry to provide fair and balanced coverage of controversial issues of public importance. Instead, journalists and station owners were allowed to use their own judgment to decide whether and how to cover such issues. In addition, the American people were expected to use their own common sense to evaluate media coverage of issues and determine what was presented fairly and what was one-sided.

Critics claim that many television news operations became less objective and more biased in their reporting in the absence of the Fairness Doctrine. Some blamed the trend toward less objectivity in TV news on the fact that the major broadcast and cable networks were owned by large parent corporations, such as Time Warner, Walt Disney, Viacom, Seagram, News Corporation, Sony, GE, and AT&T. These major corporations had financial interests in a wide variety of industries, including movies and music, alcoholic beverages, theme parks, professional sports franchises, telephone services, and nuclear power plants. The critics pointed out that the desire to earn profits in one area of the business might create a conflict with the duty to provide fair and unbiased TV news coverage. For example, a network news program might be tempted to downplay its coverage of safety problems in a product manufactured by another division of its parent company. Since television has tremendous power to influence public opinion, critics claim that increasingly biased news coverage is a major problem that the U.S. government needs to address.

Did you know...

- Conservative radio talk show host Rush Limbaugh is one of the leading opponents of the Fairness Doctrine. When the U.S. Congress considered legislation to reinstate the Fairness Doctrine in 1993, Limbaugh mobilized his 20 million listeners to help defeat the bill. Calling it the "Hush Rush" bill, Limbaugh claimed that many radio stations would take his opinion-filled program off the air rather than trying to meet the requirement to provide listeners with opposing views on controversial issues. But Limbaugh's critics say that his radio show provides clear evidence that a new Fairness Doctrine is needed. They argue that Limbaugh routinely gives his listeners false or misleading information, engages in personal attacks against people who disagree with his views, and uses his program to provide free political advertising for conservative candidates. They claim that people who endure his abuse should have the right to respond on the air. "It's mean. It's hateful. It's destructive broadcasting," communications professor Sid Savan said in the *St. Louis Journalism Review.* "At the very least, it needs to be answered. It is very, very destructive for our system of government to have the opposition characterized as an enemy."

- The Fairness Doctrine returned to the news during the 2004 presidential election campaign. The Sinclair Broadcasting Group—a large television station group whose owners openly supported Republican president George W. Bush and other conservative candidates—announced plans to air a controversial documentary called *Stolen Honor* that questioned Democratic presidential candidate John Kerry's military record during the Vietnam War. During his service in the U.S. Navy, Kerry was awarded several medals for bravery in combat, and the documentary claimed that he did not deserve them. Many people criticized Sinclair's decision to air the program shortly before the election. They argued that it amounted to a personal attack on Kerry, and free political advertising for Bush. Some people said that Sinclair had an obligation to present controversial issues in a fair and balanced way, and they demanded that Kerry be given a chance to respond to the program. The controversy surrounding the program convinced several advertisers to withdraw their support, and it also led to a 17 percent decline in the value of Sinclair's stock. The broadcaster ultimately decided not to air the full documentary, but rather to include short clips within a news program.

- As of 2005 U.S. representative Louise Slaughter of New York was the leader of an effort in Congress to bring back the Fairness Doctrine. She claimed that the repeal of the long-standing FCC rule led to an increase in one-sided political views being expressed on American radio and television stations. She said that a new law was needed to ensure that minority opinions gained access to the public airwaves. "Partisan, biased material marketed as 'news' is increasingly contaminating our airwaves and democracy," she said in *Alt Press Online*. "Our democracy depends on an informed electorate [voting public]. The media is crucial to supporting the free exchange of ideas and providing thorough coverage of the important issues facing our nation. The American public owns the airwaves. Reinstating the Fairness Doctrine would return integrity to the media and ensure that the American public is adequately informed on all points of view."

Consider the following...

- After reviewing the arguments on both sides, do you think the Fairness Doctrine should be law in the United States? Give reasons to support your answer.

- What are the main sources of news and information for your family (radio, television, newspapers, magazines, Internet sites, other)? Do you believe that these media present controversial issues in a fair and balanced way?

- A 2006 study by the *Washington Post* indicated that the conservative Fox News Channel convinced between 3 and 8 percent of its audience to shift their voting behavior toward the Republican Party. This shift was enough to swing a very close 2004 presidential election in favor of President George W. Bush (1946–; served 2001–). What would the 1949 FCC commissioners who wrote the Fairness Doctrine think about the result of this study? What do you think about it?

For More Information

BOOKS

Hilliard, Robert L., and Michael C. Keith. *The Broadcast Century: A Biography of American Broadcasting.* Boston: Focal Press, 1992.

McChesney, Robert W. *Rich Media, Poor Democracy: Communications Politics in Dubious Times.* Urbana and Chicago: University of Illinois Press, 1999.

PERIODICALS

Aufderheide, Patricia. "After the Fairness Doctrine: Controversial Broadcast Programming and the Public Interest." *Journal of Communication,* Summer 1990.

Brennan, Timothy A. "The Fairness Doctrine as Public Policy." *Journal of Broadcasting and Electronic Media,* Fall 1989.

Corrigan, Don. "Applying Fairness Doctrine to Rush Limbaugh Wouldn't Limit Speech but Expand It." *St. Louis Journalism Review,* October 2003.

Hazlett, Thomas W. "Dan Rather's Good Deed: His Critics Should Thank Him for Sinking the Fairness Doctrine." *Weekly Standard,* March 21, 2005.

Hazlett, Thomas W. "The Fairness Doctrine and the First Amendment." *Public Interest,* Summer 1989.

Matelski, Marilyn J. "Fair's Fair . . . or Is It?" *Nieman Reports,* Spring 1995.

WEB SITES

"Broadcasting Fairness Doctrine Promised Balanced Coverage." *Wisdom Fund,* July 25, 1997. http://www.twf.org/News/Y1997/Fairness.html (accessed on July 26, 2006).

Clark, Drew. "How Fair Is Sinclair's Doctrine?" *Slate,* October 20, 2004. http://www.slate.com/id/2108443 (accessed on July 26, 2006).

"The Fairness Doctrine." *The Federal Communications Commission.* http://www.fcc.gov/ftp/Bureaus/Mass_Media/Databases/documents_collection/490608.pdf (accessed on July 26, 2006).

Limburg, Val E. "Fairness Doctrine." *Museum of Broadcast Communications.* http://www.museum.tv/archives/etv/F/htmlF/fairnessdoct/fairnessdoct.htm (accessed on July 26, 2006).

"Media Groups Unveil Web Site to Support Slaughter's Fairness Doctrine Bill." *Alt Press Online,* October 21, 2004. http://www.altpressonline.com/modules.php?name=News&file=article&sid=278 (accessed on July 26, 2006).

Morin, Richard. "The Fox News Effect." *Washington Post,* May 4, 2006. http://www.washingtonpost.com/wp-dyn/content/article/2006/05/03/AR2006050302299.html (accessed on July 26, 2006).

Rendall, Steve. "The Fairness Doctrine: How We Lost It, and Why We Need It Back." *Fairness and Accuracy in Reporting (FAIR),* February 12, 2005. http://www.fair.org/index.php?page=2053 (accessed on July 26, 2006).

"What Happened to Fairness?" *NOW.* http://www.pbs.org/now/politics/fairness.html (accessed on July 26, 2006).

Edward R. Murrow

Excerpt of "Keynote Address to the Radio and Television News Directors Association"
Delivered on October 15, 1958, in Chicago, Illinois
Excerpted from RTNDA Speeches, *available at http://www.rtnda.org/resources/speeches/murrow.shtml*

"This instrument can teach, it can illuminate; yes, and it can even inspire. But it can do so only to the extent that humans are determined to use it to those ends. Otherwise it is merely wires and lights in a box."

Edward R. Murrow (1908–1965) is widely considered to be one of the greatest figures in the history of American broadcast journalism. A pioneer in both radio and television news reporting, he was known for his honesty, high standards of journalism, and courageous stands on controversial issues. Throughout his thirty-year career, he often used his influence to urge the broadcast industry to make a better effort to educate and inform the American people.

Murrow got his start in radio broadcasting. Commercial radio first became available in the United States in the 1920s. Its popularity increased rapidly, so that by the 1930s it had become the main source of news and entertainment for millions of Americans. Murrow produced a radio show during his college years, and in 1935 he accepted a full-time job with the Columbia Broadcasting System (CBS). Two years later he moved to London, England, to become director of the radio network's European news bureau.

Reporting on World War II for CBS Radio

During World War II (1939–45), Murrow served as a war correspondent for CBS Radio in Europe. He provided live reports from the rooftops of London during the series of German bombing raids known as the

Edward R. Murrow served as a war correspondent for CBS Radio in Europe during World War II. © BETTMANN/ CORBIS.

Blitzkrieg. His detailed descriptions of the war captivated American listeners and turned Murrow into a celebrity. Murrow also contributed to news coverage of the war by hiring and training a staff of talented young war correspondents to give similar reports from other cities in Europe. This team of reporters, who became known as "Murrow's Boys," included such rising stars as Eric Sevareid, Charles Collingwood, William Shirer, and Howard K. Smith. The compelling live reports broadcast by Murrow and the others revolutionized war coverage and helped radio overtake newspapers to become Americans' first choice for news and information.

When the United States entered the war in 1941, Murrow risked his life to fly with American pilots on several bombing raids. On these occasions, he recorded his thoughts and experiences so that they could be played for radio audiences later. In 1945 Murrow traveled with the U.S. ground forces that liberated the Buchenwald concentration camp in Germany, where the Nazis, under their leader Adolf Hitler, had murdered more than 50,000 Jews and political prisoners during the war. The American troops found 20,000 prisoners still at the camp—all of them weak from hunger, illness, and forced labor—as well as thousands of dead bodies. Murrow shocked many radio listeners by providing a vivid description of the horrors he encountered at Buchenwald. But he refused to apologize for his controversial report, because he believed that it was important for people to know what really happened there. In fact, he concluded his report with the words, "If I've offended you by this rather mild account of Buchenwald, I'm not in the least sorry."

After the war ended, Murrow returned to the United States. In 1946 he was promoted to vice president and director of public affairs at CBS, but he disliked working in network management and longed to return to broadcasting. In 1950 he launched a popular radio news program called *Hear It Now.* The following year he brought the series to the new medium of television as *See It Now.* The first public demonstrations of television had taken place prior to World War II, but both television development and broadcasting were put on hold for the duration of the conflict. By

1950, however, television was growing rapidly, and Murrow wanted to play a role in shaping the future of the new medium.

Using TV as a weapon

See It Now aired on CBS from 1951 to 1958. It was presented as a series of documentaries (fact-based films) that investigated serious issues affecting American society, like the relationship between cigarette smoking and lung cancer, or the unfair treatment of migrant farm workers. Many episodes presented the stories of ordinary people in a way that shed new light on social or political issues. Throughout the show's run, Murrow constantly pushed the network to use the power of television to expose problems and fight against injustice.

See It Now is probably best known for a 1954 program about Joseph McCarthy (1908–1957), a U.S. Senator from Wisconsin who had ruined the careers of many American politicians and entertainers by falsely accusing them of being Communists. McCarthy used the tensions of the Cold War (a period of intense military and political rivalry that pitted the United States and its democratic system of government against the Soviet Union and its Communist system of government) to hurt his enemies and advance his own career. Murrow's show helped turn public opinion against McCarthy, and the senator soon fell from power. Before the episode went on the air, however, CBS executives felt so nervous about the subject matter that they refused to promote it. Murrow and his producer, Fred W. Friendly (1915–1998), were forced to use their own money to purchase a full-page advertisement in the *New York Times*.

During its seven-year run, *See It Now* received four Emmy Awards as Best News or Public Affairs Program, and Murrow won four individual Emmys as Best News Commentator or Analyst for hosting the program. He also earned an Emmy as Most Outstanding Television Personality for hosting *Person to Person,* a lighter, less controversial show that aired from 1953 to 1961. On this program, Murrow conducted informal interviews with celebrities, including actress Marilyn Monroe, actor Marlon Brando, and author John Steinbeck.

Despite winning awards and earning critical praise, *See It Now* never attracted particularly high TV ratings. Furthermore, Murrow often argued with CBS owner William S. Paley about the content of the show. Murrow believed that the electronic news media should be used to promote democratic ideals, like free speech, citizen participation in government, and individual rights and liberties. He felt that Paley was too concerned

LIBRARY - CAÑADA COLLEGE

Edward R. Murrow, left, and producer Fred Friendly fought hard to keep Murrow's show, the award-winning See It Now, *on the air in the 1950s despite low ratings.* CBS PHOTO ARCHIVE/GETTY IMAGES.

about ratings and sponsors, and he complained that the boss forced him to water down the edgy, investigative aspects of the show. But Paley eventually grew tired of involving the network in controversy, and he decided to cancel *See It Now.*

Murrow made his final broadcast of *See It Now* on July 7, 1958. Three months later he gave the keynote address at the annual convention of the Radio and Television News Directors Association (RTNDA) in Chicago, Illinois. In this famous speech, which is excerpted below, Murrow strongly criticizes network executives for wasting television's potential to inform and educate the American people. He refers to television as a "weapon" that could be useful in the battle to promote greater understanding and address important social issues. But he says that the broadcast industry has failed to develop the weapon, choosing instead to focus on entertaining viewers and increasing profits.

Things to remember while reading the excerpt of the Keynote Address to the Radio and Television News Directors Association:

- Television programming in the late 1950s, when Murrow made his speech, is generally regarded as being of higher quality than most of the programming available today. For instance, Murrow suggests airing a public service program in place of *The Ed Sullivan Show,* a variety program that was tremendously popular at the time. Looking back at the show, however, modern TV critics often talk about the many big-name entertainers—like Elvis Presley and the Beatles—that the show introduced to American audiences. In fact, many people rank *The Ed Sullivan Show* among the best television programs of all time. If Murrow found that show unworthy of viewers' attention, there is little question that he would dislike the vast majority of modern TV programs.

- One of the biggest complaints Murrow makes in his speech is that television does not address the realities facing the nation and the world. He claims that the United States faces "mortal danger" and is locked in competition with "malignant forces of evil." At the time Murrow gave his address, the United States and the Soviet Union were engaged in a period of intense military and political rivalry known as the Cold War. Both of these world superpowers developed nuclear weapons capable of destroying the other. They also became involved in a series of smaller conflicts around the world in hopes of spreading their own political philosophies and systems of government to new regions, while preventing the other side from doing the same. "Murrow saw turmoil, danger, and opportunity in the world," CBS News anchor Dan Rather explained in a 1993 speech before the RTNDA, "and the best means of communicating the realities to the public—the communications innovation called television—was increasingly ignoring the realities."

- Murrow gave this speech to an audience of his peers—fellow TV and radio newscasters and network executives. Early on, he makes it clear to these industry insiders that he is expressing his own opinions rather than speaking on behalf of his employer, CBS.

Edward R. Murrow

• • •

Excerpt of "Keynote Address to the Radio and Television News Directors Association"

This just might do nobody any good. At the end of this discourse a few people may accuse this reporter of fouling his own comfortable nest, and your organization may be accused of having given hospitality to **heretical** and even dangerous thoughts. But the elaborate structure of networks, advertising agencies and sponsors will not be shaken or altered. It is my desire, if not my duty, to try to talk to you journeymen with some **candor** about what is happening to radio and television.

I have no technical advice or counsel to offer those of you who **labor in this vineyard** that produces words and pictures. You will forgive me for not telling you that **instruments** with which you work are miraculous, that your responsibility is **unprecedented** or that your aspirations are frequently frustrated. It is not necessary to remind you that the fact that your voice is amplified to the degree where it reaches from one end of the country to the other does not confer upon you greater wisdom or understanding than you possessed when your voice reached only from one end of the bar to the other. All of these things you know.

You should also know at the outset that, in the manner of witnesses before Congressional committees, I appear here voluntarily—by invitation—that I am an employee of the Columbia Broadcasting System, that I am neither an officer nor a director of that corporation and that these remarks are of a "do-it-yourself" nature. If what I have to say is responsible, then I alone am responsible for the saying of it. Seeking neither **approbation** from my employers, nor new sponsors, nor acclaim from the critics of radio and television, I cannot well be disappointed. Believing that potentially the commercial system of broadcasting as practiced in this country is the best and freest yet devised, I have decided to express my concern about what I believe to be happening to radio and television. These instruments have been good to me beyond my due. There exists in mind no reasonable grounds for personal complaint. I have no feud, either with my employers, any sponsors, or with the professional critics of radio and television. But I am seized with an abiding fear regarding what these two instruments are doing to our society, our culture and our **heritage**.

Our history will be what we make it. And if there are any historians about fifty or a hundred years from now, and there should be preserved the **kinescopes** for one week of all three networks, they will there find recorded in black and white, or color, evidence of **decadence**, escapism and **insulation** from the realities of the world in which we live. I invite your attention to the television schedules of all networks between the

Heretical: An opinion contrary to generally accepted beliefs.

Candor: Openness or honesty.

Labor in this vineyard: Work in the field of television.

Instruments: Communication media like TV and radio.

Unprecedented: Has never been seen before.

Approbation: Praise.

Heritage: Traditions passed down from previous generations.

Kinescopes: Televised images.

Decadence: Decay or decline.

Insulation: Isolation or protection.

hours of 8 and 11 P.M., Eastern Time. Here you will find only fleeting and **spasmodic** reference to the fact that this nation is in mortal danger. There are, it is true, occasional informative programs presented in that **intellectual ghetto** on Sunday afternoons. But during the daily peak viewing periods, television in the main insulates us from the realities of the world in which we live. If this state of affairs continues, we may alter an advertising slogan to read: LOOK NOW, PAY LATER.

For surely we shall pay for using this most powerful instrument of communication to insulate the citizenry from the hard and demanding realities which must be faced if we are to survive. I mean the word survive literally. If there were to be a competition in **indifference**, or perhaps in insulation from reality, then **Nero and his fiddle**, **Chamberlain and his umbrella**, could not find a place on an early afternoon **sustaining show**. If Hollywood were to run out of Indians, the program schedules would be mangled beyond all recognition. Then some courageous soul with a small budget might be able to do a **documentary** telling what, in fact, we have done—and are still doing—to the Indians in this country. But that would be unpleasant. And we must at all costs shield the sensitive citizens from anything that is unpleasant.

I am entirely persuaded that the American public is more reasonable, restrained and more mature than most of our industry's program planners believe. Their fear of controversy is not warranted by the evidence. I have reason to know, as do many of you, that when the evidence on a controversial subject is fairly and calmly presented, the public recognizes it for what it is—an effort to **illuminate** rather than to **agitate**.

Several years ago, when we undertook to do a program on **Egypt and Israel**, well-meaning, experienced and intelligent friends shook their heads and said, "This you cannot do—you will be **handed your head**. It is an emotion-packed controversy, and there is no room for reason in it." We did the program. **Zionists**, anti-Zionists, the friends of the Middle East, Egyptian and Israeli officials said, with a faint tone of surprise, "It was a fair **count**. The information was there. We have no complaints."

Our experience was similar with two half-hour programs dealing with cigarette smoking and lung cancer. Both the medical profession and the tobacco industry cooperated in a rather **wary** fashion. But in the end of the day they were both reasonably content. The subject of **radioactive fallout** and the banning of nuclear tests was, and is, highly controversial. But according to what little evidence there is, viewers were prepared to listen to both sides with reason and restraint. This is not said to claim any special or unusual competence in the presentation of controversial subjects, but rather to indicate that **timidity** in these areas is not warranted by the evidence. . . .

Spasmodic: Occasional.

Intellectual ghetto: A place where there is little stimulation for the mind.

Indifference: Lack of caring or interest.

Nero and his fiddle: A reference to a Roman emperor who casually played his fiddle while the city of Rome went up in flames.

Chamberlain and his umbrella: A reference to Neville Chamberlain, a British prime minister whose policies led German dictator Adolf Hitler to believe that he could take over Europe prior to World War II.

Sustaining show: An informational television program paid for by the station or network, rather than by a commercial sponsor.

Documentary: Fact-based film.

Illuminate: Shed light on; inform.

Agitate: Upset or annoy; cause arguments.

Egypt and Israel: Neighboring countries in the Middle East that were involved in a dispute.

Handed your head: Face harsh criticism from all sides.

Zionists: Supporters of the state of Israel.

Count: Account; version of the story.

Edward R. Murrow

Wary: Cautious or distrustful.

Radioactive fall-out: Potentially dangerous materials released through nuclear explosions.

Timidity: Fear; lack of courage.

Precedents: Examples.

Editorialize: Express opinions about controversial issues.

Unsponsored: Without support from advertisers.

Conduit: Route or path.

Libelous: An unfair written attack.

Defamatory: Harmful to someone's reputation.

Rate card: Sheet used to determine the amount charged for commercial time on a TV program.

Covey or clutch: Group.

Manifold: Many.

Quarter: Person or department.

Irate: Angry.

Potent: Important or powerful.

The oldest excuse of the networks for their timidity is their youth. Their spokesmen say, "We are young; we have not developed the traditions nor acquired the experience of the older media." If they but knew it, they are building those traditions, creating those **precedents** everyday. Each time they yield to a voice from Washington or any political pressure, each time they eliminate something that might offend some section of the community, they are creating their own body of precedent and tradition. They are, in fact, not content to be "half safe."

Nowhere is this better illustrated than by the fact that the chairman of the Federal Communications Commission publicly prods broadcasters to engage in their legal right to **editorialize**. Of course, to undertake an editorial policy, overt and clearly labeled, and obviously **unsponsored**, requires a station or a network to be responsible. Most stations today probably do not have the manpower to assume this responsibility, but the manpower could be recruited. Editorials would not be profitable; if they had a cutting edge, they might even offend. It is much easier, much less troublesome, to use the money-making machine of television and radio merely as a **conduit** through which to channel anything that is not **libelous**, obscene or **defamatory**. In that way one has the illusion of power without responsibility. . . .

One of the basic troubles with radio and television news is that both instruments have grown up as an incompatible combination of show business, advertising and news. Each of the three is a rather bizarre and demanding profession. And when you get all three under one roof, the dust never settles. The top management of the networks, with a few notable exceptions, has been trained in advertising, research, sales or show business. But by the nature of the corporate structure, they also make the final and crucial decisions having to do with news and public affairs. Frequently they have neither the time nor the competence to do this. It is not easy for the same small group of men to decide whether to buy a new station for millions of dollars, build a new building, alter the **rate card**, buy a new Western, sell a soap opera, decide what defensive line to take in connection with the latest Congressional inquiry, how much money to spend on promoting a new program, what additions or deletions should be made in the existing **covey or clutch** of vice-presidents, and at the same time—frequently on the same long day—to give mature, thoughtful consideration to the **manifold** problems that confront those who are charged with the responsibility for news and public affairs.

Sometimes there is a clash between the public interest and the corporate interest. A telephone call or a letter from the proper **quarter** in Washington is treated rather more seriously than a communication from an **irate** but not politically **potent** viewer. It is tempting enough to give away a little air time for frequently irresponsible and unwarranted utterances in an effort to temper the wind of criticism. . . .

So far, I have been dealing largely with the **deficit side of the ledger**, and the items could be expanded. But I have said, and I believe, that potentially we have in this country a **free enterprise** system of radio and television which is superior to any other. But to achieve its promise, it must be both free and **enterprising**. There is no suggestion here that networks or individual stations should operate as **philanthropies**. But I can find nothing in the Bill of Rights [section of the U.S. Constitution] or the Communications Act [of 1934] which says that they must increase their **net profits** each year, lest the Republic collapse. I do not suggest that news and information should be **subsidized** by foundations or private subscriptions. I am aware that the networks have expended, and are expending, very considerable sums of money on public affairs programs from which they cannot hope to receive any financial reward. I have had the privilege at CBS of presiding over a considerable number of such programs. I testify, and am able to stand here and say, that I have never had a program turned down by my superiors because of the money it would cost.

But we all know that you cannot reach the potential maximum audience in **marginal time** with a sustaining program. This is so because so many stations on the network—any network—will decline to carry it. Every **licensee** who applies for a grant to operate in the **public interest, convenience and necessity** makes certain promises as to what he will do in terms of program content. Many recipients of licenses have, in blunt language, **welshed** on those promises. The money-making machine somehow blunts their memories. The only remedy for this is closer inspection and **punitive** action by the F.C.C. But in the view of many this would come perilously close to supervision of program content by a federal agency.

So it seems that we cannot rely on philanthropic support or foundation subsidies; we cannot follow the "sustaining route"—the networks cannot pay all the freight—and the F.C.C. cannot or will not discipline those who abuse the facilities that belong to the public. What, then, is the answer? Do we merely stay in our comfortable nests, concluding that the obligation of these instruments has been discharged when we work at the job of informing the public for a minimum of time? Or do we believe that the preservation of the Republic is a seven-day-a-week job, demanding more awareness, better skills and more perseverance than we have yet contemplated. . . .

This nation is now in competition with **malignant** forces of evil who are using every instrument at their command to empty the minds of their subjects and fill those minds with slogans, determination and faith in the future. If we go on as we are, we are protecting the mind of the American public

Deficit side of the ledger: Problems in the TV industry.

Free enterprise: A system that allows private businesses to operate for the purpose of earning money.

Enterprising: Ambitious or energetic.

Philanthropies: Charities.

Net profits: The amount earned after subtracting expenses.

Subsidized: Paid for; given financial support.

Marginal time: Less-desirable time slots.

Licensee: Holder of a license to broadcast over the airwaves.

Public interest, convenience and necessity: A phrase from the Communications Act of 1934 describing the responsibilities of broadcasters.

Welshed: Failed to follow through.

Punitive: Discipline or punishment.

Malignant: Actively mean and terrible.

Menacing: Threatening; potentially dangerous.

Tithe: Offering or donation.

Stockholders: People who hold shares of ownership in a corporation.

Pluralistic: Large and varied.

Fill the hall: Attract an audience.

Exposition: Explanation.

Fallible: Capable of making mistakes.

Exalt: Give high praise to.

Ed Sullivan: (1901–1974) Early television personality best known for hosting a variety show on CBS.

Steve Allen: (1921–2000) Actor, comedian, and television talk show host.

Palatable: Clear and understandable.

from any real contact with the **menacing** world that squeezes in upon us. We are engaged in a great experiment to discover whether a free public opinion can devise and direct methods of managing the affairs of the nation. We may fail. But we are handicapping ourselves needlessly.

Let us have a little competition. Not only in selling soap, cigarettes and automobiles, but in informing a troubled, apprehensive but receptive public. Why should not each of the 20 or 30 big corporations which dominate radio and television decide that they will give up one or two of their regularly scheduled programs each year, turn the time over to the networks and say in effect: "This is a tiny **tithe**, just a little bit of our profits. On this particular night we aren't going to try to sell cigarettes or automobiles; this is merely a gesture to indicate our belief in the importance of ideas." The networks should, and I think would, pay for the cost of producing the program. The advertiser, the sponsor, would get name credit but would have nothing to do with the content of the program. Would this blemish the corporate image? Would the **stockholders** object? I think not. For if the premise upon which our **pluralistic** society rests, which as I understand it is that if the people are given sufficient undiluted information, they will then somehow, even after long, sober second thoughts, reach the right decision—if that premise is wrong, then not only the corporate image but the corporations are done for.

There used to be an old phrase in this country, employed when someone talked too much. It was: "Go hire a hall." Under this proposal the sponsor would have hired the hall; he has bought the time; the local station operator, no matter how indifferent, is going to carry the program—he has to. Then it's up to the networks to **fill the hall**. I am not here talking about editorializing but about straightaway **exposition** as direct, unadorned and impartial as **fallible** human beings can make it. Just once in a while let us **exalt** the importance of ideas and information. Let us dream to the extent of saying that on a given Sunday night the time normally occupied by **Ed Sullivan** is given over to a clinical survey of the state of American education, and a week or two later the time normally used by **Steve Allen** is devoted to a thoroughgoing study of American policy in the Middle East. Would the corporate image of their respective sponsors be damaged? Would the stockholders rise up in their wrath and complain? Would anything happen other than that a few million people would have received a little illumination on subjects that may well determine the future of this country, and therefore the future of the corporations? This method would also provide real competition between the networks as to which could outdo the others in the **palatable** presentation of information. It would provide an outlet for the young men of skill, and there are some even of dedication, who would like to do something other than devise methods of insulating while selling.

There may be other and simpler methods of utilizing these instruments of radio and television in the interests of a free society. But I know of none that could be so easily accomplished inside the framework of the existing commercial system. I don't know how you would measure the success or failure of a given program. And it would be hard to prove the **magnitude** of the benefit **accruing** to the corporation which gave up one night of a variety or quiz show in order that the network might **marshal** its skills to do a thoroughgoing job on the present status of **NATO**, or plans for controlling nuclear tests. But I would reckon that the president, and indeed the majority of shareholders of the corporation who sponsored such a venture, would feel just a little bit better about the corporation and the country.

It may be that the present system, with no modifications and no experiments, can survive. Perhaps the money-making machine has some kind of built-in **perpetual** motion, but I do not think so. To a very considerable extent the media of mass communications in a given country reflect the political, economic and social climate in which they flourish. That is the reason ours differ from the British and French, or the Russian and Chinese. We are currently wealthy, fat, comfortable and **complacent**. We have currently a built-in allergy to unpleasant or disturbing information. Our mass media reflect this. But unless we get up off our **fat surpluses** and recognize that television in the main is being used to distract, **delude**, amuse and insulate us, then television and those who finance it, those who look at it and those who work at it, may see a totally different picture too late.

I do not **advocate** that we turn television into a 27-inch **wailing wall**, where **longhairs** constantly moan about the state of our culture and our defense. But I would just like to see it reflect occasionally the hard, unyielding realities of the world in which we live. I would like to see it done inside the existing framework, and I would like to see the doing of it **redound** to the credit of those who finance and program it. Measure the results by **Nielsen, Trendex or Silex**—it doesn't matter. The main thing is to try. The responsibility can be easily placed, in spite of all the **mouthings** about giving the public what it wants. It rests on big business, and on big television, and it rests at the top. Responsibility is not something that can be assigned or delegated. And it promises its own reward: good business and good television.

Perhaps no one will do anything about it. I have ventured to outline it against a background of criticism that may have been too harsh only because I could think of nothing better. Someone once said—I think it was **Max Eastman**—that "that publisher serves his advertiser best who best serves his readers." I cannot believe that radio and television, or the corporations that finance the programs, are serving well or truly their viewers or listeners, or themselves.

Magnitude: Importance.

Accruing: Growing or accumulating.

Marshal: Gather or organize.

NATO: The North Atlantic Treaty Organization; a group of nations that agreed to help and protect one another.

Perpetual: Constant or never-ending.

Complacent: Lazy and satisfied; willing to accept things as they are.

Fat surpluses: Big money profits.

Delude: Fool or confuse.

Advocate: Support or argue in favor of.

Wailing wall: Place of mourning.

Longhairs: Nickname for intellectuals and hippies.

Redound: Reflect or transfer.

Nielsen, Trendex or Silex: Companies that measure television audiences and publish ratings for programs.

Mouthings: Things said without sincerity.

Max Eastman: (1883–1969) American writer.

Edward R. Murrow

Retribution: Punishment.

Appropriation: Budget.

Contagion: By example.

Stonewall Jackson: (1824–1863) Confederate general during the Civil War (real name Thomas J. Jackson).

Scabbard: A sheath to hold a sword.

I began by saying that our history will be what we make it. If we go on as we are, then history will take its revenge, and **retribution** will not limp in catching up with us.

We are to a large extent an imitative society. If one or two or three corporations would undertake to devote just a small fraction of their advertising **appropriation** along the lines that I have suggested, the procedure would grow by **contagion**; the economic burden would be bearable, and there might ensue a most exciting adventure—exposure to ideas and the bringing of reality into the homes of the nation.

To those who say people wouldn't look; they wouldn't be interested; they're too complacent, indifferent and insulated, I can only reply: There is, in one reporter's opinion, considerable evidence against that contention. But even if they are right, what have they got to lose? Because if they are right, and this instrument is good for nothing but to entertain, amuse and insulate, then the tube is flickering now and we will soon see that the whole struggle is lost.

This instrument can teach, it can illuminate; yes, and it can even inspire. But it can do so only to the extent that humans are determined to use it to those ends. Otherwise it is merely wires and lights in a box. There is a great and perhaps decisive battle to be fought against ignorance, intolerance and indifference. This weapon of television could be useful.

Stonewall Jackson, who knew something about the use of weapons, is reported to have said, "When war comes, you must draw the sword and throw away the **scabbard**." The trouble with television is that it is rusting in the scabbard during a battle for survival.

• • •

What happened next . . .

Murrow's speech did not go over well with the audience at the RTNDA convention. The members of the electronic news media attending the conference did not appreciate Murrow's harsh words about their performance. The speech also caused hard feelings between Murrow and his boss at CBS, William S. Paley. Paley finally ran out of patience with Murrow and took steps to limit his air time. "The speech Ed Murrow gave at the 1958 RTNDA convention in Chicago was a risky speech, and he knew it," Rather noted. "It was a bold shot, and he knew it. That was part of the Murrow style, and part of what has made the Murrow mystique: the bold, brave shot."

Murrow's outspoken criticism of commercial broadcasting essentially led to his being forced out of the industry. His speech received praise and admiration from people outside of television, but it created anger and resentment within the broadcasting establishment. Under increasing pressure from network executives, Murrow quit his job with CBS in 1960. The following year, he accepted an appointment from President John F. Kennedy to serve as head of the U.S. Information Agency. This agency provided the official views of the U.S. government to citizens of other nations through such organizations as the Voice of America radio network.

Edward R. Murrow died of lung cancer on April 28, 1965, at the age of fifty-seven. Shortly before his death, he received the Presidential Medal of Freedom, the highest civilian (non-military) honor in the United States. He was also made an honorary knight in England. After Murrow died, the broadcasting industry gradually let go of its anger and began recognizing his many contributions. In 1971 the RTNDA established the Edward R. Murrow Awards to honor outstanding achievements in electronic journalism. CBS placed his photograph in the lobby of its headquarters in New York City, along with a plaque that reads, "He set standards of excellence that remain unsurpassed."

Did you know . . .

- Murrow came up with his signature opening and closing lines while reporting for CBS Radio in wartime London. He started each broadcast by stating, "THIS . . . is London." The unique way he said the phrase—with added emphasis on "this," followed by a dramatic pause—caught the imagination of the public and helped make Murrow a star. Years later, the CBS television network adapted the phrase for its promotional spots, in which a narrator said, "This . . . is CBS." Throughout his career, Murrow closed each broadcast by telling the audience, "Good night, and good luck." He borrowed this phrase from London residents during World War II. They always wished each other "good luck" upon parting because they never felt certain that they would live to greet each other the following day.

- Much of Edward R. Murrow's 1958 address to the RTNDA appears in the 2005 film *Good Night, and Good Luck.* Based on interviews with Murrow's colleagues and family, the movie follows the legendary journalist's efforts to discredit anti-Communist crusader Senator Joseph McCarthy on his TV program *See It Now*. *Good Night, and Good Luck* received a number of Academy Award nominations, including one as Best Picture and one for David Strathairn as Best Actor for his performance in the role of Murrow.

Consider the following...

- Murrow argues that if television is not used to serve the public interest, it is "merely wires and lights in a box." What suggestions does Murrow make in his speech that he believes would improve the quality of television in America? If you were in charge of a major broadcast network, what changes would you make?

- According to Dan Rather in his 1993 address to the RTNDA, "Murrow was worried because he saw a trend setting in—avoiding the unpleasant or controversial or challenging. He saw the networks shortening news broadcasts, or jamming them with ever-increasing numbers of commercials—throwing out background, context, and analysis, relying just on headlines, and going for entertainment values over the values of good journalism." Rather had not seen many improvements by the time he made his speech. What is your assessment of the state of TV news today?

- Murrow's purpose in making this speech was to convince his peers to care more deeply about an issue he believed was important. Think of a social, political, environmental, or humanitarian issue you care about. Write a one-page speech to try to convince your classmates to share your concerns.

For More Information

BOOKS

Edwards, Bob. *Edward R. Murrow and the Birth of Broadcast Journalism*. New York: Wiley, 2004.

Kendrick, Alexander. *Prime-Time: The Life of Edward R. Murrow*. Boston: Little, Brown, 1969.

Murrow, Edward R., and Edward Bliss, Jr., eds. *In Search of Light: The Broadcasts of Edward R. Murrow, 1938–1961*. New York: Knopf, 1967.

Persico, Joseph E. *Edward R. Murrow: An American Original*. New York: McGraw-Hill, 1988.

Sperber, A.M. *Murrow, His Life and Times*. New York: Freundlich, 1986.

WEB SITES

Edgerton, Gary. "Edward R. Murrow." *Museum of Broadcast Communications.* http://www.museum.tv/archives/etv/M/htmlM/murrowedwar/murrowedwar. htm (accessed on July 26, 2006).

"Edward R Murrow Biography." *Edward R. Murrow Center.* Tufts University. http://fletcher.tufts.edu/murrow/murrow/biography.html (accessed on July 26, 2006).

Montagne, Renee. "Edward R. Murrow: Broadcasting History." *National Public Radio.* http://www.npr.org/templates/story/story.php?storyid=1872668 (accessed on July 26, 2006).

Murrow, Edward R. "Keynote Address to the Radio and Television News Directors Association." *RTNDA Speeches,* http://www.rtnda.org/resources/ speeches/murrow.shtml (accessed on July 26, 2006).

Rather, Dan. "Speech at 1993 RTNDA Convention, Miami, Florida." *Radio and Television News Directors Association.* http://www.rtnda.org/resources/ speeches/rather.html (accessed on May 22, 2006).

6

John F. Kennedy

"A Force That Has Changed the Political Scene"
Originally published in TV Guide, *November 14, 1959*
Excerpted from TV Guide: 50 Years of Television. *New York: Crown, 2002*

"Whether TV improves or worsens our political system, whether it serves the purpose of political education or deception, whether it gives us better or poorer candidates, more intelligent or more prejudiced campaigns—the answers to all these questions are up to you, the viewing public."

America's political leaders recognized the power of television as soon as the new medium was introduced in the 1940s. When it came time to nominate candidates for the 1948 presidential election, for instance, both the Democratic and Republican political parties decided to hold their nominating conventions in Philadelphia, because the city's TV broadcasts could be seen on fourteen stations along the East Coast.

As early as 1952, it became clear that television could make or break political candidates. The Democratic candidate for president that year, Adlai Stevenson (1900–1965), bought half an hour of network air time to broadcast a campaign speech. Unfortunately for Stevenson, his speech upset many viewers because it replaced the most popular prime-time program of the era, *I Love Lucy*. In the meantime, Republican candidate Dwight D. Eisenhower (1890–1969) aired a series of thirty-second campaign commercials that helped turn the election in his favor.

John F. Kennedy was one of the first political figures to take full advantage of the potential of television to create an image that appealed to voters. Kennedy was born into a prominent political family on May 29, 1917, in Brookline, Massachusetts. He graduated from Harvard University in 1940 with a degree in international relations. After completing his

President John F. Kennedy in 1962. © BETTMANN/CORBIS.

college education, he enlisted in the U.S. Navy to fight in World War II (1939–45). Kennedy soon gained the rank of lieutenant and became commander of a patrol-torpedo (PT) boat operating in the Pacific Ocean. In 1943, his boat was rammed and sunk by a Japanese destroyer near the Solomon Islands. Although injured, Kennedy led fellow survivors to safety and later received medals for heroism.

Once the war ended, Kennedy entered politics. In 1946, he was elected to the U.S. House of Representatives as a Democrat from a Boston district. He won reelection twice, then in 1952 he was elected to the U.S. Senate from Massachusetts. The following year Kennedy married Jacqueline Bouvier. They eventually had two children, Caroline and John Jr. In 1955, while recovering from back surgery, Kennedy wrote a nonfiction book called *Profiles in Courage,* which earned the prestigious Pulitzer Prize in history. The young senator came to national attention in 1956, when he nearly gained the Democratic Party's nomination for vice president of the United States.

In 1959, Kennedy wrote an article called "A Force That Has Changed the Political Scene" for *TV Guide.* In this article, which is reprinted below, the increasingly popular politician talks about the impact of television on campaigns, candidates, elections, and government in America. He acknowledges that "TV offers new opportunities, new challenges, and new problems." In general, Kennedy is optimistic about the impact of television on the political process. He expresses hope that television coverage will make politicians more accountable to voters and more honest in their dealings. He also predicts that the need to create a TV "image" will lead to the rise of "a new breed of candidates" who are young, intelligent, and compassionate.

Things to remember while reading "A Force That Has Changed the Political Scene":

- Around the time this article was published, Kennedy announced his intention to seek the Democratic Party's nomination for president of the United States in 1960. During his successful campaign, Kennedy provided a prime example of the "new breed" of candidate who crafted an appealing image for the TV Age.

- In his article, Kennedy mentions that President Woodrow Wilson (1856–1924; served 1913–21) undertook an "intensive cross- country tour to plead the cause of the League of Nations." This took place in 1919, shortly after the end of World War I (1914–18). The League of Nations was an international organization, similar to the United Nations, that included representatives from many countries around the world. It was intended to serve as a place for nations to settle their differences peacefully and thus avoid future wars. Wilson viewed U.S leadership in the League of Nations as a key part of his plan to secure peace and create a new world order. But the U.S. Congress did not support the idea. In order to generate public support for U.S. participation in the League, Wilson spent three weeks traveling around the country and making speeches. Before the end of the tour, however, Wilson collapsed from exhaustion and suffered a stroke. He spent the last year of his presidency in bed, relying upon his wife to conduct official business on his behalf. The United States never did join the League of Nations, and the organization was too weak to prevent World War II from erupting twenty years later.

- Kennedy also refers to the quiz show scandal that rocked the television industry during the late 1950s. Game and quiz shows were extremely popular forms of TV entertainment at that time. Many of the shows were produced by sponsors—large companies that used television programs to advertise their products. Some of the sponsors used their high level of control over the programs to "fix," or arrange, the results of the quiz shows. They provided some of the most popular contestants with answers in advance, for example, so that they would continue winning and attract the largest possible audiences for the sponsor's commercials. The quiz show scandal came to light through a highly publicized investigation by the U.S. Congress. After the corruption was revealed, most of the quiz shows were cancelled, and the television networks took greater control over the production of programs.

• • •

"A Force That Has Changed the Political Scene"

The wonders of science and technology have revolutionized the modern American political campaign. Giant electronic brains project [election] results on the basis of carefully conducted polls. Automatic typewriters

John F. Kennedy

Observation car: The caboose of a train, from which political candidates would address crowds during campaign stops.

Constituents: Members of the voting public within a politician's district.

Net: Overall.

Woodrow Wilson: Twenty-eighth president of the United States (1856–1924; served 1913–21).

League of Nations: An international organization, similar to the United Nations, that was formed following World War I.

Scrutinizes: Examines very closely.

Run roughshod over: Trample upon; disregard.

Smoke-filled room: A secretive, behind-the-scenes meeting of powerful people.

Bombastic orator: Loud-voiced speaker.

Ringing the rafters: Making the roof vibrate.

Deception: Practice of deliberately misleading, often by lying or withholding information.

Vigor: Energy, good health, mental strength.

Compassion: Feelings of sympathy for or eagerness to help a person in an unfortunate situation.

Conviction: Strongly held opinion.

Uncannily: Unbelievably.

prepare thousands of personally addressed letters, individually signed by automatic pens. Jet planes make possible a coast-to-coast speaking schedule that no **observation car** back platform could ever meet. Even wash-and-wear fabrics permit the wilted nonstop candidate to travel lighter, farther and faster.

But nothing compares with the revolutionary impact of television. TV has altered drastically the nature of our political campaigns, conventions, **constituents**, candidates, and costs. Some politicians regard it with suspicion, others with pleasure. Some candidates have been advised to avoid it. To the voter and vote getter alike, TV offers new opportunities, new challenges and new problems.

But for better or worse—and I side with those who feel its **net** effect can definitely be for the better—the impact of TV on politics is tremendous. Just 40 years ago, **Woodrow Wilson** exhausted his body and mind in an intensive cross-country tour to plead the cause of the **League of Nations**. Three weeks of hard travel and 40 speeches brought on a stroke before he had finished "taking his case to the people" in the only way available. Today, President Dwight D. Eisenhower [1890–1965; served 1953–61], taking his case to the people on the labor situation, is able to reach several million in one 15-minute period without ever leaving his office.

Many new political reputations have been made on TV—and many old ones have been broken. The searching eye of the television camera **scrutinizes** the candidates—and the way they are picked. Party leaders are less willing to **run roughshod over** the voters' wishes and handpick an unknown, unappealing or unpopular candidate in the traditional **"smoke-filled room"** when millions of voters are watching, comparing and remembering.

The slick or **bombastic orator**, pounding the table and **ringing the rafters**, is not as welcome in the family living room as he was in the town square or party hall. In the old days, many a seasoned politician counted among his most highly developed and useful talents his ability to dodge a reporter's question, evade a "hot" issue and avoid a definite stand. But today a vast viewing public is able to detect such **deception** and, in my opinion, willing to respect political honesty.

Honesty, **vigor**, **compassion**, intelligence—the presence or lack of these and other qualities make up what is called the candidate's "image." While some intellectuals and politicians may scoff at these images—and while they may in fact be based only on a candidate's TV impression, ignoring his record, views and other appearances—my own **conviction** is that these images or impressions are likely to be **uncannily** correct. I think, no matter what their defenders or **detractors** may say, that the television public has a fairly good idea of what Eisenhower is really like—or **Jimmy Hoffa** or **John McClellan** or Vice President [Richard M.] Nixon or countless others.

This is why a new breed of candidates has sprung up on both the state and national levels. Most of these men are comparatively young. Their youth may still be a handicap in the eyes of older politicians—but it is definitely an **asset** in creating a television image people like and (most difficult of all) remember.

This is not to say that all the politicians of yesteryear would have been failures in the Age of Television. The rugged vigor of **Teddy Roosevelt**, the determined sincerity of Woodrow Wilson, the quiet dignity of **Abraham Lincoln**, and the confidence-inspiring calm of **Franklin D. Roosevelt**—all would have been tremendously effective on television.

Can you imagine the effect of televising FDR's [Franklin D. Roosevelt's] **"fireside chats"**?

But political success on television is not, unfortunately, limited only to those who deserve it. It is a medium that lends itself to **manipulation, exploitation** and **gimmicks**. It can be abused by **demagogues**, by appeals to emotion and **prejudice** and ignorance. Political campaigns can actually be taken over by the public relations experts, who tell the candidate not only how to use TV but what to say, what to stand for and what "kind of person" to be. Political shows, like quiz shows, can be fixed—and sometimes are.

The other great problem TV presents for politics is the item of financial cost. It is no small item. In the 1956 campaign, the Republican National Committee, according to the Gore report [an independent analysis], spent over $3 million for television—and the Democratic National Committee, just under $2.8 million on television broadcasting.

If all candidates and parties are to have equal access to this essential and decisive campaign medium, without becoming deeply obligated to the big financial contributors from the worlds of business, labor or other major **lobbies**, then the time has come when a solution must be found to this problem of TV costs.

This is not the place to discuss alternative remedies. But the basic point is this: Whether TV improves or worsens our political system, whether it serves the purpose of political education or deception, whether it give us better or poorer candidates, more intelligent or more prejudiced campaigns—the answers to all these questions are up to you, the viewing public.

It is your power to perceive deception, to shut off gimmickry, to reward honesty, to demand legislation where needed. Without your approval, no TV show is worthwhile and no politician can exist.

Detractors: Critics.

Jimmy Hoffa: Labor union leader (1913–1975).

John McClellan: Democratic U.S. senator from Arkansas (1896–1977; served 1943–77).

Asset: Positive quality.

Teddy Roosevelt: Twenty-sixth president of the United States (1858–1919; served 1901–09).

Abraham Lincoln: Sixteenth president of the United States (1809–1865; served 1861–65).

Franklin D. Roosevelt: Thirty-second president of the United States (1882–1945; served 1933–45).

Fireside chats: Weekly radio addresses to the American people.

Manipulation: The act of changing or rearranging something, often in order to mislead.

Exploitation: The act of treating someone or something unfairly for one's own benefit.

Gimmicks: Tricks.

Demagogues: People who use false claims and promises to gain power.

Prejudice: A negative opinion or hostile attitude formed prior to experience or gathering evidence.

Lobbies: Groups that attempt to influence government officials.

That is the way it always has been and will continue to be—and that is the way it should be.

• • •

What happened next...

In the summer of 1960, the Democratic Party selected John F. Kennedy as its candidate for president of the United States. His opponent in the general election was Republican Richard M. Nixon (1913–94), who had served two terms as vice president under President Dwight D. Eisenhower. In September, the two candidates faced off in the first-ever televised presidential debates. At this point, Nixon was ahead in the polls and favored to win the election. Nixon's supporters emphasized that he had more experience, particularly in the area of foreign affairs, than his lesser-known opponent.

On the day of the first debate, Nixon was not feeling well and appeared pale and tired. Kennedy, on the other hand, looked suntanned and healthy. Nixon wore a rumpled gray suit that blended into the background, while Kennedy stood out in a crisp, dark suit. As the two candidates answered questions on stage, Kennedy seemed calm and confident. He also looked into the television cameras as he spoke, which gave viewers the impression that he was speaking directly to them. Nixon, on the other hand, sweated visibly and appeared uncomfortable as he answered questions. He addressed his responses to the journalists who had posed the questions, rather than looking at the television cameras.

An estimated 77 million viewers—or more than 60 percent of the adult population of the United States at that time—tuned in to watch the first Kennedy–Nixon debate. The substance of the two candidates' answers was evenly matched, and most people who listened to the debate on the radio felt that Nixon had won. But the TV audience was influenced by the dramatic visual differences between the two candidates, and people who watched on TV thought Kennedy performed better by a wide margin. The debates helped Kennedy convince the American people that he had the experience and maturity to be president, and he ended up winning the election a few months later. In polls conducted after the election, more than half of all voters said that the debates had influenced their opinions, and 6 percent said they based their vote on the debates alone.

John F. Kennedy and Richard Nixon during one of their presidential debates. Kennedy's calm, confident TV image helped convince voters to elect him to the presidency in 1960. © BETTMANN/CORBIS.

The Kennedy–Nixon debates are considered a landmark in the history of television and American politics. From that time on, the ability to create an appealing TV image was an important consideration for all national political candidates. "The Kennedy–Nixon debates stand out as a remarkable moment in the nation's political history, not only because they propelled an unlikely candidate to victory, but also because they ushered in an era in which television dominated the electoral process," Liette Gidlow wrote in the online journal *History Now*. Some critics argue that television's dominance of politics has resulted in a triumph of image over issues, and personality over positions.

A presidency for the TV Age

Kennedy took office as the thirty-fifth president of the United States on January 20, 1961. At the age of forty-three, he was the youngest person ever to be elected president. As president, Kennedy continued to take advantage of the broad reach of television to lead and inspire the American people. In his televised inaugural address (a speech upon taking office), for instance, Kennedy called all American citizens to public service with the stirring words, "Ask not what your country can do for you, ask what you can do for your country." Kennedy also described an optimistic vision for the future of the United States he called the New Frontier, which focused on eliminating problems such as war, poverty, and prejudice.

Shortly after taking office, President Kennedy appointed a young lawyer named Newton N. Minow (1926–) as chairman of the Federal Communications Commission (FCC), the government agency charged with regulating television. In 1961, Minow made a famous speech before the National Association of Broadcasters (NAB). (*See* Chapter 7, Newton Minow.) Minow criticized the content of TV programming as a "vast wasteland" and encouraged the networks to make a greater effort to serve the public interest. With Minow applying pressure through the FCC, the broadcast networks placed an increased emphasis on news and information programming.

As president, Kennedy supported the civil rights movement. During this time, millions of African Americans participated in marches and protests with the goal of ending segregation (the forced separation of people by race) and gaining equal rights and opportunities in American society. Kennedy sent federal troops into the South to enforce U.S. Supreme Court orders to end the segregation of public schools. He also called upon the U.S. Congress to pass new civil rights legislation. Furthermore, Kennedy is known for launching an ambitious space program, with the goal of sending an American astronaut to the Moon before the end of the decade. He also created the Peace Corps, an organization that sends American volunteers to developing countries to provide education and other forms of aid.

In terms of foreign policy, many of Kennedy's decisions were driven by the fact that the United States and the Soviet Union were engaged in a period of intense military and political rivalry known as the Cold War (1945–91). Each of these world superpowers developed nuclear weapons capable of destroying the other. They also became involved in a series of smaller conflicts around the world in hopes of spreading their own political philosophies and systems of government to new regions, while preventing the other side from doing the same. Shortly after taking office, for instance, Kennedy supported an invasion of Cuba (an island nation located ninety miles from the southern coast of Florida) by a group of rebels hoping to overthrow the government of Communist dictator Fidel Castro (1926–). The poorly executed Bay of Pigs invasion failed to unseat Castro and resulted in an embarrassment for the Kennedy administration.

In 1962, the U.S. government discovered that the Soviet Union was trying to install nuclear weapons in Cuba. During a tense confrontation between the superpowers, Kennedy ordered the U.S. Navy to prevent Soviet ships from reaching Cuban ports. His strong stand forced the Soviet Union to back down and remove its weapons from Cuba. In 1963, Kennedy began working toward international arms control agreements designed to stop the spread of nuclear weapons.

The Kennedy assassination

On November 22, 1963—shortly after he had completed his first thousand days in office—President Kennedy was shot and killed as he rode through Dallas, Texas, in the back seat of an open car. The untimely and violent death of a popular president had a traumatic impact on the entire United States. All of the television networks suspended regular programming to provide viewers with nonstop coverage of the events that took place over the next four days. Television drew people together in their shock and grief, and an amazing 90 percent of American citizens tuned in to the TV news over the course of that weekend.

The aftermath of the Kennedy assassination marked the first time that the presence of television cameras changed the course of history. Lee Harvey Oswald (1939–63) was quickly captured and charged with murdering the president. Recognizing the high level of media interest in the case, law enforcement officials arranged to move the prisoner to the county jail at a convenient time for news coverage. As police officers escorted Oswald through a hallway jammed with reporters, a Dallas nightclub owner named Jack Ruby (1911–67) stepped out of the crowd and shot and killed the suspect. The murder of Oswald was the first dramatic news event to be shown live on TV. Afterward, many people blamed the decision to allow television cameras at Oswald's transfer for making the murder possible.

The extensive coverage of the events surrounding Kennedy's assassination and funeral helped turn TV into a dominant source of news and information. Over the course of a single weekend, millions of Americans made the switch from radio and newspapers to TV as their main link to current events. Kennedy's strong leadership qualities, combined with his mastery of television and his tragic death, helped make him one of the most popular presidents in U.S. history. While historians generally grade his performance above average, polls of average Americans consistently rank him among the greatest U.S. presidents.

Did you know...

- John F. Kennedy took full advantage of his youth, good looks, charm, strong speaking skills, and attractive family to create an appealing television image throughout his campaign and presidency. While Kennedy undoubtedly possessed strong leadership qualities, in some ways his TV image did not reflect reality. Kennedy took great care to appear vigorous and athletic on TV, for instance, when he really had serious health problems. He suffered from Addison's disease (a condition in which the adrenal glands—located near the kidneys—fail to produce enough hormones), which caused weakness and digestive problems. He also suffered from severe back pain that required several surgeries and constant pain medication. On the surface, Kennedy and his glamorous wife, Jacqueline, seemed to have a perfect life. Their personal popularity exceeded that of any other president and first lady, and they were often treated like celebrities—posing for photo spreads in leading magazines and setting new fashion trends. But others point out that, behind the scenes, Kennedy had a series of extramarital affairs. Some historians argue that Kennedy succeeded in maintaining his positive image because television news operations were more respectful toward politicians at that time, and less likely to air details of their personal lives.
- In his *TV Guide* article, Kennedy provides figures for television spending by the two major political parties during the 1956 presidential campaign: $3 million by the Republicans; and $2.8 million by the Democrats. He describes the high cost of TV exposure as a "great problem" in the political process, because it forces candidates to accept money from businesses and political interest groups that expect favors in return. Yet these figures seem tiny

in comparison to the 2004 presidential campaign, when Democratic senator John Kerry (1943–) and Republican president George W. Bush (1946–) spent a combined $600 million on television and radio advertising. Counting the money spent by the political parties and various advocacy groups to support the candidates, the total advertising spending during the presidential race topped $1 billion, according to the Center for Responsive Politics. Clearly, the high cost of television advertising remains a major issue in American politics.

Consider the following...

- Choose a prominent political figure and describe his or her "image." What does the person do or say to reinforce that image? To what extent do you think the image reflects reality?

- In his article, Kennedy claims that television coverage of politics will allow voters to hold politicians more accountable for their actions. He argues that TV viewers are "able to detect...deception" and "willing to respect political honesty." Do you think that modern TV coverage has made politicians more or less honest? Cite examples to support your answer.

- Kennedy became president partly because he adapted quickly to the new medium of television and used it to his advantage. Some experts suggest that, in the near future, the Internet may challenge television as the main source of contact and information between political candidates and voters. How do you think this will affect who succeeds in politics?

For More Information

BOOKS

Bliss, Edward J., Jr. *Now the News: The Story of Broadcast Journalism.* New York: Columbia University Press, 1991.

Dallek, Robert. *An Unfinished Life: John F. Kennedy.* Boston: Little, Brown, 2003.

Garner, Joe. *Stay Tuned: Television's Unforgettable Moments.* Kansas City: Andrews McMeel Publishing, 2002.

Hilliard, Robert L., and Michael C. Keith. *The Broadcast Century: A Biography of American Broadcasting.* Boston: Focal Press, 1992.

Lasswell, Mark. *TV Guide: 50 Years of Television.* New York: Crown, 2002.

McChesney, Robert W. *Rich Media, Poor Democracy: Communications Politics in Dubious Times.* Urbana and Chicago: University of Illinois Press, 1999.

O'Brien, Michael. *John F. Kennedy: A Biography.* New York: Thomas Dunne Books, 2005.

Stark, Steven D. *Glued to the Set: The 60 Television Shows and Events That Made Us Who We Are Today.* New York: The Free Press, 1997.

WEB SITES

Allen, Erika Tyner. "Kennedy-Nixon Debates." *Museum of Broadcast Communications.* http://www.museum.tv/archives/etv/K/htmlK/kennedy-nixon/kennedy-nixon.htm (accessed on July 26, 2006).

Gidlow, Liette. "The Great Debate: Kennedy, Nixon, and Television in the 1960 Race for the Presidency." *History Now,* September 2004. http://www.historynow.org/historian2.html (accessed on July 26, 2006).

"John F. Kennedy Biography." *The White House.* http://www.whitehouse.gov/history/presidents/jk35.html (accessed on July 26, 2006).

Kierstead, Phillip. "Network News." *Museum of Broadcast Communications.* http://www.museum.tv/archives/etv/N/htmlN/newsnetwork/newsnetwork.htm (accessed on July 26, 2006).

7

Newton N. Minow

Excerpt of "Television and the Public Interest"
   A speech delivered before the National Association of Broadcasters, May 9, 1961
   Excerpted from Abandoned in the Wasteland: Children, Television, and the First Amendment.
      New York: Hill and Wang, 1995.

"I invite you to sit down in front of your television set when your station goes on the air ... and keep your eyes glued to that set until the station signs off. I can assure you that you will observe a vast wasteland."

The Federal Communications Commission (FCC) is the U.S. government agency responsible for regulating all types of communication that use radio waves. Radio waves are a form of electromagnetic energy that travels through the air. The waves exist in a range of frequencies called the radio spectrum. Only a limited number of frequencies can be used to carry communication signals. Since the usable frequencies are scarce, they are also very valuable.

Since the beginning of the communication age, the U.S. government has taken a strong interest in controlling the use of the airwaves and assigning the usable radio frequencies. The Radio Act of 1927 said that the airwaves belong to the American people and required broadcasters to apply for a license to use this public property. The Communications Act of 1934, which established the FCC, said that broadcasters using the public airwaves had a duty to serve the "public interest, convenience, and necessity." The law used somewhat vague language, however, and it did not describe exactly what broadcasters needed to do in order to meet this obligation to the American people.

The U.S. television industry officially got its start in 1941, when the FCC recognized the new medium for the first time. Television broadcasting was suspended when the United States entered World War II in December 1941. After the war ended in 1945, however, the television industry entered a period of rapid growth. TV ownership increased from 10 percent of American homes in 1950 to 87 percent in 1960. The number of commercial television stations exploded as well—from 9 immediately after the war ended to 500 by 1960.

The rapid growth of television broadcasting created a challenge for the FCC. The agency had to determine how to divide up the usable frequencies among various technologies, such as radio and television broadcasting, police and fire department dispatches, telephone and telegraph messages, and even walkie-talkies. The FCC also had to decide which of the many individuals and companies that applied for television broadcasting licenses were most deserving of space in the scarce radio spectrum.

From the beginning, the FCC's stated goals were to use the airwaves to serve the public interest and to prevent any individual or corporation from gaining exclusive control of them. Since the term "public interest" was not fully explained in the Communications Act of 1934, however, the FCC often struggled to decide how to enforce the rule. For instance, the agency left most decisions about the content of TV programs to the national broadcast networks (ABC, CBS, and NBC).

Some people felt that the government had limited power to control TV program content. They argued that the First Amendment to the U.S. Constitution, which guaranteed citizens the right to free speech, should protect broadcasters from government censorship (a policy of examining creative works prior to distribution and removing any material considered improper or offensive). But other people believed that the vague "public interest" clause of the Communications Act of 1934 gave the FCC broad power to regulate TV, including program content.

In order to avoid possible action by the FCC, the networks established their own rules to guide program content. The National Association of Broadcasters (NAB), which included representatives from the three national television networks, adopted a set of guidelines called the Code of Practices for Television Broadcasters in 1951. The code established rules for the networks to follow regarding various issues, including acceptable content and the number of commercials aired per hour of programming. Stations that voluntarily followed the rules earned the right to display the NAB's Seal of Good Practice. Over time, though, it became increasingly clear that the code was not effective in regulating the networks' behavior.

Newton Minow shortly after being appointed chairman of the Federal Communications Commission, January 1961.
AP IMAGES.

As the popularity of television increased rapidly during the 1950s, network programmers competed fiercely to create shows that would attract high ratings. The more viewers that tuned into a given show, the higher the show would place in the weekly TV ratings, and the more money the network could charge advertisers to air commercials during that show. Advertising dollars provided a major source of funding for the networks, allowing them to stay in business and continue producing programs. By the end of the decade, however, critics were beginning to complain that the networks sacrificed quality in their quest for high ratings and big advertising money.

Minow becomes head of the FCC

This was the situation in the television industry in 1960, when Democrat **John F. Kennedy** (1917–1963; served 1961–63; see Chapter 6) was elected president of the United States. Kennedy was one of the first political figures to understand and take advantage of the power of television. In fact, his strong performance in the first-ever televised presidential debate was believed to be a deciding factor in his election victory over Republican candidate Richard M. Nixon (1913–1994).

During his inaugural address (a speech upon taking office) in January 1961, Kennedy called all American citizens to public service with the stirring words, "Ask not what your country can do for you, ask what you can do for your country." Kennedy also described an optimistic vision for the future of the United States he called the New Frontier, which focused on eliminating problems such as war, poverty, and prejudice.

Shortly after taking office, Kennedy appointed a relatively unknown, thirty-four-year-old lawyer named Newton N. Minow to be chairman of the FCC. Newton Norman Minow was born on January 17, 1926, in Milwaukee, Wisconsin. He earned a law degree from Northwestern University in Chicago in 1950, and then he spent a year serving as a law clerk for Fred M. Vinson, the Chief Justice of the U.S. Supreme Court. Minow's interest in public service began when he worked as a legal counsel for Illinois governor Adlai Stevenson (1900–1965), who unsuccessfully ran for president of the United States in 1952 and 1956. In 1960, Minow joined Kennedy's presidential campaign, and the two men found that they shared similar ideas about the future of American television.

A few weeks after taking over as head of the FCC, Minow made a famous speech before the National Association of Broadcasters. In this speech, which is excerpted below, Minow outlines his views about the FCC's role in regulating television. He also provides insight into his personal philosophy as chairman of the FCC. Most importantly, though, Minow sharply criticizes the content of television programming as a "vast wasteland" and encourages broadcasters to work harder to meet their obligation to inform and educate the American people.

Minow's speech, delivered May 9, 1961, was officially titled "Television and the Public Interest," but it is better known as the "Wasteland Speech." It is widely considered to be one of the landmark addresses in the history of the television industry. Minow was the first FCC chairman to criticize broadcasters in public, and his words sparked a national debate over the future of television.

Things to remember while reading the excerpt of "Television and the Public Interest":

- In 1961 the only television broadcast stations available were on channels two through thirteen.

- Many significant events in U.S. and world history took place during the 1960s. For instance, the United States and the Soviet Union were engaged in a period of intense military and political rivalry known as the Cold War (1945–91). Each of these world super-powers developed nuclear weapons capable of destroying the other. They also became involved in a series of smaller conflicts around the world in hopes of spreading their own political philoso-phies and systems of government to new regions, while preventing the other side from doing the same. The Cold War thus provided an important reason why the United States became involved in the Vietnam War (1954–1975) during this time. Finally, the 1960s also saw the beginning of the civil rights movement in the United States. Millions of African Americans participated in marches and protests as a means to end segregation (the forced separation of people by race) and gain equal rights and opportunities in American society. Minow mentions some of these things in his speech. He argues that television should do a better job of educating and informing viewers about such important issues and world events.

- Minow also refers to the quiz show scandal that rocked the televi-sion industry during the late 1950s. Game and quiz shows were ex-tremely popular forms of TV entertainment at that time. Many of the shows were produced by sponsors—large companies that used television programs to advertise their products. Some of the sponsors used their high level of control over the programs to "fix," or determine, the results of the quiz shows. They provided some of the most popular contestants with answers in advance, for example, so that they would continue winning and attract the largest possible audiences for the sponsor's commercials. The quiz show scandal came to light through a highly publicized investigation by the U.S. Congress. After it was revealed, most of the quiz shows were cancelled, and the television networks took greater control over the production of programs. In his speech, Minow says that the problems exposed by the scandal have been addressed, and he expresses his determination to move on to more pressing concerns.

• • •

Excerpt of "Television and the Public Interest"

It may . . . come as a surprise to some of you, but I want you to know that you have my admiration and respect. Yours is a most honorable profession.

Newton N. Minow

Tough row to hoe: A difficult job or task to do.

Bread: Income or money.

Trustees: People legally responsible for taking care of property belonging to someone else.

Beneficiary: A person who benefits from another' work.

Return: Profit or benefit.

Gross broadcast revenues: Total money earned from broadcasting.

Recession: Period of reduced economic activity.

New Frontier: Vision for the future of the United States, introduced by President John F. Kennedy in 1961, that focused on eliminating war, prejudice, and poverty.

Censor: The process of examining a creative work prior to distribution and removing any material considered improper or offensive.

Anyone who is in the broadcasting business has a **tough row to hoe**. You earn your **bread** by using public property. When you work in broadcasting you volunteer for public service, public pressure, and public regulation. You must compete with other attractions and other investments, and the only way you can do it is to prove to us every three years that you should have been in business in the first place.

I can think of easier ways to make a living.

But I cannot think of more satisfying ways.

I admire your courage—but that doesn't mean I would make life any easier for you. Your license lets you use the public's airwaves as **trustees** for 180 million Americans. The public is your **beneficiary**. If you want to stay on as trustees, you must deliver a decent **return** to the public—not only to your stockholders. So, as a representative of the public, your health and your product are among my chief concerns.

As to your health: let's talk only of television today. 1960 **gross broadcast revenues** of the television industry were over $1,268,000,000; profit before taxes was $243,900,000, an average return on revenue of 19.2 percent. Compared with 1959, gross broadcast revenues were $1,163,900,000, and profit before taxes was $222,300,000, an average return on revenue of 19.1 percent. So, the percentage increase of total revenues from 1959 to 1960 was 9 percent, and the percentage increase of profit was 9.7 percent. This, despite a **recession**. For your investors, the price has indeed been right.

I have confidence in your health.

But not in your product.

It is with this and much more in mind that I come before you today.

One editorialist in the trade press wrote that "the FCC of the **New Frontier** is going to be one of the toughest FCC's in the history of broadcast regulation." If he meant that we intend to enforce the law in the public interest, let me make it perfectly clear that he is right—we do. If he meant that we intend to muzzle or **censor** broadcasting, he is dead wrong. It would not surprise me if some of you had expected me to come here today and say in effect, "Clean up your own house or the government will do it for you." Well, in a limited sense, you would be right—I've just said it.

But I want to say to you earnestly that it is not in that spirit that I come before you today, nor is it in that spirit that I intend to serve the FCC. I am in Washington to help broadcasting, not to harm it; to strengthen it, not weaken it; to reward it, not punish it; to encourage it, not threaten it; to stimulate it, not censor it. Above all, I am here to uphold and protect the public interest.

What do we mean by "the public interest"?

Some say the public interest is merely what interests the public. I disagree. So does your distinguished president, **Governor [LeRoy] Collins**. In a recent speech he said,

> Broadcasting, to serve the public interest, must have a soul and a **conscience**, a burning desire to excel, as well as to sell; the urge to build the character, citizenship and intellectual stature of people, as well as to expand the **gross national product**.... By no means do I imply that broadcasters disregard the public interest.... But a much better job can be done, and should be done.

I could not agree more.

And I would add that in today's world, with chaos in **Laos** and the **Congo** aflame, with **Communist tyranny** on our **Caribbean doorstep** and relentless pressure on our **Atlantic alliance**, with social and economic problems at home of the gravest nature, yes, and with technological knowledge that makes it possible, as our President [John F. Kennedy] has said, not only to destroy our world but to destroy poverty around the world—in a time of **peril** and opportunity, the old complacent, unbalanced fare of action-adventure and situation comedies is simply not good enough.

Your industry possesses the most powerful voice in America. It has an inescapable duty to make that voice ring with intelligence and with leadership. In a few years, this exciting industry has grown from a novelty to an instrument of overwhelming impact on the American people. It should be making ready for the kind of leadership that newspapers and magazines assumed years ago, to make our people aware of their world.

Ours has been called the jet age, the atomic age, the space age. It is also, I submit, the television age. And just as history will decide whether the leaders of today's world employed the **atom** to destroy the world or rebuild it for mankind's benefit, so will history decide whether today's broadcasters employed their powerful voice to enrich the people or **debase** them.

If I seem today to address myself chiefly to the problems of television, I don't want any of you radio broadcasters to think we've **gone to sleep at your switch**—we haven't. We still listen. But in recent years most of the controversies and cross-currents in broadcast programming have swirled around television. And so my subject today is the television industry and the public interest.

Like everybody, I wear more than one hat. I am the chairman of the FCC. I am also a television viewer and the husband and father of other television viewers. I have seen a great many television programs that seemed to me eminently worthwhile and I am not talking about the much bemoaned good old days of *Playhouse 90* and *Studio One*.

I am talking about this past season. Some were wonderfully entertaining, such as *The Fabulous Fifties*, *The Fred Astaire Show*, and *The Bing*

Governor LeRoy Collins: (1909–1991) Former governor of Florida and president of the National Association of Broadcasters (NAB) from 1961 to 1964.

Conscience: An inner sense of right and wrong.

Gross National Product: The total value of goods and services produced by a country in a year.

Laos: A country in southeast Asia that experienced a civil war during the 1960s.

Congo: A country in central Africa that experienced a civil war during the 1960s.

Communist tyranny: A reference to Fidel Castro, a Communist dictator who came to power in Cuba in 1959.

Caribbean doorstep: A reference to Cuba, located 90 miles from the southern tip of Florida in the Caribbean Sea.

Atlantic alliance: The North Atlantic Treaty Organization (NATO), a group of nations that pledged to defend one another.

Peril: Danger.

Atom: A unit of matter that provides the source of nuclear weapons and nuclear energy.

Debase: Destroy the character or value of.

Gone to sleep at your switch: Stopped paying attention.

Newton N. Minow

Playhouse 90 and Studio One: Minow is referring to two high-quality programs from the 1950s.

Crosby Special; some were dramatic and moving, such as [novelist Joseph] Conrad's *Victory* and *Twilight Zone*; some were marvelously informative, such as *The Nation's Future, CBS Reports,* and *The Valiant Years.* I could list many more—programs that I am sure everyone here felt enriched his own life and that of his family. When television is good, nothing—not the theater, not the magazines or newspapers—nothing is better.

But when television is bad, nothing is worse. I invite you to sit down in front of your television set when your station goes on the air and stay there without a book, magazine, newspaper, profit and loss sheet or rating book to distract you—and keep your eyes glued to that set until the station signs off. I can assure you that you will observe a vast **wasteland.**

Wasteland: A space that is desolate and spiritually barren or empty.

You will see a procession of game shows, violence, audience participation shows, formula comedies about totally unbelievable families, blood and thunder, mayhem, violence, sadism, murder, western bad men, western good men, private eyes, gangsters, more violence, and cartoons. And, endlessly, commercials—many screaming, cajoling, and offending. And most of all, boredom. True, you will see a few things you will enjoy. But they will be very, very few. And if you think I exaggerate, try it.

Is there one person in this room who claims that broadcasting can't do better?

Well, a glance at next season's proposed programming can give us little heart. Of 73 and 1/2 hours of prime evening time, the networks have tentatively scheduled 59 hours to categories of action-adventure, situation comedy, variety, quiz, and movies.

Is there one network president in this room who claims he can't do better?

Well, is there at least one network president who believes that the other networks can't do better?

Trust accounting with your beneficiaries: Minow is telling broadcasters that he feels they need to justify their programming decisions to TV viewers.

Gentlemen, your **trust accounting with your beneficiaries** is overdue.

Never have so few owed so much to so many.

Why is so much of television so bad? I have heard many answers: demands of your advertisers; competition for ever higher ratings; the need always to attract a mass audience; the high cost of television programs; the insatiable appetite for programming material—these are some of them. Unquestionably, these are tough problems not susceptible to easy answers.

But I am not convinced that you have tried hard enough to solve them.

I do not accept the idea that the present overall programming is aimed accurately at the public taste. The ratings tell us only that some people have their television sets turned on and of that number, so many are tuned to one channel and so many to another. They don't tell us what the public might watch if they were offered half-a-dozen additional choices. A rating, at best, is an indication of how many people saw what you gave them. Unfortunately, it does not reveal the depth of the penetration, or the intensity of reaction, and it never reveals what the acceptance would have been if what you gave them had been better—if all the forces of art and creativity and daring and imagination had been unleashed. I believe in the people's good sense and good taste, and I am not convinced that the people's taste is as low as some of you assume.

My concern with the rating services is not with their accuracy. Perhaps they are accurate. I really don't know. What, then, is wrong with the ratings? It's not been their accuracy—it's been their use.

Certainly, I hope you will agree that ratings should have little influence where children are concerned. The best estimates indicate that during the hours of 5 to 6 P.M. sixty percent of your audience is composed of children under twelve. And most young children today, believe it or not, spend as much time watching television as they do in the schoolroom. I repeat—let that sink in—most young children today spend as much time watching television as they do in the schoolroom. It used to be said that there were three great influences on a child: home, school, and church. Today, there is a fourth great influence, and you ladies and gentlemen control it.

If parents, teachers, and ministers conducted their responsibilities by following the ratings, children would have a steady diet of ice cream, school holidays, and no Sunday school. What about your responsibilities? Is there no room on television to teach, to inform, to uplift, to stretch, to enlarge the **capacities** of our children? Is there no room for programs deepening their understanding of children in other lands? Is there no room for a children's news show explaining something about the world to them at their level of understanding? Is there no room for reading the great literature of the past, teaching them the great traditions of freedom? There are some fine children's shows, but they are drowned out in the massive doses of cartoons, violence, and more violence. Must these be your trademarks? Search your consciences and see if you cannot offer more to your young beneficiaries whose future you guide so many hours each and every day.

What about adult programming and ratings? You know, newspaper publishers take popularity ratings too. The answers are pretty clear: it is almost always the comics, followed by the advice to the lovelorn columns. But, ladies and gentlemen, the news is still on the front page of all newspapers; the editorials are not replaced by more comics; the newspapers have not become one long collection of advice to the lovelorn. Yet newspapers do not need a license from the government to be in business—they do not use **public property.** But in television, where your responsibilities as

Capacities: Knowledge or ability to learn.

Public property: Referring to the airwaves, which are owned by the public.

Coaxial cable: A type of high-speed wire used to carry television signals since the birth of television in the 1930s.

public trustees are so plain, the moment that the ratings indicate that westerns are popular there are new imitations of westerns on the air faster than the old **coaxial cable** could take us from Hollywood to New York. Broadcasting cannot continue to live by the numbers. Ratings ought to be the slave of the broadcaster, not his master. And you and I both know that the rating services themselves would agree.

Let me make clear that what I am talking about is balance. I believe that the public interest is made up of many interests. There are many people in this great country and you must serve all of us. You will get no argument from me if you say that, given a choice between a western and a symphony, more people will watch the western. I like westerns and private eyes too, but a steady diet for the whole country is obviously not in the public interest. We all know that people would more often prefer to be entertained than stimulated or informed. But your obligations are not satisfied if you look only to popularity as a test of what to broadcast. You are not only in show business; you are free to communicate ideas as well as relaxation. You must provide a wider range of choices, more diversity, more alternatives. It is not enough to cater to the nation's whims; you must also serve the nation's needs.

Persist: Continue despite warnings.

Lowest common denominator: A decline in quality that results from producing television shows that can be understood by the simplest or least educated audience.

And I would add this: that if some of you **persist** in a relentless search for the highest rating and the **lowest common denominator**, you may very well lose your audience. Because, to paraphrase a great American who was recently my law partner [former Illinois governor and presidential candidate Adlai Stevenson], the people are wise, wiser than some of the broadcasters—and politicians—think.

Intervention: Action or involvement.

As you may have gathered, I would like to see television improved. But how is this to be brought about? By voluntary action by the broadcasters themselves? By direct government **intervention**? Or how?

Let me address myself now to my role not as a viewer but as chairman of the FCC. I could not if I would, chart for you this afternoon in detail all of the actions I contemplate. Instead, I want to make clear some of the fundamental principles which guide me.

First: the people own the air. They own it as much in prime evening time as they do at six o'clock Sunday morning. For every hour that the people give you—you owe them something. I intend to see that your debt is paid with service.

Payola: Bribery.

Rehashing the cliches: Going over old mistakes again and again.

Second: I think it would be foolish and wasteful for us to continue any worn-out wrangle over the problems of **payola**, rigged quiz shows, and other mistakes of the past. There are laws on the books which we will enforce. But there is no chip on my shoulder. We live together in perilous, uncertain times; we face together staggering problems; and we must not waste much time now by **rehashing the cliches** of past controversy.

To quarrel over the past is to lose the future.

Third: I believe in the **free enterprise system** system. I want to see broadcasting improved, and I want you to do the job. I am proud to champion your cause. It is not rare for American businessmen to serve a public trust. Yours is a special trust because it is imposed by law.

Fourth: I will do all I can to help educational television. There are still not enough educational stations, and major centers of the country still lack usable educational channels. If there were a limited number of printing presses in this country, you may be sure that a fair proportion of them would be put to educational use. Educational television has an enormous contribution to make to the future, and I intend to give it a hand along the way. If there is not a nationwide educational television system in this country, it will not be the fault of the FCC.

Fifth: I am unalterably opposed to governmental censorship. There will be no **suppression** of programming which does not meet with **bureaucratic** tastes. Censorship strikes at the **taproot** of our free society.

Sixth: I did not come to Washington to idly observe the **squandering** of the public's airwaves. The squandering of our airwaves is no less important than the lavish waste of any precious natural resource. I intend to take the job of chairman of the FCC very seriously. I believe in the **gravity** of my own particular sector of the New Frontier. There will be times perhaps when you will consider that I take myself or my job *too* seriously. Frankly, I don't care if you do. For I am convinced that either one takes this job seriously—or one can be seriously taken.

Now, how will these principles be applied? Clearly, at the heart of the FCC's authority lies its power to license, to renew or fail to renew, or to **revoke** a license. As you know, when your license comes up for renewal, your performance is compared with your promises. I understand that many people feel that in the past licenses were often renewed **pro forma**. I say to you now: renewal will not be pro forma in the future. There is nothing permanent or sacred about a broadcast license....

There is your challenge to leadership. You must reexamine some fundamentals of your industry. You must open your minds and open your hearts to the limitless horizons of tomorrow.

I can suggest some words that should serve to guide you:

Television and all who participate in it are jointly accountable to the American public for respect for the special needs of children, for community responsibility, for the advancement of education and culture, for the acceptability of the program materials chosen, for decency and **decorum** in production, and for **propriety** in advertising. This responsibility cannot be discharged by any given group of programs, but can be discharged only through the highest standards of respect for the American home,

Free enterprise system: An economic system in which private businesses compete for profits with little government interference.

Suppression: Strict control or limits.

Bureaucratic: Official government rules.

Taproot: Base or foundation.

Squandering: Wasting.

Gravity: Serious significance.

Revoke: Take away.

Pro forma: Routinely; automatically.

Decorum: Standards of polite behavior.

Propriety: Appropriateness.

applied to every moment of every program presented by television. Program materials should enlarge the horizons of the viewer, provide him with wholesome entertainment, afford helpful stimulation, and remind him of the responsibilities which the citizen has towards his society.

These words are not mine. They are yours. They are taken literally from your own **Television Code**. They reflect the leadership and aspirations of your own great industry. I urge you to respect them as I do. And I urge you to respect the intelligent and farsighted leadership of Governor LeRoy Collins, and to make this meeting a creative act. I urge you at this meeting and, after you leave, back home, at your stations and your networks, to strive **ceaselessly** to improve your product and to better serve your viewers, the American people.

I hope that we at the FCC will not allow ourselves to become so bogged down in the mountain of papers, hearings, memoranda, orders, and the daily routine that we close our eyes to the wider view of the public interest. And I hope that you broadcasters will not permit yourselves to become so absorbed in the chase for ratings, sales, and profits that you lose this wider view. Now more than ever before in broadcasting's history the times demand the best of all of us.

We need imagination in programming, not **sterility**; creativity, not imitation; experimentation, not conformity; excellence, not mediocrity. Television is filled with creative, imaginative people. You must strive to set them free.

Television in its young life has had many hours of greatness—its *Victory at Sea*, its **Army–McCarthy hearings**, its *Peter Pan*, its *Kraft Theaters*, its *See It Now*, its *Project 20*, the World Series, its political conventions and campaigns, the Great Debates—and it has had its endless hours of mediocrity and its moments of public disgrace. There are estimates that today the average viewer spends about 200 minutes daily with television, while the average reader spends 38 minutes with magazines and 40 minutes with newspapers. Television has grown faster than a teenager, and now it is time to grow up.

What you gentlemen broadcast through the people's air affects the people's taste, their knowledge, their opinions, their understanding of themselves and of their world. And their future.

The power of instantaneous sight and sound is without **precedent** in mankind's history. This is an awesome power. It has limitless capabilities for good—and for evil. And it carries with it awesome responsibilities, responsibilities which you and I cannot escape.

In his stirring inaugural address our President [John F. Kennedy] said, "And so, my fellow Americans: ask not what your country can do for you; ask what you can do for your country."

Television Code: Rules of conduct for members of the National Association of Broadcasters.

Ceaselessly: Continuously, without stopping.

Sterility: Lifelessness; plainness.

Army–McCarthy hearings: A 1954 Congressional inquiry into the behavior of anti-communist senator Joseph McCarthy.

Precedent: An earlier, similar case.

Ladies and Gentlemen:

Ask not what broadcasting can do for you. Ask what you can do for broadcasting.

I urge you to put the people's airwaves to the service of the people and the cause of freedom. You must help prepare a generation for great decisions. You must help a great nation fulfill its future.

Do this, and I pledge you our help.

• • •

What happened next...

For the most part, people in the audience at the National Association of Broadcasters convention did not like Minow's speech. They were hurt by his criticism of the quality of TV programming, and they worried that the FCC under Minow would enact new regulations to force broadcasters to serve the "public interest." Minow's speech was widely quoted and reprinted, though, and it got a better reception outside the NAB. To his dismay, however, much of the media coverage focused on the fact that the head of the FCC had dared to describe American television programming as a "vast wasteland." Many people seemed to miss his main point—that television should work harder to educate and inform viewers.

During his two years as head of the FCC, Minow continued to give speeches and interviews about television's responsibility to serve the public interest. His tough stance toward broadcasters launched a national debate about the direction of television and the role of the FCC. It also made him one of the most controversial figures ever to serve in that position. In fact, some historians claim that the outspoken Minow received more press coverage in the early 1960s than any public figure besides President Kennedy.

Despite all this attention, however, Minow's efforts to make positive changes met with stiff opposition from the powerful broadcasting industry. As a result, his FCC never imposed specific guidelines for program content on the networks. But some analysts claim that the quality of television programming improved during Minow's tenure anyway, simply because the networks knew that he was keeping an eye on them. For example, all three networks increased their news and information programming during this time.

The major accomplishment of Minow's term as FCC chairman was securing passage of the All-Channel Receiver Act of 1962. This legislation required all TV sets sold in the United States to be equipped with tuners capable of receiving ultra-high-frequency (UHF) channels. Before this time, most TV sets only received the stronger very-high-frequency (VHF) channels, and viewers had to purchase a separate tuner if they wanted to watch UHF channels. Since the three major broadcast networks and their affiliate stations controlled most of the available VHF channels across the United States, increasing public access to UHF gave viewers more options. UHF channels tended to feature more local and regional programming than VHF, and many UHF stations aired high-quality cultural and educational programming from the newly formed Public Broadcasting Service (PBS).

President Kennedy was assassinated in November 1963. A short time later, Newton N. Minow resigned from his position as chairman of the FCC and returned to private law practice in the field of communications. He remained influential in the broadcasting industry by serving on the PBS board of governors, teaching communications at Northwestern University, giving speeches, and writing books.

Did you know . . .

- Shortly after making his "Wasteland Speech," Newton N. Minow received a supportive telephone call from veteran journalist **Edward R. Murrow** (1908–1965; see Chapter 5). Murrow started his career as a CBS Radio reporter, then moved into television as the host of a hard-hitting news program called *See It Now*. In 1958, Murrow had made a similar speech criticizing the state of television news reporting. According to Minow's book *Abandoned in the Wasteland*, Murrow raised Minow's spirits by saying, "Good for you—you'll get a lot of heat and criticism, but don't lose your courage."

- The 1960s television situation comedy *Gilligan's Island*, about a group of castaways shipwrecked on a deserted island, featured a veiled reference to FCC chairman Newton N. Minow. The program's producers disagreed with Minow's assessment of the quality of television programming. To express their view, they named the doomed ship on the show the *S.S. Minnow* after him.

- On May 9, 1991—the thirtieth anniversary of his famous "Wasteland Speech"—Newton N. Minow gave an updated speech called "How Vast the Wasteland Now" at the Freedom Forum Media Studies Center, Columbia University. He expressed some disappointment about how his earlier talk has been remembered. "The two words I wanted people to remember from that speech were not 'vast wasteland,'" he noted. "The two words I cared about were 'public interest.'" Minow also told listeners that he believes the quality of TV programming has grown worse, rather than better, over time. "In 1961 I worried that my children would not benefit much from television," he stated, "but in 1991 I worry that my grandchildren will actually be harmed by it."

Consider the following...

- After reading Minow's speech, describe what you think he meant by the term "public interest." How has the meaning of the term changed over time? How would you define it today?

- How much responsibility do you think modern television networks have to serve the public interest? What role should the FCC play in ensuring that broadcasters meet this responsibility? What if "public interest" programming is not what most TV viewers want to watch?

- Make a list of the ways you think television serves the public interest. Make a second list of the ways you think TV programming is harmful to the public interest.

- The most-quoted phrase from Minow's 1961 address to the NAB is his criticism of TV programming as a "vast wasteland." Do you think the quality of television programming has improved or grown worse over time? Give examples to support your answer.

- Minow's famous speech was included on several lists of the best American speeches of the twentieth century. Considering your answers to the preceding questions, do you think the speech was a success or a failure?

For More Information

BOOKS

Hilliard, Robert L., and Michael C. Keith. *The Broadcast Century: A Biography of American Broadcasting.* Boston: Focal Press, 1992.

Minow, Newton N. *Abandoned in the Wasteland: Children, Television, and the First Amendment.* New York: Hill and Wang, 1995.

PERIODICALS

Landay, Jerry M. "Thoughts from Another Newt on Free Speech." *Christian Science Monitor,* September 5, 1995.

"Vast Wasteland Speech Revisited." *Federal Communications Law Journal* (special issue), May 2003.

WEB SITES

Curtin, Michael. "Newton Minow." *Museum of Broadcast Communications.* http://www.museum.tv/archives/etv/M/htmlM/minownewton/minownewton.htm (accessed on July 27, 2006).

8

Lyndon B. Johnson

Excerpt of "Remarks of Lyndon B. Johnson upon Signing the Public Broadcasting Act of 1967,"
delivered November 7, 1967

Available online at Corporation for Public Broadcasting, *http://www.cpb.org/aboutpb/act/remarks.html*

> "The Corporation [for Public Broadcasting] will assist stations and producers who aim for the best in broadcasting good music, in broadcasting exciting plays, and in broadcasting reports on the whole fascinating range of human activity. It will try to prove that what educates can also be exciting."

In the early days of television, many people believed that the new technology could become a valuable tool for informing and educating the American people. The first laws affecting the television industry tried to make sure that TV lived up to this potential. The Communications Act of 1934, for example, stated that the airwaves used for transmitting TV signals belonged to the American people. Since television broadcasters used the public airwaves to distribute their programs, they had a duty to create programs that served the public interest.

When commercial television broadcasting began in the 1940s, however, a combination of factors allowed three major networks (ABC, CBS, and NBC) to gain control of the airwaves. As the popularity of television increased rapidly during the 1950s, these networks competed fiercely to create shows that would attract high ratings. The more viewers that tuned into a given show, the higher the show would place in the weekly TV ratings, and the more money the network could charge advertisers to air commercials during that show. Advertising dollars provided a major source of funding for the networks, allowing them to stay in business and continue producing programs. By the end of the decade, critics were beginning to complain that the networks served their own interests rather than the public interest, and often sacrificed quality in their quest for high ratings and big advertising money.

TV evolves under Kennedy and Johnson

In 1960, Democrat **John F. Kennedy** (1917–1963; served 1961–63; see Chapter 6) was elected president of the United States. Kennedy was one of the first political figures to understand and take advantage of the power of television. In fact, his strong performance in the first-ever televised presidential debate was believed to be a deciding factor in his election victory over Republican candidate Richard M. Nixon. Shortly after taking office in 1961, Kennedy appointed **Newton Minow** (1926–; see Chapter 7) as chairman of the Federal Communications Commission (FCC), the U.S. government agency responsible for regulating television. Minow outlined his views about the television industry in a famous 1961 speech before the National Association of Broadcasters, called "Television and the Public Interest." In this speech, which is excerpted in this volume, Minow sharply criticized the content of television programming as a "vast wasteland" and encouraged broadcasters to work harder to meet their obligation to inform and educate the American people. Many people believed that the Kennedy administration would challenge the television networks to improve the quality of programming.

In November 1963, Kennedy was shot and killed while riding in the back of an open car in Dallas, Texas. Two hours later, Vice President Lyndon Baines Johnson (1908–1973; served 1963–68) took the oath of office to become the thirty-sixth president of the United States. Johnson was born on August 27, 1908, in Stonewall, Texas. The son and grandson of men who had served in the Texas legislature, he was a born politician. Johnson attended Southwest Texas State Teachers' College and worked as a high-school teacher for several years. In 1931, he moved to Washington, D.C., to serve as an assistant to a newly elected U.S. congressman from Texas.

Once he got a glimpse of the inner workings of government, Johnson became determined to run for office himself. In 1937, he was elected to fill the seat of a Texas congressman who died, and he won reelection to the U.S. House of Representatives in 1938 and 1940. Although he was defeated in a race for the U.S. Senate in 1941, he won the seat in 1948. Johnson was a master of the legislative process and moved up quickly through the ranks of the Senate to become majority leader (highest-ranking member of the political party holding the most seats) in 1955. Johnson considered running for president in 1960, but he believed he would lose

The Public Broadcasting Act of 1967

In the introduction to the Public Broadcasting Act of 1967—which President Lyndon Johnson signed into law on November 7, 1967—legislators explain the purpose of the bill:

> The Congress hereby finds that—it is in the public interest to encourage the growth and development of public radio and television broadcasting, including the use of such media for instructional, educational, and cultural purposes; ... it furthers the general welfare to encourage public telecommunications services which will be responsive to the interests of people both in particular localities and throughout the United States, which will constitute [provide] an expression of diversity and excellence, and which will constitute a source of alternative telecommunications services for all citizens of the nation; it is in the public interest to encourage the development of programming that involves creative risks and that addresses the needs of unserved and underserved audiences, particularly children and minorities; [and] it is necessary and appropriate for the Federal Government to complement, assist, and support a national policy that will most effectively make public telecommunications services available to all citizens of the United States.

the Democratic nomination to the more popular Kennedy. Once Kennedy became the presidential candidate, however, Johnson agreed to serve as his vice presidential running mate.

After Kennedy was assassinated, Johnson emerged as a skillful leader who was determined to fulfill Kennedy's vision for the future. Johnson supported the civil rights movement, in which millions of African Americans participated in marches and protests to end segregation (the forced separation of people by race) and gain equal rights and opportunities in American society. He also introduced programs designed to improve education, eliminate poverty, and help senior citizens. Thanks to the success of his ambitious programs, Johnson was reelected president in 1964 by one of the largest margins in history.

The Public Broadcasting Act of 1967

Although Minow had stepped down as head of the FCC following Kennedy's assassination, Johnson continued to press for improvements in the quality of television programming. In 1967, the U.S. Congress responded by passing the Public Broadcasting Act. This law established the Corporation for Public Broadcasting (CPB), a private, nonprofit corporation intended to promote and provide funding for public television and radio

The children' program Sesame Street *debuted on PBS in 1970 and continued to educate and entertain young fans into the 2000s.* BILL PIERCE/TIME LIFE PICTURES/GETTY IMAGES.

services. The act also provided $38 million to build new educational television and radio facilities, and set aside additional funds to conduct a study of educational broadcasting.

After Congress passed the Public Broadcasting Act of 1967, President Johnson signed the bill into law. The signing took place on November 7 in a special ceremony at the White House, and Johnson gave a speech to mark the occasion. In his remarks, which are excerpted below, Johnson expresses his hope that public broadcasting will improve the quality of television programming and enrich the lives of American viewers.

Things to remember while reading the excerpt of "Remarks of President Lyndon B. Johnson upon Signing the Public Broadcasting Act of 1967":

- In his remarks, Johnson talks about some of the "miracles" of communication technology. He mentions that telephone and telegraph signals were being sent around the world using cables beneath the ocean and satellites above Earth. In addition, the majority of television programs were being broadcast in color rather than black and white for the first time. The president believes that the next challenge facing the U.S. government and the American people is to figure out how to best use these new technologies to improve people's lives.

- The president presents a forward-thinking view of the future of communication technology. He proposes using radio, television, computer, and satellite technologies to "build a great network for knowledge" that connects people around the world to educational resources. Although Johnson would not live to see it (he died in 1973), the network he describes is very similar to the modern Internet.

- The Public Broadcasting Act of 1967 established the Corporation for Public Broadcasting (CPB) to provide funding for public television and radio services. The CPB is not a government agency, but a private, independent enterprise that receives funding from the federal government. The act specifically made the CPB a separate, nonprofit organization so that it would not be influenced by political pressures. Of the nine-person board of directors appointed by the president, only five were allowed to be from the same political party. Johnson says that he intends to choose highly qualified individuals to serve as CPB directors to ensure that public broadcasting reaches its full potential.

• • •

Excerpt of "Remarks of Lyndon B. Johnson upon Signing the Public Broadcasting Act of 1967"

It was in 1844 that Congress authorized $30,000 for the first telegraph line between Washington and Baltimore. Soon afterward, **Samuel Morse** sent a stream of dots and dashes over that line to a friend who was waiting. His message was brief and **prophetic** and it read: "**What hath God wrought**?"

Samuel Morse: (1791–1872) Inventor of the telegraph and the system of Morse code used to send telegraph messages.

Prophetic: An accurate prediction of the future.

What hath God wrought: A Bible verse (Numbers 23:23) meaning, "Look what God has made."

Lyndon B. Johnson

Morality: Standards of good behavior.

Every one of us should feel the same awe and wonderment here today.

For today, miracles in communication are our daily routine. Every minute, billions of telegraph messages chatter around the world. They interrupt law enforcement conferences and discussions of **morality**. Billions of signals rush over the ocean floor and fly above the clouds. Radio and television fill the air with sound. Satellites hurl messages thousands of miles in a matter of seconds.

Ponder: Think about or consider.

Today our problem is not making miracles—but managing miracles. We might well **ponder** a different question: What hath man wrought—and how will man use his inventions?

The law that I will sign shortly offers one answer to that question.

Chicken in every pot: Food to meet all people's basic needs.

It announces to the world that our Nation wants more than just material wealth; our Nation wants more than a "**chicken in every pot**." We in America have an appetite for excellence, too.

While we work every day to produce new goods and to create new wealth, we want most of all to enrich man's spirit.

That is the purpose of this act.

It will give a wider and, I think, stronger voice to educational radio and television by providing new funds for broadcast facilities.

It will launch a major study of television's use in the Nation's classrooms and their potential use throughout the world.

Finally—and most important—it builds a new institution: the Corporation for Public Broadcasting.

The Corporation will assist stations and producers who aim for the best in broadcasting good music, in broadcasting exciting plays, and in broadcasting reports on the whole fascinating range of human activity. It will try to prove that what educates can also be exciting.

It will get part of its support from our Government. But it will be carefully guarded from Government or from [political] party control. It will be free, and it will be independent—and it will belong to all of our people.

Television is still a young invention. But we have learned already that it has immense—even revolutionary—power to change, to change our lives.

Trivial: Minor; not important.

I hope that those who lead the Corporation will direct that power toward the great and not the **trivial** purposes.

Replica: Copy.

At its best, public television would help make our Nation a **replica** of the old Greek marketplace, where public affairs took place in view of all the citizens.

But in weak or even in irresponsible hands, it could generate controversy without understanding; it could mislead as well as teach; it could appeal to passions rather than to reason.

If public television is to fulfill our hopes, then the Corporation must be representative [of all citizens' viewpoints], it must be responsible—and it must be long on **enlightened** leadership.

I intend to search this Nation to find men that I can nominate, men and women of outstanding ability, to this board of directors. . . .

What hath man wrought? And how will man use his miracles?

The answer just begins with public broadcasting.

In 1862, the **Morrill Act** set aside lands in every State—lands which belonged to the people—and it set them aside in order to build the land-grant colleges of the Nation.

So today we **rededicate** a part of the airwaves—which belong to all the people—and we dedicate them for the enlightenment of all the people.

I believe the time has come to stake another claim in the name of all the people, **stake a claim** based upon the combined resources of communications. I believe the time has come to **enlist** the computer and the satellite, as well as television and radio, and to enlist them in the cause of education.

If we are up to the obligations of the next century and if we are to be proud of the next century as we are of the past two centuries, we have got to quit talking so much about what has happened in the past two centuries and start talking about what is going to happen in the next century beginning in **1976**.

So I think we must consider new ways to build a great network for knowledge—not just a broadcast system, but one that employs every means of sending and storing information that the individual can use.

Think of the lives that this would change:

- the student in a small college could tap the resources of a great university. . . .
- The country doctor getting help from a distant laboratory or a teaching hospital;
- a scholar in Atlanta might draw instantly on a library in New York;
- a famous teacher could reach with ideas and inspirations into some far-off classroom, so that no child need be neglected.

Eventually, I think this electronic knowledge bank could be as valuable as the **Federal Reserve Bank**.

And such a system could involve other nations, too—it could involve them in a partnership to share knowledge and to thus enrich all mankind.

A wild and visionary idea? Not at all. Yesterday's strangest dreams are today's headlines and change is getting swifter every moment.

I have already asked my advisers to begin to explore the possibility of a network for knowledge—and then to draw up a suggested **blueprint** for it.

Enlightened: Wise and open-minded.

Morrill Act: A law enacted during the Civil War era that granted each state that remained in the Union a certain amount of federal land. The states sold the land in order to raise money to establish a system of 70 "land-grant" colleges.

Rededicate: Set aside or commit for a second time.

Stake a claim: Demand a portion or share.

Enlist: Use or gain the support of.

1976: The nation's bicentennial, or 200th birthday.

Federal Reserve Bank: The central bank of the United States, established by Congress in 1913 to create a more stable monetary system.

Blueprint: Design or map.

Henry Thoreau: (1817–1862) Author and naturalist who promoted a simple way of life.

Skeptical: Doubting or questioning.

In 1844, when **Henry Thoreau** heard about Mr. Morse's telegraph, he made his sour comment about the race for faster communication. "Perchance," he warned, "the first news which will leak through into the broad, flapping American ear will be that Princess Adelaide has the whooping cough."

We do have **skeptical** comments on occasion. But I don't want you to be that skeptic. I do believe that we have important things to say to one another—and we have the wisdom to match our technical genius.

In that spirit this morning, I have asked you to come here and be participants with me in this great movement for the next century, the Public Broadcasting Act of 1967....

• • •

What happened next...

In 1968, Lyndon Johnson announced that he would not seek reelection as president of the United States. But the move toward public broadcasting continued after he left office. In 1969, the CPB established the Public Broadcasting Service (PBS) to create and distribute public television programs. PBS first went on the air in October 1970. It eventually grew to include more than 350 member stations across the United States. Many of these stations operated out of colleges and universities. Instead of selling commercial time to make money, PBS stations received funding from individual viewers, businesses, charities, and the CPB. This arrangement freed the PBS stations from worrying about ratings and thus enabled them to air innovative, high-quality educational and cultural programs that did not attract large enough audiences to interest the commercial broadcast networks.

"Our purpose is not to sell to the public. Our mission and purpose is to serve the public—in Lyndon Johnson's words, to manage miracles for the public good," PBS president Pat Mitchell explained to the *Carnegie Reporter*. "It's not just about using media to sell something or promote something. It's about using the power of our public airwaves to educate, to inform, and to inspire, while giving all of our citizens the opportunity to know more, to achieve more, and be more. There is no better use for the modern miracles of communication than that."

While PBS has developed a number of award-winning programs over the years, it has also created some controversy. Politicians occasionally try to discontinue government funding for PBS, claiming that it should be able to support itself through private donations rather than taxpayer money. Other people argue that PBS should receive more

Mister Roger's Neighborhood, *a TV program for children and their parents, ran on PBS for thirty-one years.* AP IMAGES.

government funding so that it does not have to depend on corporate sponsorships. They claim that corporate sponsors could influence programming choices, which would make PBS move away from educational shows and toward shows with more commercial appeal.

The Public Broadcasting Act of 1967 expired in 1996, although the federal government continued to provide funding for the CPB each year.

In 2004, U.S. senator John McCain of Arizona introduced a bill to reauthorize the act, but it was never put to a vote and did not become law.

Did you know...

- The U.S. government supplies about 15 percent of the total funding for the PBS. In terms of tax dollars, this means that each American citizen pays only about $1 per year to support public television. In contrast, TV viewers in the United Kingdom pay an annual fee of more than $200 per year to support the British Broadcasting Corporation (BBC).

- The total budget for PBS's national program service—which provides funding for member stations to create more than 2,000 hours of programming each year—is about the same as the amount that the premium cable channel HBO spends on advertising for just one of its original series.

- Despite its financial limitations, PBS still manages to reach American television audiences. Surveys show that 70 percent of U.S. households tune in to watch PBS at some point every week. On an average evening, the total audience for PBS member stations is twice as large as the national audience for the top-rated cable channel.

Consider the following...

- After reading Johnson's speech, do you think that public broadcasting in the United States has lived up to his expectations? Explain why or why not.

- In many ways, the Public Broadcasting Act of 1967 grew out of FCC chairman Newton Minow's 1961 "Wasteland Speech," in which he challenged the broadcast industry to improve the quality of American television. Review the excerpt from Minow's speech in Chapter 7. Do you think that PBS was the solution he had in mind?

- PBS operates as a non-commercial alternative to the traditional broadcast networks. It receives all of its funding from private donations and taxes, so it does not have to worry about earning high ratings, pleasing advertisers, or making a profit. Think about the programs you've watched on PBS. How do they differ from what's available on the commercial networks? Based on your answer, do you think it makes sense to have two separate systems of television in the United States?

For More Information

BOOKS

Barsamian, David. *The Decline and Fall of Public Broadcasting: Creating Alternative Media.* Cambridge, MA: South End Press, 2001.

Ledbetter, James. *Made Possible By: The Death of Public Broadcasting in the United States.* New York and London: Verso, 1998.

McCauley, Michael P., ed. *Public Broadcasting and the Public Interest: Media, Communication, and Culture in America.* Armonk, NY: M. E. Sharpe, 2003.

Witherspoon, John, et al. *History of Public Broadcasting,* revised edition. Takoma Park, MD: Current, 2000.

PERIODICALS

McGraw, Dan. "Is PBS Too Commercial?" *U.S. News and World Report,* June 15, 1998.

Mitchell, Pat. "The Digital Future Initiative: PBS Envisions Tomorrow." *Carnegie Reporter,* Fall 2005.

WEB SITES

"American Experience: The Presidents." *PBS.* http://www.pbs.org/wgbh/amex/presidents/36_l_johnson/index.html (accessed on July 27, 2006).

Aufderheide, Patricia. "Public Television." *Museum of Broadcast Communications.* http://www.museum.tv/archives/etv/P/htmlP/publictelevi/publictelevi.htm (accessed on July 27, 2006).

"Investing in Public TV." *Public Radio Exchange,* July 22, 2004. http://about.prx.org/archives/000047.php (accessed on July 27, 2006).

Johnson, Lyndon B. "Remarks of Lyndon B. Johnson upon Signing the Public Broadcasting Act of 1967." *Corporation for Public Broadcasting,* http://www.cpb.org/aboutpb/act/remarks.html (accessed on July 27, 2006).

9

Vladimir Zworykin

Excerpt of an interview with Vladimir Zworykin

Conducted by Mark Heyer and Al Pinsky, IEEE History Center, Rutgers University, New Brunswick,
New Jersey, July 4, 1975
Available online at http://www.ieee.org/web/aboutus/history_center/oral_history/abstracts/zworykinab.html

"Of course the picture was very primitive," Zworykin recalled of the first demonstration of his electronic television system in the 1920s. "We were able to transmit some geometric figures and move them before the photographic camera and receive them on the Kinescope."

Electrical engineer Vladimir Zworykin is one of the most important figures in the creation and development of television technology. During his twenty-five years as the director of television research at the Radio Corporation of America (RCA), he helped make the television industry a reality in the United States.

Zworykin was born in Russia in 1889. He first became interested in television as a student at the St. Petersburg Institute of Technology in Russia during the 1910s. Zworykin served as an assistant to Professor Boris Rosing, a respected physicist (a scientist who studies the behavior of energy and matter). At this time, scientists around the world were just beginning to develop systems for transmitting live, moving pictures across a distance. Like most other researchers working on the problem in these early years, Rosing and Zworykin developed a mechanical television transmitter. Mechanical TV systems used spinning metal disks with holes in them to continuously measure the amount of light reflected off a moving image. The holes sent electrical signals, which varied in strength depending on the amount of light hitting them, across a wire to a similar device at the other end. The second device reversed the

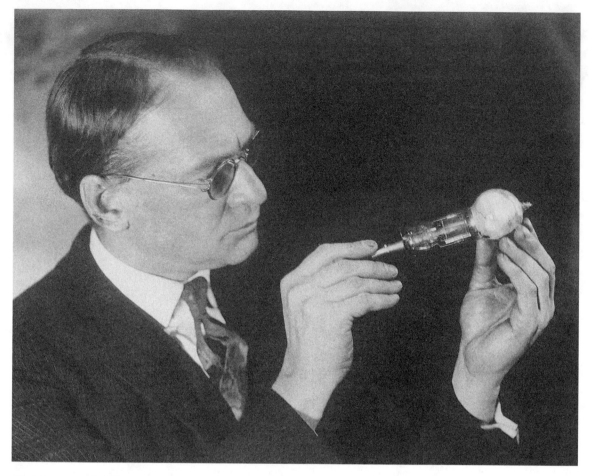

Vladimir Zworykin holds an early version of his invention, the Iconoscope. © BETTMANN/CORBIS.

process and turned the electrical signals back into light, creating a crude representation of the moving image at the other end of the wire.

Rosing was one of the first researchers to develop an electronic device (one that had no moving parts, and instead worked entirely by using the properties of electricity) called a cathode ray tube to receive and display television signals. A cathode is a filament inside a sealed glass tube, sort of like those found in lightbulbs. When the filament is heated, it forms a vacuum, or an empty space that does not contain any matter. A cathode ray is a stream of electrons that pours off the cathode into the vacuum. Rosing and Zworykin used electrical circuits to focus these electrons into a beam and shoot them toward a flat screen at one end of the tube. The inside of the screen was coated in phosphor, a substance that emits light, or glows, when struck by a beam of radiation.

After studying X-ray technology with physicist Paul Langevin in Paris, Zworykin moved to the United States in 1919. He took a job as a researcher with the Westinghouse Electric Corporation in Pittsburgh, Pennsylvania. Over the next several years, he helped develop radio technology and worked on ways to improve the light sensitivity and electrical output of photoelectric cells. Zworykin also worked toward a doctoral degree in electrical engineexring at the University of Pittsburgh during this time, receiving his Ph.D. in 1926.

Inventing the Iconoscope and Kinescope

Around 1923, Zworykin created an all-electronic television camera tube he called the Iconoscope. The Iconoscope worked by reflecting the light from a moving image onto a special plate. This plate was coated with tiny dots, or pixels, of a chemical that was sensitive to light. When the light swept across the pixels, they would become electrically charged. The charge varied in strength depending on the amount of light that hit each pixel. In this way, Zworykin's Iconoscope television camera converted a visual image into an electrical signal without the need for the spinning wheels used in mechanical television systems.

Zworykin demonstrated an early version of the Iconoscope for his bosses at Westinghouse. They were not impressed with the small, hazy image the camera supposedly created, however, and suggested that he find a more practical topic for his research. But Zworykin continued pursuing his interest in television, even if he had to conduct experiments in the laboratory at night or on weekends.

In 1928 Zworykin invented an improved version of the cathode ray television picture tube he called the Kinescope. He successfully used this device to receive and display the TV signals from his Iconoscope camera. One of the people who heard about Zworykin's television research was **David Sarnoff** (1891–1971; see Chapter 1), an ambitious businessman who had recently become the acting president of RCA. RCA was the leading producer of radios in the United States, and Sarnoff was determined to make it a leader in the television industry as well.

Going to work for RCA

In 1929 Sarnoff hired Zworykin as the head of television research at RCA. The following year, the U.S. government awarded a patent (a form of legal protection for an invention) to American inventor Philo T. Farnsworth (1906–1971) for an all-electronic television system.

Who Really Invented Television?

Historians still debate about who should receive the credit for inventing electronic television technology. Although many scientists and researchers made important contributions, the controversy usually comes down to RCA engineer Vladimir Zworykin and independent inventor Philo T. Farnsworth. Zworykin first applied for a patent on his Iconoscope television camera tube in 1923. But the U.S. Patent Office did not grant the patent to Zworykin, because the inspectors decided there was not enough proof that this early camera system ever worked.

In 1930, the agency awarded a patent to Farnsworth for a similar television camera tube called the Image Dissector. Farnsworth had originally come up with the idea in 1920, when he was fourteen years old, and showed detailed drawings of the device to his high school science teacher. He had also conducted a well-documented successful test of his system on September 7, 1927.

Shortly after Farnsworth received his patent, Zworykin visited the young inventor's laboratory and examined his invention. The following year, RCA decided to challenge Farnsworth's patent in court. Although the court finally ruled in favor of Farnsworth and forced RCA to pay one million dollars for the right to use his technology, RCA president David Sarnoff continued to give his engineers full credit for inventing television. Author Paul Schatzkin outlined the ongoing controversy in *The Farnsworth Chronicles*:

> The historical record with regard to "who invented television" remains fuzzy at best, deliberately distorted at worst. The debate often comes down to a simple question: Does any single individual deserve to be remembered as the sole inventor of television? Can we create for television the kind of mythology of individual, creative genius that history has bestowed on [telegraph inventor Samuel] Morse, [electric light inventor Thomas] Edison, [telephone inventor Alexander Graham] Bell, or [airplane inventors] the Wright brothers?
>
> The question may be simple, but clearly the answer is not. Before Uncle Milty [early TV variety show host Milton Berle], before [TV journalist and news anchor] Walter Cronkite, before Lucy and Desi and Ethel and Fred [of the 1950s TV comedy I Love Lucy], literally hundreds of scientists and engineers contributed to the development of the appliance that now

A short time later, Sarnoff sent Zworykin to visit Farnsworth's laboratory and check out his inventions. Farnsworth gladly gave the prominent engineer a tour and let Zworykin examine a model of his television camera, called the Image Dissector.

Following an unsuccessful attempt to buy Farnsworth's invention, Sarnoff decided to challenge Farnsworth's patents in court. RCA filed a lawsuit claiming that Zworykin had invented his electronic television system first. They asked the court to throw out Farnsworth's TV patents and award the rights to the invention to Zworykin instead. The patent battles dominates our "living room dreams." How can we single out any individual and say, "It all started here?"

The historical record is sadly devoid of [lacking] references to Farnsworth. Though the oversight has begun to improve in recent years, it is still entirely possible to open an encyclopedia and read that electronic television began when "Vladimir Zworykin invented the Iconoscope for RCA in 1923".... Some historians have gone so far as to suggest that Farnsworth and Zworykin should be regarded as "co-inventors." But that conclusion ignores Zworykin's 1930 visit to Farnsworth's lab, where many witnesses heard Zworykin say "I wish that I might have invented it." Moreover, it ignores the conclusion of the patent office, in its 1935 decision..., which states quite clearly "priority of invention awarded to Farnsworth." These misinterpretations of the historical record are precisely what more than sixty years of corporate public relations wants us to believe—that television "was too complex to be invented by a single individual"....

That said, there is no question that much credit for refining all aspects of television technology goes to RCA

engineers. There were hundreds, maybe thousands, of individuals who contributed to the development of electronic video before television broadcasting reached the general public in the 1950s, and thousands more who have contributed to its advancement in the decades since. But refinement is not invention, though that is precisely what the proponents of the "co-inventor" theory of the origins of television would like us to accept.

Why is any of this important? Who really cares who invented television? What difference does it make whether electronic television was first developed by a Russian émigré [immigrant] or a Mormon farm boy? And should it still matter seventy years after the fact?

It matters because the suppression [hiding] of the true story deprives us of some important knowledge of the human character. It tempts us to believe that progress is the product of institutions [large organizations like companies, universities, and the government], not individuals. It tempts us to place our faith in those institutions, rather than in ourselves.

between Farnsworth and RCA continued throughout the 1930s. After hearing testimony from Farnsworth's high school science teacher—to whom Farnsworth, at age fourteen, had shown his original drawing of an electronic television system—the U.S. Patent Office concluded that Farnsworth had indeed invented electronic television before Zworykin. For the first time in its history, RCA was forced to pay a fee (called a royalty) for the right to use technology created by an independent inventor.

Despite the fact that RCA lost the patent battle, Zworykin continued making important contributions to the development of television. In the late 1930s he introduced an improved type of television camera called the Image Orthicon. Since this camera was more sensitive than the Iconoscope, television performers were no longer required to work under extremely bright, hot lights. Zworykin retired from active research at RCA in 1954, but he remained with the company as a technical consultant. By the time of his retirement, around 30 million television sets in use across the United States included parts that he had helped develop. Zworykin also began pursuing a new area of interest—medical electronics—at Rockefeller University in New Jersey at this time.

In 1975, Zworykin agreed to be interviewed for the IEEE (Institute of Electrical and Electronics Engineering) Oral History Project. In his talk with interviewers Mark Heyer and Al Pinsky, which is excerpted below, Zworykin discusses his career at Westinghouse and RCA. He recalls his creation of the Iconoscope television camera and the Kinescope television receiver. Zworykin also talks about studying under Boris Rosing and Paul Langevin, which helped give him an early interest in television research. He remembers meeting with David Sarnoff of RCA in 1929, and the first public demonstrations of TV broadcasting a decade later. Finally, Zworykin acknowledges his disappointment with the quality of television programming, and expresses concern about the image of the United States that TV projects to the rest of the world.

Things to remember while reading the excerpt of the interview with Vladimir Zworykin:

- Some of Zworykin's phrasing may seem a bit unusual to modern readers, for a number of reasons. Since he was born in Russia, English was not his first language. In addition, this document is a transcript from an interview, and many people are not able to express their thoughts clearly in that kind of situation. Some of Zworykin's statements include technical terms that may not be familiar to people who are not trained in electrical engineering. Finally, Zworykin was eighty-five years old at the time he gave this interview, and many of the events he mentions took place five decades earlier.

- When Zworykin first began experimenting with television systems, many people questioned the value of his research. Even his bosses at Westinghouse did not see much point in pursuing television

*Vladimir Zworykin with
one of the first facsimile
transmitters, or fax machines,
created at Westinghouse in
1929.* © BETTMANN/CORBIS.

technology. In response to critics who doubted whether television
would ever serve a useful purpose, Zworykin once predicted that
television cameras someday would be used to allow people on
Earth to see the surface of the Moon. The engineer saw his prediction come true in 1969, when American astronaut Neil Armstrong became the first person to walk on the Moon. The
historic event was broadcast live on television, and it was watched
by 130 million people in the United States and 600 million more
around the world.

• • •

Excerpt of the IEEE Vladimir Zworykin interview

Mark Heyer: In the first television work, what were the first problems that you worked on when you came to [RCA laboratories in] Camden [New Jersey]? You started working on television? Were you working on developing a picture tube?

Nipkow disk: A system of spinning metal disks, invented by German scientist Paul G. Nipkow in 1884, that scanned the light reflected by a moving image, turned it into an electrical signals, and transmitted it across a wire.

Pick-up: Scanning system.

Probe: Metal point that makes contact with an electrical circuit.

Aperture: The opening in a lens that allows light to enter.

Kliegs: Bright lamps used in early motion pictures.

Sensitivity in the receiving curve: The device's sensitivity to light.

Mosaic: The tiny particles in a camera tube that convert light into electrical signals.

Optics: Camera lenses.

Amplification: Increase in strength.

Braun tube: An early cathode-ray tube invented by the German scientist Karl Ferdinand Braun in 1897.

Cathode-ray tube: A vacuum tube that shoots a beam of electrons toward a light-sensitive screen.

Vladimir Zworykin: Yes. The first fall [1929], it was to find out why the mechanical television seemed like the **Nipkow disk**, where they were unable to [transmit signals wirelessly through the air] by radio [wave] or by wire. Then we found out an old mechanical **pick-up** was not sufficient because they were transmitting the light only when the **probe**, whatever it is, the **aperture** for instance, was transmitting the light from the point of the image during the time that the system coincided with this point. Since we have to transmit the whole picture thirty times at least per second [to make the human eye perceive it as continuous movement], and divide the picture many hundred thousand times [into points of light or pixels to display on the screen], the light becomes in the millionth of the seconds. Therefore, the signal was very weak and we were unable to transmit a satisfactory picture, even under the **kliegs**, the most powerful light at that time. So, I found out that solution can be done if the time of receiving this pulse [of electricity] is for one-thirtieth of a second instead of one-millionth second and therefore theoretically gain a million times more [strength in the signal] without changing **sensitivity in the receiving curve**. Just the time element [of the equation] changed. For that we constructed at Westinghouse a **mosaic** where the image was focused with regular **optics** like in a movie and the picture information in this mosaic was all in one-thirtieth of a second. It means a theoretical gain by the number of picture elements, of several hundred thousand times. Of course, we never got a complete hundred percent efficiency but you do get tremendous **amplification** and sensitivity. Starting from the first tube constructed when we were at Westinghouse, we were able to start to transmit the picture under normal light, under conditions without artificial light.

Heyer: So that was...?

Zworykin: Then I called this tube the Iconoscope.

Heyer: How was the Kinescope different from the Iconoscope?

Zworykin: The Kinescope of course has its origin in the **Braun tube**. Braun about ten years before us constructed a **cathode-ray tube** for the recording of very fast events by using the **electron beam** and applying to the **deflection** of the electron beam magnetic or **electrostatic** fields. Well, we used a cathode-ray tube and a fluorescent screen with the corresponding **amplitude** of the cathode-ray tube **intensity** in the light, and deflected the beam magnetically or electrostatically by the signals we received from an Iconoscope through the proper **amplifier**. This type of combination of the Iconoscope and receiving tube, we called Kinescope from two Greek words. *Kine* is movement, and *scope* is target. The first demonstration was in the fall or beginning of the winter of 1923 at Westinghouse Research Laboratory.

Heyer: The first demonstration of a complete [television] system?

Zworykin: Yes, of the laboratory **prototype**. Of course the picture was very primitive. We were able to transmit some **geometrical figures** and move them before the photographic camera and receive them on the Kinescope....

Al Pinsky: You might go back a little bit to where you went to school and tell us about Professor **[Boris] Rosing**.

Zworykin: I came to Westinghouse from Russia in 1918. Before that I was in France working with **Paul Langevin**, who is a very well-known **theoretical physicist**, a **Nobel Prize** winner in theoretical physics. Before that I graduated from the Institute of Technology in St. Petersburg [Russia]. When I was there I came under the influence of Professor Boris Rosing, who I consider one of the earlier pioneers of realizing the difficulty with mechanical television and starting to use electronic television. Of course, his system and the system I was helping him with during my spare time from earning my degree was **hybrid**. The transmitter was similar to Nipkow's, by a series of rotating mirrors. But for receiving [TV signals] he used a cathode-ray tube. Since for receiving it is essential to get the light only at the moment when the system coincides with this point of the picture, the picture was very unsatisfactory.

Heyer: Sounds like the **holograms** that I've seen.

Zworykin: Well, it's always [like that] when you start with something.

Heyer: So you were actually working on it as early as the early 1920s?

Zworykin: First I worked with the WD11 tube [an amplifier for radio broadcasting that was his first project at RCA]. From there I went to the transmission of the picture by **facsimile**. From there I went to the development of the more sensitive **photocell**. I have quite a number of patents there. From there I went to the **sound movie** and from sound then to television. That was sometime in 1925. When I came to this country, I didn't find [anyone] very receptive [to the idea of television for a while]....

Heyer: Now tell us about your talk with **David Sarnoff**.

Zworykin: That was in 1929 in connection with this transfer of television [research from Westinghouse to RCA]. I got an invitation to come to New York and talk to Sarnoff and I told him what we can do (of course what we did) and how much we accomplished. This [what follows] has been

Electron beam: A stream of tiny, negatively charged particles.

Deflection: Bouncing or bending in a new direction.

Electrostatic: Static electricity.

Amplitude: Strength.

Intensity: Brightness or force.

Amplifier: A device for increasing the strength of a signal.

Prototype: Model.

Geometrical figures: Basic shapes.

Boris Rosing: (1869–1933) Russian scientist and inventor.

Paul Langevin: (1872–1946) French physicist.

Theoretical physicist: A scientist who comes up with possible explanations for complex problems involving matter and energy.

Nobel Prize: Prestigious annual awards presented to individuals and organizations that make notable contributions in the areas of physics, chemistry, medicine, economics, literature, and world peace.

Hybrid: A combination of two or more different things.

Holograms: Three-dimensional pictures made of light.

Vladimir Zworykin

Facsimile: An exact reproduction sent electronically over a wire or wirelessly using radio waves.

Photocell: An electrical device that is changed through interaction with light.

Sound movie: Theatrical films that included sound (as opposed to silent movies).

David Sarnoff: (1891–1971) Longtime president of the Radio Corporation of America (RCA).

Practical: Work well enough for widespread use.

Novel: New and unusual.

Chronology: Timeline.

mentioned in his speech many times. He asked me how much it would cost to make [television] **practical**. Well, how can you tell? I figured it out and I had three men already working with me. . . . I thought I needed about two more men and two rooms and without knowing much about the financial end, I estimated $100,000. So Sarnoff always says, "See how he cheated me!" because RCA cost $40,000,000 before they got a dollar out of television [chuckling].

Heyer: But when the dollars started coming up they really gained. That was in 1929, right?

Zworykin: Well, in 1930 we first started broadcasting . . . from the City Hall in Camden, and then when we came here in 1941 from [the] Empire State Building [in New York City].

Heyer: I understand David Sarnoff opened the World's Fair in 1939 with a television broadcast.

Zworykin: That was not exactly a broadcast. That was short-wave television. Short-distance television.

Pinsky: Were you there?

Zworykin: Yes. That was in San Francisco and then later on we had a demonstration here in New York.

Heyer: What was the reaction of people that saw these demonstrations?

Zworykin: Well, in the first measure usually someone made a speech and showed equipment.

Heyer: Had people heard about television? Did they have an idea what it was? Was it a big surprise?

Zworykin: Not much. It was very little known of at that time.

Heyer: It was **novel** at that time.

Zworykin: But then as the Second World War started, all the [electronic research] efforts were very concentrated on military applications, including television. . . .

Heyer: Okay, so in our **chronology** here we've gotten up to about the end of the war and the beginning of commercial broadcasting. . . . So what were you working on at RCA after the war?

Zworykin: Mostly, for quite a long time, on television, but in general producing electronic devices for [other purposes]. We developed many things. . . .

Pinsky: I think you were the first person to predict that man would see the moon via television.

Zworykin: I didn't know it for certain. I spoke of that in self-defense because the great concern about television was what to put on it and why put in so much work on it. I had to defend myself by saying, "You can see the opposite side of the moon if someone sends a rocket there with a television camera. You will maybe have to wait for fifty years." But I didn't know that [it would happen in the 1960s].

Heyer: All the astronauts mentioned how it changed their view of the trip.

Zworykin: Yes, when they came back here and saw themselves on television walking on the moon. One time the picture was very clear. You see yourself, you know, at that particular important moment.

Heyer: Have you seen a lot of the pictures [of the earth] the satellites have been sending back [from orbit in the earth's atmosphere]?

Zworykin: Yes. That was the most interesting contribution from broadcasting, to my mind.

Heyer: Did you want to talk a little bit about the future?

Zworykin: Yes. I am not presently satisfied with the programs. Of course, I think everybody is doing what they think they have to do. Our programs are **commercial**, and therefore the income from broadcasting depends upon the number of people viewing. By taking surveys of this, right or wrong, they conclude that lower-quality programs appeal to more people. Therefore, they put in a lot of broadcasted violence and murder. They sometimes teach youngsters to do them in **actuality**. They can repeat them exactly. Rating systems are not good for the population, the younger generation in general. It also makes us look bad **abroad**. They see the ugly face of America. I think it partially produces our current unpopularity abroad. Only twenty to thirty years ago we were heroes in Soviet Russia, for example. . . . Westinghouse and Edison were heroes from an engineering point of view, also. That was not true just for Russia, but also for Europe when I was a student. That was the general impression—America was very admired from the outside.

Then all the actors in Hollywood were using the **Rolls Royce**. Therefore, Europe's impression of America was that everyone was a multimillionaire. Everybody used Rolls Royces. About ten years ago I was in a Moscow taxi, and the driver found out that I was American who could speak Russian. He said I must be breeding cattle. I asked him why and he said he got that from films. Now you see the vision of America. Of course that is only part of it. Television [programs] from satellites go everywhere; pictures from satellites can hit Africa in seconds. If we continue to transmit these kinds of programs it will not improve our image.

Heyer: Do you think that having this satellite transmission and more communication will bring pressure [to change]?

Zworykin: Certainly they are already talking about installing low-power transmission, which was good for receiving on television receivers. We can

Commercial: For the purpose of making money.

Actuality: Real life.

Abroad: Overseas; in foreign countries.

Rolls Royce: A very expensive brand of luxury automobile.

Vladimir Zworykin

Video disk: Digital video disk (DVD).

Sound disks: Compact disks (CDs).

Pornographic: Offensive sexual material.

Free enterprise: A system in which privately owned businesses are allowed to compete to earn money without interference from the government.

Censorship: A policy in which the government or other authorities review the content of creative works and remove anything that might be considered offensive.

receive broadcasts from and send them to any part of the world. I feel very guilty for [sending such bad programming] even indirectly, having a part in it.

Heyer: Do you think the same kind of programming we are doing now will be sent then?

Zworykin: That's what I tried to stop. We need to start thinking about this aspect.

Pinsky: Also on **video disk**.

Zworykin: That's another thing that will send our image abroad. In a couple of years the market will have cheap disks very similar to the **sound disks**. That will be different from the broadcasts because it doesn't depend on being sent by some group who has big [television transmission] equipment. It will be done by anybody who wants to record like they record music now. So, you can collect a library of whatever you want. We can make programs of our books that way, which will be easier to read than regular books. But at the same time, it can be used for bad things. You can use it for **pornographic** pictures and violent pictures and selling them around the world.

Heyer: So we'll have the same old problems with new technology.

Zworykin: It is not controllable.

Heyer: The classic dilemma—**free enterprise** and all the problems, or **censorship**.

Zworykin: All technology can be used for bad or good [purposes]. It's up to you how to use it.

• • •

What happened next...

Zworykin received many prestigious awards for his inventions over the years, particularly his contributions to the development of television. In 1952, for instance, he received the Edison Medal from the American Institute of Electrical Engineers. He received the National Medal of Science in 1967, and a decade later he was inducted into the National Inventors Hall of Fame. Zworykin died in 1982.

Did you know...

- Many people have referred to Vladimir Zworykin as the "Father of Television." But Zworykin always refused to accept sole credit for inventing the technology. Instead, he insisted that television grew out of the work of hundreds of researchers and inventors.

- Zworykin received more than 120 U.S. patents over the course of his career. He contributed to the development of many important technologies besides television, including infrared night-vision goggles, the electron microscope, electric-eye cameras used in security systems, and electronic controls for vehicles and weapons systems.
- Like Philo T. Farnsworth, a prominent inventor of early television systems, Zworykin disliked television programming and would not allow his children to watch TV.

Consider the following...

- In his interview, Vladimir Zworykin says that "all technology can be used for bad or good. It's up to you how to use it." Do you think the impact of television has been primarily positive or negative? Choose a side and debate with other members of the class.
- Think about some of your favorite television shows. What image do you think these programs project about the United States to viewers in other countries?
- The U.S. Patent Office awarded inventor Philo T. Farnsworth the first patent for an all-electronic television system. Yet Vladimir Zworykin, as the director of television research at RCA, oversaw the development of television broadcasting into a powerful medium of mass communication and the development of TV sets that were used in millions of American homes. Which man do you feel is most deserving of the title "Father of Television"?

For More Information

BOOKS

Abramson, Albert. *Zworykin: Pioneer of Television*. Urbana: University of Illinois Press, 1995.

Fisher, David E., and Marshall J. Fisher. *Tube: The Invention of Television*. Washington, DC: Counterpoint, 2002.

WEB SITES

Benjamin, Louise. "Vladimir Zworykin." *Museum of Broadcast Communications*. http://www.museum.tv/archives/etv/Z/htmlZ/zworykinvla/zworykinvla. htm (accessed on July 27, 2006).

Schatzkin, Paul. "Who Invented What—and When?" *The Farnsworth Chronicles.* http://farnovision.com/chronicles/tfc-who_invented_what.html (accessed July 27, 2006).

"Vladimir Zworykin" and "Iconoscope Camera Tube." *IEEE Virtual Museum.* http://www.ieee-virtual-museum.org/collection/tech.php?taid= &id=2345791&lid=1 (accessed July 27, 2006).

"Vladimir Zworykin Interview (July 4, 1975)" *IEEE Virtual Museum.* http://www. ieee.org/web/aboutus/history_center/oral_history/abstracts/zworykinab. html (accessed on July 27, 2006).

10

"An Appeal to Hollywood"

First presented and published on July 21, 1999
Reprinted from Vulgarians at the Gate: TV Trash and Raunch Radio,
  written by Steve Allen and published in 2001.

"By making a concerted effort to turn its energies to promoting decent, shared values and strengthening American families, the entertainment industry has it within its power to help make an America worthy of the third millennium."

According to the American Academy of Pediatrics, as of 2005 American children watched an average of three to four hours of television per day. Watching TV offers children some potential benefits. Educational programs can help them succeed in school, for example, by introducing such subjects as math, reading, and science. TV shows can also help teach children important social skills, like sharing, cooperating, and accepting differences.

However, television programs can also have a negative influence on kids. Many shows include racial and gender stereotypes (generalized, often negative ideas about a group of people), violent behavior, sexual situations, and language that are not appropriate for young viewers. Even programs specifically aimed at children feature commercials, and studies show that young people cannot always tell the difference between entertainment and advertisements. Finally, many critics argue that kids could put the time spent watching television to better use—by reading, interacting with their families, doing homework, and engaging in physical activity.

Since the 1950s, many people have conducted studies on the effects television has on young people. One of the main issues that has grown out of this research concerns children's exposure to violence on television. In 1972, for instance, the U.S. government released the results of a large-scale study about the effects of TV violence on children. This research showed that viewing violent programs on television tended to increase children's aggressive behavior, make them less sensitive to the pain and suffering of others, and cause them to become more fearful of the world around them. Many later studies confirmed these effects of children's exposure to TV violence. Nevertheless, the TV networks continued to air programming with violent content because it grabbed viewers' attention and received high ratings.

In response to growing concerns about children's exposure to TV violence, in 1992 the broadcast networks adopted a ratings system that provides on-screen advisories for all programs. Modeled after the ratings system used for theatrical films, it is intended to inform parents about program content that might be inappropriate for younger viewers. The ratings appear in newspaper TV listings, in cable and satellite program descriptions, and on the screen during the first fifteen seconds of shows. In addition to age-group ratings, the system uses code letters to indicate whether a program contains violence (V), sexual situations (S), strong language (L), or suggestive dialogue (D). The Telecommunications Policy Act of 1996 took the effort to protect children from violence on television a step further by requiring all new TV sets to be equipped with a V-chip—a device that can detect program ratings and be set to block programs that contain an unacceptable level of violence.

Despite such measures, critics continued to complain about the content of television programming. In May 1999, the Parents Television Council (PTC) released the results of a study showing that the broadcast industry's voluntary ratings system had failed to reduce the levels of violence, sex, and offensive language in prime-time programs. In fact, the PTC found that this sort of content had increased by 30 percent between November 1996, when the ratings system was first introduced, and November 1998.

The PTC also noted that the television ratings did not always reflect the true content of programs. For instance, a study of TV shows broadcast during the early evening hours found that 65 percent of the programs containing foul language did not carry the "L" label, while 76 percent of the programs containing discussion of sexual topics did not receive a "D" rating for suggestive dialogue. The PTC complained that the ratings system did not go far enough to help parents protect children from inappropriate TV program content.

American children watch an average of three to four hours of television per day.
© ROYALTY-FREE/CORBIS.

On July 21, 1999, a group of around sixty prominent Americans released a document called "An Appeal to Hollywood," which is reprinted below. They presented the text at a news conference in Washington, D.C., published it as a full-page advertisement in major newspapers across the country, and sent copies to the heads of all the major

President Bill Clinton, center; vice president Al Gore, right; and Jack Valenti, head of the Motion Picture Association of America, discuss the launch of the television ratings advisory system in 1996. CYNTHIA JOHNSON/TIME LIFE PICTURES/GETTY IMAGES.

companies in the entertainment industry. The document calls on the entertainment industry to establish a new set of guidelines regarding violent and sexual material in television programs, movies, music, and video games. It also asks broadcasters to include more family-friendly entertainment on television.

Things to remember while reading "An Appeal to Hollywood":

- This document was released about three months after a tragedy occurred at Columbine High School near Littleton, Colorado. Two high-school students, Dylan Klebold and Eric Harris, used guns and explosive devices to kill twelve classmates and one teacher—and wound twenty-four other people—before committing suicide. Some analysts suggested that Klebold and Harris's actions may have been influenced, in part, by their exposure to violent video games, music, and movies. In the months afterward, the impact of violent entertainment on teens was a big topic for discussion across the country.

- The document mentions the National Association of Broadcasters (NAB) Code of Practices for Television Broadcasters, which guided program content for thirty years. This code was adopted in the early 1950s. It encouraged broadcasters to think of television as a guest in viewers' homes that had an obligation to treat the host with respect. It emphasized that the TV industry had a responsibility to advance education and culture, provide fair coverage of news and controversial issues, and follow basic rules of good taste and decency in creating programs. The code even provided specific examples of subject matter that broadcasters should avoid including in program content. For instance, it said that programs should not contain attacks on religion and should always portray religious leaders in a positive way. It also said that broadcasters should avoid presenting greed, cruelty, or selfishness as worthy motivations. The NAB Code was thrown out during the 1980s following a court ruling that stated competing television networks had worked together illegally to create it. "An Appeal to Hollywood" recommends that the entertainment industry establish a new code of acceptable program content based on the old Television Code. But supporters of free speech argue that such a code might place unacceptable limitations on television programming. For instance, they claim that the restrictions mentioned above could prevent news programs from reporting on allegations of sexual abuse by Catholic priests and could spell the end of competition-based reality shows such as *Survivor*.

• • •

"An Appeal to Hollywood"

American parents today are deeply worried about their children's exposure to an increasingly **toxic** popular culture. The events in **Littleton, Colorado**, are only the most recent reminder that something is deeply **amiss** in our media age. Violence and explicit content in television, films, music, and video games have escalated sharply in recent years. Children of all ages now are being exposed to a barrage of images and words that threaten not only to rob them of normal childhood innocence but also to distort their view of reality and even undermine their character growth.

Toxic: Harmful or poisonous.

Littleton, Colorado: Site of the 1999 Columbine High School tragedy, in which two students shot and killed twelve classmates and a teacher before committing suicide.

Amiss: Wrong.

"An Appeal to Hollywood"

Partisan: Showing firm support of a political party or position.

These concerns know no political or **partisan** boundaries. According to a recent CNN–USA Today–Gallup poll, 76 percent of adults agree that TV, movies, and popular music are negative influences on children, and 75 percent report that they make efforts to protect children from such harmful influences. Nearly the same number say shielding children from the negative influences of today's media culture is "nearly impossible."

Degrading: Harmful to moral character.

En masse: Together in large groups.

Disintegration: Breaking apart.

Negligent: Extremely careless.

Adversely: Negatively

Moreover, there is a growing public appreciation of the link between our excessively violent and **degrading** entertainment and the horrifying new crimes we see emerging among our young: schoolchildren gunning down teachers and fellow students **en masse**, killing sprees inspired by violent films, and teenagers murdering their babies only to return to dance at the prom.

Clearly, many factors are contributing to the crisis—family **disintegration**, ineffective schools, **negligent** parenting, and the ready availability of firearms. But, among researchers, the proposition that entertainment violence **adversely** influences attitudes and behavior is no longer controversial; there is overwhelming evidence of its harmful effects. Numerous studies show that degrading images of violence and sex have a desensitizing effect.

Susceptible: Open or responsive.

Nowhere is the threat greater than to our at-risk youth—youngsters whose disadvantaged environments make them **susceptible** to acting upon impulses shaped by violent and dehumanizing media imagery.

In the past, the entertainment industry was more conscious of its unique responsibility for the health of our culture. For thirty years, television lived by the National Association of Broadcasters (NAB) Television Code, which detailed responsibilities to the community, children, and society and **prescribed** specific programming standards. For many years, this voluntary code set boundaries that enabled television to thrive as a creative medium without causing undue damage to the **bedrock** values of our society.

Prescribed: Established or set forth; assigned.

Bedrock: Basic or core.

Standards: Rules or guidelines.

Desirability: Potential benefits.

Affirmation: Recognition or acknowledgment.

In recent years, several top entertainment executives have spoken out on the need for minimum **standards** and, more recently, on the **desirability** of more family-friendly programming. But to effect real change, these individual expressions must transform into a new, collective **affirmation** of social responsibility on the part of the media industry as a whole.

Undersigned: People who signed this document, giving it their approval.

Compact: Agreement.

We, the **undersigned**, call on executives of the media industry—as well as CEOs [chief executive officers] of companies that advertise in the electronic media—to join with us and with America's parents in a new social **compact** aimed at renewing our culture and making our media environment more healthy for our society and safer for our children. We call on industry leaders in all media—television, film, video, and electronic games—to band together to develop a new voluntary code of conduct, broadly modeled on the NAB code.

The code we envision would affirm in clear terms the industry's vital responsibilities for the health of our culture; establish certain minimum standards for violent, sexual, and degrading material for each medium, below which producers can be expected not to go; commit the industry to an overall reduction in the level of entertainment violence; ban the practice of targeting of adult-oriented entertainment to youth markets; provide for more accurate information to parents on media content; commit to the creation of "windows" or "safe havens" for family programming, including a revival of TV's "family hour"; and, finally, pledge significantly greater creative efforts to develop family-oriented entertainment.

We strongly urge parents to express their support for this voluntary code of conduct directly to media executives and advertisers with telephone calls, letters, faxes, or e-mails. . . . And we call on all parents to fulfill their part of the compact by responsibly supervising their children's media exposure.

We are not **advocating censorship** or wholesale **strictures** on artistic creativity. We are not demanding that all entertainment be geared to young children. Finally, we are not asking government to police the media.

Rather, we are urging the entertainment industry to assume a decent minimum of responsibility for its own actions and take **modest** steps of self-restraint. And we are asking parents to help in this task by shielding their own children and also by making their concerns known to media executives and advertisers.

Hollywood has an enormous influence on America, particularly the young. By making a **concerted** effort to turn its energies to promoting decent, shared values and strengthening American families, the entertainment industry has it within its power to help make an America worthy of the **third millennium**. We, as leaders from government, the religious community, the **nonprofit world**, and the **private sector**, along with members of the entertainment community, challenge the entertainment industry to this great task. We appeal to those who are **reaping** great profits to give something back. We believe that by choosing to do good, the entertainment industry can also **make good**, and both the industry and our society will be richer and better as a result.

• • •

Advocating: Promoting or arguing in favor of.

Censorship: A policy of reviewing creative works and removing any material considered offensive.

Strictures: Limits.

Modest: Small.

Hollywood: City in southern California that serves as the capital of the entertainment industry.

Concerted: Strong.

Third millennium: The time in which we live; the one thousand years beyond 2000.

Nonprofit world: Organizations and groups that do not attempt to make money, such as charities.

Private sector: World of privately owned business.

Reaping: Collecting.

Make good: Prosper; make money.

What happened next . . .

"An Appeal to Hollywood" attracted a fair amount of media attention, but it did not result in significant changes to the content of television programming. The broadcast industry did not immediately launch any major initiatives to reduce the amount of sex, violence, and profanity on TV.

Steve Allen: The Father of TV Talk Shows

One of the driving forces behind "An Appeal to Hollywood" was Steve Allen, a comedian, actor, writer, and musician with fifty years of experience in the television industry. He was born Stephen Valentine Patrick William Allen on December 26, 1921, in New York City. He launched his career as an entertainer in the 1940s by working as a comedian and radio disc jockey. In the early years of television, he served as the host of a variety program called *The Steve Allen Show,* which aired on CBS from 1950 to 1952 and on NBC from 1956 to 1960.

Allen is probably best known as the creator and first host of *The Tonight Show,* a late-night comedy, talk, and variety program. He launched the show on a local station in New York and then took it national in 1953. During his four years as host of the show, Allen introduced several features that have remained a part of late-night TV talk shows ever since. For instance, he pioneered the "man on the street" comedy segment, in which a comedian and camera crew ventured outside of the studio and joked around with the people passing by. He also used some of the first audience-participation skits and comedy routines.

Allen created and hosted several other game and talk shows from the 1960s through the 1980s, including the award-winning PBS series *Meeting of the Minds.* In this show, which aired from 1977 to 1981, notable historic figures (portrayed by actors) debated current issues in a talk show format. Allen's many contributions to the talk show format helped earn him the nickname "Father of TV Talk Shows." It also helped secure him a place in the Television Arts and Sciences Hall of Fame in 1986.

During his long and varied career, Allen composed thousands of songs, published more than fifty books, novels, and plays, and wrote articles for newspapers and magazines on topics ranging from comedy to religion to education. Late in his life, Allen became an outspoken critic of the quality of television programming. He worked together with the Parents Television Council to launch several major protests against what he saw as increasing levels of violent and sexual content in TV programs, including the highly publicized 1999 "Appeal to Hollywood." Steve Allen died on October 30, 2000, at age 78. His last book, *Vulgarians at the Gate: Trash TV and Raunch Radio,* was published after his death.

As of 2000, all new television sets sold in the United States were required to contain a V-chip to allow parents to block programs electronically based on their content ratings. But critics pointed out that V-chip technology was only as effective as the TV ratings system. They complained that the program ratings did not always provide a full and accurate reflection of content, and that many types of programs were not rated—including news broadcasts, sporting events, and commercials.

Censorship vs. the First Amendment

A new fight developed over the content of TV programs in 2004. In one highly publicized incident, Bono—lead singer of the rock band U2—used profanity during an acceptance speech on the televised Golden Globe Awards. An even bigger controversy surrounded an incidence of nudity during the 2004 Super Bowl telecast. The Super Bowl regularly attracts some of the largest TV audiences of the year. It is typically broadcast during the early evening hours, when millions of children are watching television. The halftime entertainment usually features big-name musical acts that hold strong appeal to young viewers. The 2004 halftime show featured a concert by the popular artists Justin Timberlake and Janet Jackson. Toward the end of their performance, as the two singers danced together on stage, Timberlake pulled on Jackson's costume and exposed her breast.

Although the entertainers claimed that the incident was an accident, and the CBS network issued an apology, many viewers were upset. Responding to viewer complaints, the Federal Communications Commission (the government agency responsible for regulating television) fined CBS a record $550,000 and warned broadcasters to watch and evaluate program content more closely. The FCC even encouraged broadcasters to create a new industry-wide code of conduct, like that proposed in "An Appeal to Hollywood." The incident also prompted the U.S. Congress to increase the maximum fines allowed for violating television content standards. In an attempt to avoid future problems, the networks introduced a time-delay of a few seconds on live broadcasts, to give technical crews time to remove any nudity or profanity.

In 2006, however, all of the major broadcast networks and their affiliate stations filed a lawsuit against the FCC, claiming that the fine against CBS was illegal because the agency did not apply clear and consistent standards of decency. Brent Bozell, president of the Parents Television Council (PTC), argued that broadcasters were using the case to challenge the government's authority to regulate TV content. "It's an industry that is just a profitable assembly line of garbage, and wants the 'right' to offend many millions of families, using the public airwaves owned by those families to do so," he wrote in an online editorial.

By contrast, supporters of free speech complain that the PTC and similar groups engage in censorship (a policy of reviewing creative works and removing any material considered offensive). They believe that individuals should be free to decide for themselves what kind of content is appropriate to watch on TV, rather than allowing the PTC or the government to decide for everyone. Opponents of censorship also claim that efforts to eliminate sex, violence, and profanity from television will limit artistic development and lead to bland and predictable programming. They believe that adults should not be forced to accept a level of entertainment that is suitable for children and that parents should take greater responsibility for monitoring their children's TV viewing.

The PTC responded to these arguments by saying that people who criticize the content of TV programming are merely exercising their own right to free speech. They also claimed that parental responsibility can only go so far in protecting children from unsuitable entertainment material. Since television is such a powerful medium, they argued, it can drive changes in customs, speech, and attitudes throughout an entire society. When society as a whole is affected by sex and violence on TV, it becomes impossible for even the most responsible parents to protect their children from exposure.

In the end, some analysts believe that the major television networks may bend to pressure from critics and the FCC and make an effort to refine program content. As broadcast programming becomes more safe and predictable, however, they expect that more viewers will abandon the networks in favor of the edgy, creative offerings available on cable and satellite.

Did you know...

- "An Appeal to Hollywood" was signed by around sixty prominent people from the worlds of politics, business, religion, education, and entertainment. The diverse group of signers included former presidents Jimmy Carter and Gerald Ford; senators John McCain of Arizona, Kay Bailey Hutchinson of Texas, Sam Brownback of Kansas, and Joe Lieberman of Connecticut; military leaders Colin Powell and Norman Schwartzkopf; religious leaders Bill Bright and Jim Wallis; academics Elizabeth Fox-Genovese and Elie Wiesel; and entertainers Steve Allen and Naomi Judd.

- The Parents Television Council (PTC) was founded in 1995 "to ensure that children are not constantly assaulted by sex, violence, and profanity on television and in other media," according to the organization's Web site. It is a national organization with nearly one million members across the United States. The PTC works with broadcasters, advertisers, government agencies, and parents to raise awareness of TV content issues and reduce the flow of negative messages to children. The organization also conducts research into program content and publishes the *Family Guide to Prime-Time Television* to help parents choose family-friendly entertainment.

Consider the following . . .

- The First Amendment to the U.S. Constitution guarantees freedom of speech to all citizens. Are there limits to free speech under the law? Should there be limits? Come up with some examples of cases where the interests of society might be best served by restricting this constitutional right.

- Who should decide what sort of material is acceptable for broadcast over the public airwaves—the government, the FCC, the television networks, voters, or individual viewers? How should the interests of the other groups factor into the decisions?

- Following singer Janet Jackson's breast-baring incident during the 2004 broadcast of the Super Bowl, Congress and the FCC took steps to increase the penalties for broadcasters who violate standards of decency. Some critics complained that the authorities treated a brief glimpse of a normal female body part as a major offense, while they routinely ignored graphic depictions of violence, torture, and mutilation in highly rated fictional programs like *CSI*. What standards should be used to judge the content of TV programs?

- Imagine if there was a television program that half of American viewers found to be of exceptionally high quality and interest, and that the other half found to be deeply offensive. Should this program be allowed on the air? Argue both sides of the question.

For More Information

BOOKS

Allen, Steve. *Vulgarians at the Gate: Trash TV and Raunch Radio.* New York: Prometheus Books, 2001.

PERIODICALS

Dessart, George. "Of Tastes and Times: Some Challenging Reflections on Television's Elastic Standards and Astounding Practices." *Television Quarterly,* 1992.

Jarvis, Jeff. "Can the FCC Shut Howard Up?" *Nation,* May 17, 2004.

Strode, Tom. "Carter, Ford, Others Ask Hollywood for Code on Media Violence, Sex." *Presbyterian Layman,* July 23, 1999.

WEB SITES

Alexander, Allison. "Children and Television." *Museum of Broadcast Communications.* http://www.museum.tv/archives/etv/C/htmlC/childrenand/childrenand. htm (accessed on July 31, 2006).

Bozell, Brent. "The Two-Faced Networks." *Parents Television Council,* April 27, 2006. http://www.parentstv.org/PTC/publications/lbbcolumns/2006/0427.asp (accessed on July 31, 2006).

Dessart, George. "Standards and Practices." *Museum of Broadcast Communications.* http://www.museum.tv/archives/etv/S/htmlS/standardsand/standardsand.htm (accessed on July 31, 2006).

"Steve Allen: Complete Biography." *Steve Allen Home Page.* http://www.steveallen.com (accessed July 31, 2006).

11

Don Hewitt

Excerpt of *Tell Me a Story: Fifty Years and 60 Minutes in Television*
Published in 2001

"Today, a lot of what passes for news on television couldn't hold its own with [the tabloid magazines at] a supermarket checkout counter."

Don Hewitt is the creator and longtime producer of television's most acclaimed investigative news program, the long-running CBS series *60 Minutes*. Hewitt joined CBS in 1948, during the earliest years of commercial television. He started out working in the control room on a news show hosted by Douglas Edwards. He also worked with legendary broadcast journalist **Edward R. Murrow** (1908–1965; see Chapter 5) on the influential public affairs program *See It Now*. Throughout the early years of his career, Hewitt came up with several innovative ideas that proved he had a flair for the visual presentation of the news.

In 1960, Hewitt directed the first-ever televised presidential debates between Vice President Richard M. Nixon and his lesser-known opponent, Massachusetts senator **John F. Kennedy** (1917–1963; see Chapter 6). Kennedy's strong performance on television helped convince the American people that he had the experience and maturity to be president, and he ended up winning the election a few months later. In 1962, Hewitt became executive producer of *The CBS Evening News with Walter Cronkite*.

In 1968, Hewitt came up with an innovative format for a new show—an hour-long "newsmagazine." Each episode would feature several different segments, like the articles in a print magazine. Some segments would provide news, such as detailed investigative reports, while others would offer feature stories, like celebrity interviews. The show would use several correspondents, with each focusing on a separate

Executive producer of 60 Minutes, *Don Hewitt, in 2003.* © CHRIS FARINA/CORBIS.

story. Hewitt believed that, unlike the nightly news, the show would be able to devote enough time to cover many angles of a story, providing in-depth analysis of political, social, and cultural issues that appealed to viewers.

Hewitt filmed a pilot (initial test) episode of the show, which would become *60 Minutes,* with reporters Harry Reasoner (1923–1991) and Mike Wallace (1918–). It made its debut on September 24, 1968. Critics immediately recognized that the show represented a new kind of broadcast journalism. Over the first few seasons, however, *60 Minutes* struggled to find an audience. Although it received poor ratings, CBS was willing to stick with it because the newsmagazine cost far less to produce than a situation comedy or drama.

Under Hewitt's guidance, *60 Minutes* soon gained a reputation for covering difficult and controversial stories. For many viewers, it was regarded as a voice for the average citizen fighting against powerful corporate and government interests. In 1970, the show added a regular

Don Hewitt, right, and Senator John F. Kennedy, center, discuss plans for the first televised presidential debate, which was held in September 1960. © BETTMANN/CORBIS.

segment called "Point/Counterpoint"—a three-minute debate about an important issue of the day between experts who held opposing political viewpoints. This debate format was later adopted by a number of other news programs, including CNN's *Crossfire* and the Fox News Channel's *Hannity and Colmes*. After nine years, however, *60 Minutes* dropped the "Point/Counterpoint" segment in favor of a lighter feature—a humorous commentary by reporter Andy Rooney.

CBS moved *60 Minutes* around the weekly schedule, placing it in seven different time slots during its first nine seasons. The show finally began to gain popularity in 1975, when it moved to 7 P.M. on Sunday nights. By the late 1970s, *60 Minutes* had grown into one of the most popular shows on television. In September 1978, it hit the top spot in the weekly TV ratings, marking the first time that a regularly scheduled nonfiction program ranked number one in the history of television.

By the 2000s, *60 Minutes* was considered one of the most successful news programs of all time. It spent twenty-three straight years (1977–2000) ranked among the top ten prime-time series, and it is the only show to hold the number-one position in the annual TV ratings in three different decades. Although the correspondents have varied through the years it has been on the air, the format has essentially remained the same. Hewitt is regarded as the visionary behind the show, and he has received widespread praise—and many awards—for his innovations to the field of television news.

In his 2001 memoir *Tell Me a Story: Fifty Years and 60 Minutes in Television,* which is excerpted below, Hewitt looks back at his long career with CBS News. He also analyzes the impact that the phenomenal success of *60 Minutes* had on television journalism. Hewitt notes that *60 Minutes* proved that "television news, done with flair, can be worthwhile and profitable at the same time." But he claims that other networks copied the newsmagazine format in hopes of achieving high ratings and profits, rather than in order to provide viewers with worthwhile news and information. Hewitt complains that this focus on profits has caused the quality of television news programs to decline over time. He calls on broadcast journalists to use good judgment, respect people's privacy, and take responsibility for reporting only the truth.

Things to remember while reading the excerpt of *Tell Me a Story*:

- In his memoir, Hewitt mentions broadcast journalist Edward R. Murrow. Hewitt worked as a producer on Murrow's hard-hitting 1950s CBS News program *See It Now.* Although this show tackled such important topics as the connection between cigarette smoking and lung cancer, it was too serious-minded and factual to earn high ratings. In order to get CBS to commit to keeping *See It Now* on the air, Murrow had to agree to host a lighter, entertainment-oriented program called *Person to Person,* which featured celebrity interviews. Some TV critics—and even Hewitt himself—have described *60 Minutes* as a combination of *See It Now* and *Person to Person.*

- Hewitt discusses how the success of *60 Minutes* encouraged the other major broadcast networks, as well as emerging cable networks, to launch their own shows using the newsmagazine format.

Don Hewitt, right, along with the 60 Minutes *news correspondents celebrate the twenty-fifth anniversary of the program in 1993.*
BOB STRONG/AFP/GETTY IMAGES.

By 1993, for instance, *60 Minutes* faced competition from six other newsmagazines. A number of similar shows still existed in the 2000s, including *Dateline NBC, Prime Time,* and *Hard Copy.*

- Although Hewitt criticizes the state of television journalism, his own show, *60 Minutes,* has generated its share of controversy over the years. Some critics have claimed that the show's producers and correspondents used questionable interview tactics, for instance, attacking subjects with unfair questions or surprising them by revealing new facts on camera.

- Hewitt talks about television ratings and the importance of "sweeps weeks." TV programs receive ratings based on the number of viewers who watch them. The more viewers a program attracts, the higher the rating it receives. Ratings are very important in the broadcast industry because they are used to determine the amount of money that TV networks can charge advertisers to buy commercial time during various programs. "Sweeps" periods occur several times per year. TV networks compete fiercely to attract viewers during these important periods, when commercial rates are established.

• • •

Excerpt of *Tell Me a Story*

Economics: Financial realities.

The sad fact of life about television today is that the **economics** of commercial broadcasting have in large measure driven the networks out of the expensive and high-risk entertainment business, which they used to be very serious about and did very well, and into the less expensive and less risky news business, which they're not very serious about and don't do very well.

Now don't get me wrong. I'm not talking about [network news anchors like] Dan Rather [(1931–); longtime anchor of *CBS Evening News*], Peter Jennings [(1938–2005); longtime anchor of *ABC World News Tonight*], Tom Brokaw [(1940–); longtime anchor of *NBC Nightly News*]. I'm not talking about [network news hosts and programs like] Ted Koppel [(1940–); broadcast journalist and longtime host of the ABC News program *Nightline*] and *Nightline,* or Bob Schieffer's [(1937–); broadcast journalist and host of the CBS News program *Face the Nation*] *Face the Nation,* Tim Russert's [(1950–); political analyst and host of the NBC News program *Meet the Press*] *Meet the Press,* or *This Week* with Sam Donaldson [(1934–); broadcast journalist and host of the ABC News program *This Week.*] and Cokie Roberts [(1943–); broadcast journalist and host of the ABC News program *This Week*]. What I am talking about are the so-called newsmagazines that came along in our [*60 Minutes'*] wake, which the networks use as filler when the ratings gods don't smile on a sitcom or an hour-long drama. If it's true, and it is, that behind every great man there's a woman, then behind almost every TV newsmagazine there's a failed sitcom. Had that sitcom not failed, that newsmagazine wouldn't be there.

Kudos: Praise.

Traveling the high road: Providing high-quality service or moral value.

The networks used to measure success by the **kudos** they got from the public and the recognition from colleagues and competitors for doing as well as they did. **Traveling the high road** was what made you proud to be a broadcast journalist, back in the days when broadcast journalism could hold its own with the best of print [newspaper and magazine journalism]. Today, a lot of what passes for news on television couldn't hold its own with [the tabloid magazines at] a supermarket checkout counter.

Today, the only measure that counts is what kind of **promotable** nonsense you can come up with to draw people away from the sitcom that's opposite you on another channel. News competing with entertainment has to mean cutting corners. You can't compete with a sitcom unless you have no **compunction** about being something you aren't, or at the very least, something you shouldn't be.

There's a line that separates news biz [business] from show biz. The trick is to walk up to that line, touch it with your toe, but don't cross it. If you don't go near it, you're going to lose your viewership or your readership. If you step over it, you'll lose your **conscience**. For more than thirty years, *60 Minutes* has walked up to that line but never crossed it.

So what is it that's happened to TV news? **Andy Rooney** says, "Most of the decisions made in television news are not about news, they're about money," and "Corporate America was late discovering there was a profit to be made with news, and it's trying to make up for a slow start...."

When I came to CBS in 1948, what was called news and public affairs was a service, not a business—a service that broadcasters were **obligated** by the **Federal Communications Commission** to provide on a more or less regular basis. And they did it more often than not on what was called a **sustaining** basis, **devoid of** commercials.

When a news or public-affairs broadcast did **go commercial**, it was often with institutional messages that **eschewed** the hard sell and dwelt on corporate responsibility. It was a time when the FCC ruled broadcasting with an iron fist, deciding what broadcasters could do and couldn't do and **decreeing** which time periods—early Sunday evening, for example—had to be devoted to public affairs or children. Network news operations were the price we paid for use of the public airwaves; they were hardly money makers—loss leaders were more like it. So much so that even [legendary broadcast journalist Edward R.] Murrow had to enter the entertainment arena with *Person to Person* to make a fraction of what Rather, Brokaw, Jennings, and even I make today.

What **turned the tide** was the enormous profit *60 Minutes* made before television got split into so many channels. *60 Minutes* proved that television news, done with flair, can be worthwhile and profitable at the same time, in fact, very profitable. In that regard, no one honestly believes that the heads of the networks woke up one morning and said to themselves, "You know, I don't think we are doing enough to inform the American people." What they woke up and said to themselves was, "Can you believe the money that *60 Minutes* makes?"

My biggest surprise in fifty-plus years at CBS was the day somebody came to me and told me that [*60 Minutes* was] in the top ten. This whole bit about moving up into the top ten was a new country and a foreign

Promotable: Easy to advertise or sell.

Compunction: Feelings of anxiety or guilt.

Conscience: Sense of right and wrong that promotes good decisions.

Andy Rooney: (1919–) Longtime *60 Minutes* commentator.

Obligated: Required.

Federal Communications Commission: The U.S. government agency responsible for regulating television.

Sustaining: Paid for by a TV network or station, rather than by advertisers.

Devoid of: Without.

Go commercial: Accept paid advertisements.

Eschewed: Avoided.

Decreeing: Ordering or commanding.

Turned the tide: Changed the situation.

language. All of a sudden, one day we were number one—four times, once in the '70s, once in the '80s, and twice in the '90s we were the number-one broadcast in America. And this was against [such popular entertainment programs as] *M*A*S*H* and *Cheers* and *Roseanne*. We are the only news show that has ever been in the top ten. . . .

Our twenty-two consecutive years in the top ten is a record we're proud of, and a record the network is more than proud of. For a while we were the single most profitable hour in the history of television, so it's our bottom line everybody's trying to **clone**, not necessarily the broadcast. . . . [Hewitt relates a story about a new CBS News program that network management referred to as a "gold mine."]

Clone: Copy.

In TV-speak, a "gold mine" is a broadcast in which commercial spots sell for a fortune. The determination of how much to charge for a spot is made during what television calls **"sweeps weeks,"** which is complete and utter **lunacy**. The networks load up their schedules with what they hope will be ratings blockbusters, then try to convince themselves and their advertisers—not to mention TV columnists—that the phony baloney is a legitimate **gauge** of how many people are watching when it's *not* sweeps week. The truth is, it's not a legitimate gauge of anything. The network executives know it. The sponsors, whose ad rates are set by this idiotic practice, know it. And yet no one comes up with a way to get rid of it. . . .

Sweeps weeks: Important ratings periods when TV networks set their advertising rates for the following season.

Lunacy: Craziness.

Gauge: Measure or indicator.

News and truth are not always the same thing. That's because the truth isn't always knowable. . . . Truth can be behind the story, the forces that animate individuals and institutions, the raw stuff that gets at the ways people behave and conduct their lives. . . . Truth and accuracy mean different things to different people. The only thing I ask of a reporter is: "Have you ever knowingly done violence to what you believe is the truth? And do you believe the story you're reporting is an honest and accurate representation of what the viewer or listener or reader thinks it is?" If a reporter can answer those two questions to my satisfaction, that, in essence, is all I need to know.

Standards and practices: Guidelines for acceptable program content.

Don't amount to a hill of beans: Are meaningless.

Maimonides: (1135–1204) Influential Jewish philosopher of the medieval period.

To me, all the do's and don'ts in the CBS News bible of **standards and practices don't amount to a hill of beans** compared with those two questions. If, as **Maimonides** said, "Do unto others is the law" and "all the rest is commentary," then for journalists "never knowingly do violence to the truth is also the law" and "all the rest is commentary." But let's face it, we [journalists] do behave sometimes as if we're the only ones with rights, and that those rights entitle us to go anywhere with our cameras or pencils or laptops, poking into a person's most private matters and broadcasting or publishing what we get.

Even though the phrase does not appear in the Constitution, I think there is such a thing as a right to privacy. And, while we're at it, neither does the phrase, "the right to know," appear in the Constitution. That's a phrase journalists use to justify **feathering their own nests** when they should be exercising judgment and restraint. If the public has a "right to know," constitutionally or otherwise, this does not translate into the media's *obligation* to publish or broadcast....

Exercising our freedom to publish or broadcast should further the cause of something worthwhile. The best way to ensure our continuing the freedom to publish and broadcast is to guard against self-indulgence, a trait as unattractive and undesirable in the press as anywhere else in our society....

Feathering their own nests: Serving their own interests.

• • •

What happened next...

In 2004, Hewitt stepped down from his role as executive producer of *60 Minutes*. But the show continued broadcasting new episodes as it neared its fortieth year on the air. Hewitt, meanwhile, assumed new responsibilities as an executive producer for CBS News.

Did you know...

- *60 Minutes* is one of the few television programs without theme music. Instead, each weekly episode opens with a simple image of a ticking stopwatch.
- *60 Minutes* has served as the target of a number of comedians over the years. The show's format and content have been the subject of parodies on TV comedy programs such as *Saturday Night Live, The Simpsons, The Family Guy,* and *Seinfeld.*
- Stories appearing on *60 Minutes* have influenced viewer behavior on a number of occasions. For example, a story about the positive health effects of drinking moderate amounts of red wine led to a significant increase in sales of the product. Similarly, a negative story about the Audi 5000 luxury automobile—which claimed that the vehicle had a defect that caused it to accelerate without warning—led to a huge drop in sales of the car in the United States. Even after government tests attributed the problem to driver error rather than a product defect, Audi sales did not recover for fifteen years.
- Longtime correspondent Mike Wallace retired from *60 Minutes* in 2006. He had been with the program for thirty-seven years—the

longest any person had appeared continuously on any news show in the history of television. At the age of eighty-seven, Wallace was also the oldest television personality at the time of his retirement.

Consider the following...

- During his long career with CBS News, Don Hewitt worked with some of the most respected broadcast journalists in the nation, including Edward R. Murrow, Walter Cronkite, Mike Wallace, Dan Rather, and Diane Sawyer. In his memoir, he indicates that the only question he ever asked of his reporters was "Have you ever knowingly done violence to what you believe is the truth?" What do you think he means by this? Provide an example of a news story that you believe "did violence" to the truth.

- Broadcast and cable television networks are businesses that exist for the purpose of making money. Hewitt claims that the success of *60 Minutes* proved that news could be a source of profit for television networks. Make a list of some of the arguments for and against television networks operating their news divisions in such a way as to achieve the highest possible ratings and profits.

- Hewitt mentions that some TV news programs use the public's "right to know" to justify their decisions to broadcast private and potentially hurtful things about people. Do you believe that you have a right to know intimate details about the lives of celebrities, politicians, and other public figures? Or do you think that individuals have a right to privacy, even if they make their living in the public eye? How should TV news producers decide what they should and should not broadcast?

For More Information

BOOKS

Blum, David. *Tick, Tick, Tick: The Long Life and Turbulent Times of 60 Minutes.* New York: HarperCollins, 2004.

Hewitt, Don. *Minute by Minute.* New York: Random House, 1985.

Hewitt, Don. *Tell Me a Story: Fifty Years and 60 Minutes in Television.* New York: Public Affairs, 2001.

Madsen, Axel. *60 Minutes: The Power and the Politics of America's Most Popular TV News Show.* New York: Dodd, Mead, 1984.

PERIODICALS

Shales, Tom. "Still Ticking at 25: The Great Granddaddy of Magazine Shows." *Washington Post,* November 13, 1993.

Stein, Harry. "How *60 Minutes* Makes News." *New York Times,* May 6, 1979.

WEB SITES

Bartone, Richard. "60 Minutes." *Museum of Broadcast Communications.* http://www.museum.tv/archives/etv/S/htmlS/60minutes/60minutes.htm (accessed on July 31, 2006).

"Don Hewitt." *Museum of Broadcast Communications.* http://www.museum.tv/archives/etv/H/htmlH/hewittdon/hewittdon.htm (accessed on July 31, 2006).

Ted Turner

Excerpt of "My Beef with Big Media"

Published in the Washington Monthly, *July/August 2004*
Also available at http://www.washingtonmonthly.com/features/2004/0407.turner.html

"The FCC says that we have more media choices than ever before. But only a few corporations decide what we can choose. That is not choice."

When the U.S. system of broadcasting first developed in the early twentieth century, it was based on the idea that the airwaves belonged to the American people. Broadcasters were allowed to use this public property through a system of licenses. Since the Communications Act of 1934 created the Federal Communications Commission (FCC), this government agency has issued rules and regulations to guide the broadcasting industry and ensure that it operates in the public interest.

Early on, the FCC decided that the public interest would be best served through diversity in ownership of radio and television stations. The agency placed strict limits on the total number of stations any individual or company could own. It also limited the number of stations that anyone could own in a single community or market. Finally, the FCC restricted cross-ownership of different types of communications media. This restriction meant, for instance, that one company could not own both a TV station and a major newspaper in the same city. The FCC made these rules in order to prevent a few large companies from dominating the flow of news and information. The agency felt that this would benefit the public by exposing people to a wide variety of viewpoints on important issues.

The FCC has made a number of changes to its media ownership regulations over the years. The agency has changed the rules in response to

Massive Media

As of 2005, Viacom was one of the largest media corporations in the world. It held interests in virtually every part of the American communications and entertainment industries. For example, Viacom owned the CBS and UPN broadcast television networks. It also owned numerous popular cable TV channels, including MTV, VH1, Nickelodeon, Noggin, TNN, BET, Comedy Central, TV Land, and Showtime. Through its Infinity Broadcasting division, Viacom owned more than 180 radio stations in major markets across the United States. It also owned the movie production companies Paramount Pictures and DreamWorks SKG, as well as the television production company King World. Viacom was also the parent company for the book publishers Simon & Schuster and Scribner, and was part-owner of the video game manufacturer Sega. Finally, Viacom operated one of the nation's largest outdoor advertising businesses.

The structure of today's massive media corporations changes frequently, as managers try to respond to new business conditions and government regulations. In December 2005, Viacom decided to split into two separate companies, Viacom Inc. and CBS Corporation. This split effectively undid the 1999 merger between Viacom and CBS. The new CBS Corporation focused on broadcasting. It owned the CBS television and radio networks and the King World television production company. The new Viacom kept its cable TV channels, outdoor advertising business, and movie production companies.

technological advances affecting the broadcast industry, such as the introduction of cable television systems. It has also made some changes in response to political pressure from industry leaders, various presidents, and Congress. In general, the FCC regulations on media ownership have been relaxed over time to allow individuals and companies to control more media outlets (radio and TV stations, cable TV systems, newspapers, and magazines). The rule changes have contributed to greater consolidation (merging or grouping together) of American broadcasting in the hands of a few large companies.

The Telecommunications Act of 1996

A number of media ownership restrictions were reduced or eliminated with the passage of the Telecommunications Act of 1996. This legislation took away many of the barriers separating different parts of the communications industry—including radio and television broadcasters, cable TV service providers, and long-distance telephone companies—in an attempt to increase competition and stimulate the development of new services. The act also extended the terms of radio and television broadcast licenses from three years to eight years and made it easier for stations to renew their licenses.

The 1996 law also relaxed the limits on ownership of television and radio stations. It eliminated the cap (maximum limit) on the number of television or radio stations one company could own nationwide. It also increased the cap on the portion of the national audience a single broadcast company could serve from 25 percent to 35 percent of the U.S. population.

The effects of the new law could be seen almost immediately in the radio industry. Before the Telecommunications Act of 1996 took effect, a single company could own a maximum of forty radio stations nationwide. After the act passed, radio broadcasting entered a period of rapid consolidation. An amazing 60 percent of radio stations across the country changed owners over the next few years, resulting in the loss of 1,700 independent radio stations. Most of these stations were purchased by four large broadcasting companies. Clear Channel Communications, for instance, grew to own more than 1,200 radio stations in all fifty states, reaching 110 million listeners.

One of the main goals of the Telecommunications Act of 1996 was to lower the rates that Americans paid for cable television service. The law was supposed to increase competition, and decrease costs, by allowing companies in other parts of the communications industry to become cable providers. Over the next five years, however, the seven largest cable operators purchased smaller systems until they controlled more than 75 percent of the national market. The consolidation of the cable industry contributed to a 30 percent overall increase in cable rates for consumers during this period.

Media consolidation

According to the PBS program *NOW with Bill Moyers,* North America contains around 2,000 television stations, 11,000 radio stations, 1,800 daily newspapers, 11,000 magazines, and 3,000 book publishers. In 1984, these media outlets were controlled by fifty different companies. By 1996, consolidation had reduced the number of companies that held a controlling interest in these media outlets to ten. The Telecommunications Act of 1996 resulted in even further consolidation. By 2002, most of the thousands of American broadcast and print media sources were controlled by only six large corporations. These major corporations had financial interests in a wide variety of other industries as well,

Ted Turner, pictured in 1985, purchased a small, independent TV station in 1976 and within a few years transformed it into the highly successful "Superstation" WTBS. © BETTMANN/CORBIS.

including movies and music, alcoholic beverages, theme parks, professional sports franchises, telephone services, and nuclear power plants.

In 2002, the FCC launched a major review of its media ownership rules. Specifically, the agency considered weakening or eliminating regulations that limited ownership of cable television systems and prohibited cross-ownership of broadcast media and newspapers in the same market. Several large media corporations filed formal requests with the FCC to eliminate all of the remaining ownership rules. These companies claimed that the regulations were outdated and no longer necessary. After all, the FCC had put the rules in place at a time when space on the airwaves was limited, so the government had to limit ownership in order to ensure diversity in broadcasting. But the media giants argued that this was no longer a problem in the age of cable TV and the Internet, which gave the American people access to news and information from a wide variety of sources. In this new competitive atmosphere, they claimed that it was not possible for any one company to dominate the flow of information.

There is no question that it makes good business sense for large media companies to be involved in all aspects of mass communications. It is much easier and less expensive for the big corporations to control all aspects of television broadcasting, for instance, rather than contracting with separate, independent companies to produce programs and operate local TV stations. The media giants had such a strong financial interest in eliminating FCC ownership rules, in fact, that the broadcast industry spent nearly $250 million lobbying (working to persuade) the federal government between 1998 and 2004.

But opponents of media consolidation have a number of reasons to think that further deregulation (reduction or elimination of rules) of ownership is a bad idea. While critics admit that advances in technology have created new sources of news and information, they claim that most of these sources are controlled by the same handful of giant corporations. They point out that the desire to earn profits in one area of the business might create a conflict with these corporations' duty to provide fair and unbiased TV news coverage. For example, a network news program might be tempted to downplay its coverage of safety problems in a product manufactured by another division of its parent company. The media giants might also tend to provide more favorable coverage to the government in order to convince the president and members of Congress to support their efforts at deregulation. In general, the critics worried that media consolidation would create a situation in which the media would be used to serve corporate interests rather than the public interest.

In June 2003, the FCC announced the results of its review. The agency decided to increase the audience-reach cap for broadcasters to 45 percent of the U.S. population. It also decided to ease the restrictions on newspaper/broadcast cross-ownership. These changes pleased many people in the broadcast industry, but they ran into a great deal of opposition from Congress and various consumer groups. In fact, the FCC received two million letters and electronic mail messages opposing the rule changes. One opposition group filed a lawsuit to prevent the changes from taking effect, and in September 2003 a federal court ruled in the group's favor and ordered the FCC to start the review process over again. When the U.S. Supreme Court refused to hear the broadcast industry's appeal in the case, it was considered an important victory for consumer groups and a blow to the large media corporations.

Ted Turner speaks out

One high-profile opponent of the FCC's proposed rule changes was Ted Turner, who made a name for himself in broadcasting by forming some of the first national cable TV networks and offering innovative cable programming. Born in 1938, Turner started his career by working in his father's billboard advertising business. After purchasing several radio stations in the late 1960s, Turner bought his first television station in 1970. This station, WTCG in Atlanta, was located at Channel 17 on the lesser quality UHF portion of the broadcast spectrum. At that time, stations affiliated with the Big Three national broadcast networks (ABC, CBS, and NBC) occupied the scarce VHF channels in nearly every important television market. But Turner disliked network programming and believed that independent stations could succeed by providing more wholesome options. He began showing old movies, cartoons, and sporting events to give viewers an alternative to the network offerings.

In 1976, Turner turned his small, independent station into a national cable network by arranging to deliver his signal to cable systems across the country via satellite. He changed his call letters to WTBS (for Turner Broadcasting System) and referred to it as a "Superstation." He soon convinced a number of national advertisers to begin placing their commercials on his cable network.

In 1980, Turner launched the Cable News Network (CNN) to provide viewers with news and information twenty-four hours per day. When promoting the new network, he claimed that he wanted to provide the American people with a source of news that was independent of the powerful broadcast networks. "Back in the Dark Ages, only the church and politicians had knowledge, and the people were kept in the dark," he declared in Ken Auletta's biography *Media Man*. "Information is power. I see CNN as the democratization of information."

The broadcast networks criticized CNN's low-budget production methods and called it the "Chicken Noodle Network." At first it appeared that CNN would be a short-lived experiment, as the network lost $20 million in its first year. But Turner's all-news format gradually attracted viewers and became profitable. It moved to the forefront of international news coverage during the 1991 Persian Gulf War, when CNN reporters provided live coverage of U.S.-led bombing raids from a hotel balcony in downtown Baghdad, Iraq. CNN thus launched a revolution in up-to-the-minute television news coverage.

Ted Turner (left), pictured with President Bill Clinton at CNN's headquarters in 1994.
© WALLY MCNAMEE/CORBIS.

After the 2003 court ruling that forced the FCC to reconsider its media ownership rule changes, Turner began speaking out against further consolidation of the American media. He expressed his opinion in speeches and in articles for major newspapers and magazines. One of these articles, "My Beef with Big Media," is excerpted below.

Turner starts out by talking about his early career in television broadcasting, when he created Superstation TBS and CNN. He acknowledges that some FCC regulations helped him, as an independent broadcaster, compete with the established broadcast networks. For instance, the All-Channel Receiver Act of 1962 required all new television sets sold in the United States to be equipped to receive UHF channels. Before this time, viewers had to purchase a separate tuner to receive these weaker channels. This rule change made it possible for more viewers to watch Turner's Atlanta-based UHF station. In 1972, the FCC issued another ruling that allowed cable TV operators to give their customers access to TV channels that originated in other cities. Before this time, cable providers could only retransmit the signals from local TV stations. This ruling aided the growth of cable television and allowed Turner to offer a wider variety of programs on TBS.

But Turner also argues that more recent FCC rule changes regarding station ownership have allowed too much media consolidation. He claims that a handful of large companies own most sources of information in the United States, including broadcast and cable networks, local TV stations, production companies that create TV programs, cable service providers, and book publishers. He says that this type of consolidation is harmful to broadcasting because it reduces the level of risk taking and the development of new ideas. He also claims that media consolidation has had a negative impact on the quality of television news. Turner acknowledges that his company, Turner Broadcasting, was big enough to benefit from some of the ownership rule changes. But he concludes by encouraging readers to urge the government to prevent further consolidation and break up some of the largest media corporations.

Things to remember while reading the excerpt of "My Beef with Big Media":

- In 1986, Turner took advantage of relaxed media ownership rules to purchase MGM—a major movie production company with a huge film library—in order to gain access to content for his cable TV networks. In 1995, however, media consolidation forced him to sell Turner Broadcasting to Time Warner Inc. He became vice chairman of Time Warner's board of directors and head of its cable TV networks division. In 2001, Time Warner merged with the Internet service provider America Online (AOL) to become AOL Time Warner. A short time later, Turner fell out of favor with corporate management. He resigned from his position as vice chairman in 2003, and in 2006 he announced that he would no longer serve on the AOL Time Warner board of directors. These experiences may have influenced his opinions on the subject of media consolidation.

• Turner blames media consolidation for the declining quality of American journalism. But some critics hold CNN partly responsible for the decline in TV news. They claim that the need to provide round-the-clock news pushed the American media toward sensational "tabloid journalism," which emphasized sleazy, celebrity-centered stories instead of important, but more complex, national and international news events.

• • •

Excerpt of "My Beef with Big Media"

In the late 1960s, when Turner Communications was a business of billboards and radio stations and I was spending much of my energy ocean racing [in sailboats], a UHF-TV station came up for sale in Atlanta. It was losing $50,000 a month and its programs were viewed by fewer than 5 percent of the market.

I **acquired** it.

When I moved to buy a second station in Charlotte [North Carolina]—this one worse than the first—my accountant quit in protest, and the company's board [of directors] **vetoed** the deal. So I **mortgaged** my house and bought it myself. The Atlanta purchase turned into the Superstation; the Charlotte purchase—when I sold it 10 years later—gave me the **capital** to launch CNN.

Both purchases played a role in revolutionizing television. Both required a streak of independence and a taste for risk. And neither could happen today. In the current climate of consolidation, independent broadcasters simply don't survive for long. That's why we haven't seen a new generation of people like me or even **Rupert Murdoch**—independent television **upstarts** who challenge the big boys and force the whole industry to compete and change.

It's not that there aren't **entrepreneurs** eager to make their names and fortunes in broadcasting if given the chance. If nothing else, the 1990s **dot-com boom** showed that the spirit of entrepreneurship is alive and well in America, with plenty of investors willing to put real money into new media ventures. The difference is that [the U.S. government in] Washington has changed the rules of the game. When I was getting into the television

Acquired: Bought.

Vetoed: Refused to approve.

Mortgaged: Borrowed money against.

Capital: Money.

Rupert Murdoch: (1931–) Australian businessman who launched the Fox network.

Upstarts: People who rise suddenly from a low position to one of power.

Entrepreneurs: People who start their own businesses.

Dot-com boom: A period when people rushed to create new Internet-based businesses, known as "dot-com" businesses after the extension ".com" used for commercial Web sites.

Ted Turner

Localism: Attention to local and community issues.

Foothold: Starting point.

Import: Receive from other places and send to local areas.

RCA: Radio Corporation of America, one of the early manufacturers of broadcasting equipment.

Concentrated: Gathered closely into one large group.

Tilt the playing field: Change conditions to give an advantage to one side.

business, lawmakers and the Federal Communications Commission (FCC) took seriously the commission's mandate to promote diversity, **localism**, and competition in the media marketplace. They wanted to make sure that the big, established networks—CBS, ABC, NBC—wouldn't forever dominate what the American public could watch on TV. They wanted independent producers to thrive. They wanted more people to be able to own TV stations. They believed in the value of competition.

So when the FCC received a glut of applications for new television stations after World War II, the agency set aside dozens of channels on the new UHF spectrum so independents could get a **foothold** in television. That helped me get my start 35 years ago. Congress also passed a law in 1962 requiring that TVs be equipped to receive both UHF and VHF channels. That's how I was able to compete as a UHF station, although it was never easy. (I used to tell potential advertisers that our UHF viewers were smarter than the rest, because you had to be a genius just to figure out how to tune us in.) And in 1972, the FCC ruled that cable TV operators could **import** distant signals. That's how we were able to beam our Atlanta station to homes throughout the South. Five years later, with the help of an **RCA** satellite, we were sending our signal across the nation, and the Superstation was born.

That was then.

Today, media companies are more **concentrated** than at any time over the past 40 years, thanks to a continual loosening of ownership rules by Washington. The media giants now own not only broadcast networks and local stations; they also own the cable companies that pipe in the signals of their competitors and the studios that produce most of the programming. To get a flavor of how consolidated the industry has become, consider this: In 1990, the major broadcast networks—ABC, CBS, NBC, and Fox—fully or partially owned just 12.5 percent of the new series they aired. By 2000, it was 56.3 percent. Just two years later, it had surged [grown suddenly] to 77.5 percent.

In this environment, most independent media firms either get gobbled up by one of the big companies or driven out of business altogether. Yet instead of balancing the rules to give independent broadcasters a fair chance in the market, Washington continues to **tilt the playing field** to favor the biggest players. Last summer, the FCC passed another round of sweeping pro-consolidation rules that, among other things, further raised the cap on the number of TV stations a company can own.

In the media, as in any industry, big corporations play a vital role, but so do small, emerging ones. When you lose small businesses, you lose big ideas. People who own their own businesses are their own bosses. They are independent thinkers. They know they can't compete by imitating the big guys—they have to **innovate**, so they're less obsessed with earnings than they are with ideas. They are quicker to seize on new technologies and new product ideas. They steal **market share** from the big companies, spurring them to adopt new approaches. This process promotes competition, which leads to higher product and service quality, more jobs, and greater wealth. It's called **capitalism**.

But without the proper rules, healthy capitalist markets turn into sluggish **oligopolies**, and that is what's happening in media today. Large corporations are more profit-focused and **risk-averse**. They often kill local programming because it's expensive, and they push national programming because it's cheap—even if their decisions run **counter** to local interests and community values. Their managers are more **averse** to innovation because they're afraid of being fired for an idea that fails. They prefer to sit on the sidelines, waiting to buy the businesses of the risk-takers who succeed.

Unless we have a climate that will allow more independent media companies to survive, a dangerously high percentage of what we see [on television]—and what we don't see—will be shaped by the profit motives and political interests of large, **publicly traded conglomerates**. The economy will suffer, and so will the quality of our public life. Let me be clear: As a business proposition, consolidation makes sense. The **moguls** behind the mergers are acting in their corporate interests and playing by the rules. We just shouldn't have those rules. They make sense for a corporation. But for a society, it's like **over-fishing the oceans**. When the independent businesses are gone, where will the new ideas come from? We have to do more than keep media giants from growing larger; they're already too big. We need a new set of rules that will break these huge companies to pieces.

The Big Squeeze

In the 1970s, I became convinced that a 24-hour all-news network could make money, and perhaps even change the world. But when I invited two large media corporations to invest in the launch of CNN, they turned me down. I couldn't believe it. Together we could have launched the network for a fraction of what it would have taken me alone; they had all the **infrastructure**, contacts, experience, knowledge. When no one would go in with me, I risked my personal wealth to start CNN. Soon after our launch in 1980, our expenses were twice what we had expected and revenues half what we had projected. Our losses were so high that our loans were **called in**. I **refinanced** at 18 percent interest, up from 9, and stayed just a step ahead of the bankers. Eventually, we not only became profitable, but also changed the nature of news—from watching something that happened to watching it as it happened.

But even as CNN was getting its start, the climate for independent broadcasting was turning hostile. This trend began in 1984, when the FCC raised the number of stations a single **entity** could own from

Innovate: Be creative; come up with new ideas.

Market share: The percentage of total customers served by each business within an industry.

Capitalism: An economic system in which private businesses compete against one another in a free market.

Oligopolies: Economic systems in which a few large businesses control the market.

Risk-averse: Unwilling or afraid to take risks or be exposed to dangerous situations.

Counter: Against or opposite.

Averse: Resistent to; likely to avoid.

Publicly traded: A business that sells shares of ownership to the public on the stock market.

Conglomerates: Very large corporations involved in a variety of businesses.

Moguls: Wealthy and powerful individuals.

Over-fishing the oceans: Catching so many fish that they all disappear; using up a resource.

Infrastructure: Basic equipment or framework.

Called in: Canceled; had to be repaid immediately.

Refinanced: Borrowed more money from someone else.

Entity: Individual or company.

Audience-reach cap: Upper limit on the percentage of American viewers one owner's TV stations could serve.

Achieved scale: Grown large enough to compete.

seven—where it had been capped since the 1950s—to 12. A year later, it revised its rule again, adding a national **audience-reach cap** of 25 percent to the 12 station limit—meaning media companies were prohibited from owning TV stations that together reached more than 25 percent of the national audience. In 1996, the FCC did away with numerical caps altogether and raised the audience-reach cap to 35 percent. This wasn't necessarily bad for Turner Broadcasting; we had already **achieved scale**. But seeing these rules changed was like watching someone knock down the ladder I had already climbed. . . .

Today, the only way for media companies to survive is to own everything up and down the media chain—from broadcast and cable networks to the sitcoms, movies, and news broadcasts you see on those stations; to the production studios that make them; to the cable, satellite, and broadcast systems that bring the programs to your television set; to the Web sites you visit to read about those programs; to the way you log on to the Internet to view those pages. Big media today wants to own the faucet, pipeline, water, and the reservoir. The rain clouds come next. . . .

The FCC says that we have more media choices than ever before. But only a few corporations decide what we can choose. That is not choice. That's like a **dictator** deciding what candidates are allowed to stand for parliamentary elections, and then claiming that the people choose their leaders. Different voices do not mean different viewpoints, and these huge corporations all have the same viewpoint—they want to shape government policy in a way that helps them maximize profits, drive out competition, and keep getting bigger. . . .

Dictator: Ruler who holds absolute power.

Monopoly: Complete control over all business within an industry.

News-sharing: A situation where print and broadcast news organizations use the same group of reporters in order to save money.

Bureaus: Branch offices of news organizations located in major cities.

Downsizing: Reducing; laying off.

Accountable: Responsible for their actions.

A few media conglomerates now exercise a near-**monopoly** over television news. There is always a risk that news organizations can emphasize or ignore stories to serve their corporate purpose. But the risk is far greater when there are no independent competitors to air the side of the story the corporation wants to ignore. More consolidation has often meant more **news-sharing**. But closing **bureaus** and **downsizing** staff have more than economic consequences. A smaller press is less capable of holding our leaders **accountable**. . . .

Naturally, corporations say they would never suppress speech. But it's not their intentions that matter; it's their capabilities. Consolidation gives them more power to tilt the news and cut important ideas out of the public debate. And it's precisely that power that the rules should prevent.

Independents' Day

This is a fight about freedom—the freedom of independent entrepreneurs to start and run a media business, and the freedom of citizens to get news, information, and entertainment from a wide variety of sources, at least some of which are truly independent and not run by people facing the pressure of **quarterly earnings reports**. No one should underestimate the danger. Big media companies want to eliminate all ownership limits. With the removal of these limits, immense media power will pass into the hands of a very few corporations and individuals.

What will programming be like when it's produced for no other purpose than profit? What will news be like when there are no independent news organizations to go after stories the big corporations avoid? Who really wants to find out? **Safeguarding** the welfare of the public cannot be the first concern of a large publicly traded media company. Its job is to seek profits. But if the government writes the rules in a way that encourages the entry into the market of entrepreneurs—men and women with big dreams, new ideas, and a willingness to take long-term risks—the economy will be stronger, and the country will be better off.

Quarterly earnings reports: Financial information that public companies release four times per year.

Safeguarding: Protecting.

• • •

What happened next . . .

The issue of media consolidation continued to generate debate after Turner wrote his article. After completing its court-ordered review, the FCC planned to propose a new set of media ownership regulations in the fall of 2006.

Did you know . . .

- In September 2002, the FCC announced that it would conduct a major review of media ownership rules. According to a PBS survey, the only network television news program to cover the announcement was ABC's *World News This Morning,* which aired a three-sentence report at 4:40 A.M. Opponents of media consolidation pointed to the lack of coverage as evidence that the large media corporations did not want the public to know about their efforts to eliminate all restrictions on media ownership. As former FCC chairman Reed Hundt noted in a panel discussion covered by the Freedom Forum, "It's not clear to me that the media is going to lead a reasonable debate about the consolidation of the media."
- In early 2003, President George W. Bush prepared to launch a U.S. military invasion of the Middle Eastern nation of Iraq. He said that the attack was necessary to prevent Iraqi dictator Saddam Hussein from providing weapons of mass destruction to terrorist groups. In an effort to gain international support for a war against Iraq,

Secretary of State Colin Powell appeared before the United Nations in early February. Powell presented evidence that he said proved Iraq possessed chemical and biological weapons. He also suggested that a link existed between Saddam Hussein and Al Qaeda, the terrorist group responsible for the September 11, 2001, attacks against the United States. The media watchdog organization Fairness and Accuracy in Reporting (FAIR) conducted a survey of media coverage of the Iraq situation during the week before and the week after Powell's presentation. FAIR found that only 3 out of 393 interviews that aired on the ABC, CBS, NBC, and PBS television networks during this period were with people who opposed starting a war with Iraq. Critics claimed that television news slanted its coverage to support the president's position on the issue. "These are not media that are serving a democratic society, where a diversity of views is vital to shaping informed opinions," Amy Goodman and David Goodman wrote in the *Seattle Times*.

- Ted Turner has an amazingly varied list of lifetime achievements. For example, he is an accomplished sailor who won the America's Cup—the most prestigious yacht-racing event in the world—in 1977. He is also known as a successful owner of professional sports teams, such as the Atlanta Hawks basketball team and the Atlanta Braves baseball team, as well as the World Championship Wrestling series. Finally, Turner owns approximately 200 million acres of land in six western states, making him the largest private landowner in America. He maintains a herd of 40,000 bison on his property and runs a chain of restaurants featuring bison meat.

Consider the following...

- Visit the Web site for a large U.S. media corporation—such as Time Warner, Walt Disney, Viacom, Seagram, News Corporation, Sony, General Electric, or AT&T—and find a list of all of the media outlets it owns. Do you think that the public interest is best served by allowing these companies to control so many media outlets? Keep in mind that the public also includes people who work for and hold stock in these corporations.

- Research the ownership of a local television station or your favorite cable television channel. Is it connected to one of the large U.S. media corporations? What other media outlets does its parent company own? What similarities or differences do you notice in the way that these media outlets present information?

- Make lists of the potential problems and benefits associated with allowing one company to own television stations, radio stations, and daily newspapers in the same city. If you were an FCC commissioner, what action would you support regarding cross-ownership of broadcast and print media outlets?

For More Information

BOOKS

Auletta, Ken. *Media Man: Ted Turner's Improbable Empire.* New York: W. W. Norton, 2004.

McChesney, Robert W. *Rich Media, Poor Democracy: Communications Politics in Dubious Times.* Urbana and Chicago: University of Illinois Press, 1999.

PERIODICALS

Davies, Jennifer. "FCC Chief Calls for New Approach to Telecommunications Regulation." *Knight-Ridder/Tribune Business News,* December 10, 2003.

Goodman, Amy, and David Goodman. "Why Media Ownership Matters." *Seattle Times,* April 3, 2005.

Miller, Mark Crispin. "What's Wrong with This Picture?" *Nation,* January 7, 2002.

Turner, Ted. "Monopoly or Democracy?" *Washington Post,* May 30, 2003.

Turner, Ted. "My Beef with Big Media" *Washington Monthly,* July/August 2004.

WEB SITES

"Big Media: Media Regulation Timeline." *NOW with Bill Moyers,* January 30, 2004. http://www.pbs.org/now/politics/mediatimeline.html (accessed on July 31, 2006).

"FCC Consumer Facts: Review of the Broadcast Ownership Rules." *Federal Communications Commission,* December 1, 2005. http://www.fcc.gov/cgb/consumerfacts/reviewrules.html (accessed on July 31, 2006).

Finney, Robert. "Ownership: U.S. Regulatory Patterns." *Museum of Broadcast Communications.* http://www.museum.tv/archives/etv/O/htmlO/ownership/ownership.htm (accessed on July 31, 2006).

"Guide to FCC Rules on Media Ownership." *Center for Digital Democracy.* http://www.democraticmedia.org/issues/mediaownership/chart.html (accessed on July 31, 2006).

"Massive Media." *NOW with Bill Moyers,* April 26, 2002. http://www.pbs.org/now/politics/media.html (accessed on July 31, 2006).

"Speaking with One Voice: Does Media Cross-Ownership Stifle Diversity?" *Freedom Forum Online,* December 15, 2000. http://www.freedomforum.org/templates/document.asp?documentID=3183 (accessed on July 31, 2006).

Stohr, Greg. "Media Industry Rejected by Top U.S. Court on Station Ownership." *Bloomberg.com,* June 13, 2005. http://www.bloomberg.com/apps/news?pid=10000087&sid=abgsaV4QV41c&refer=top_world_news (accessed on July 31, 2006).

13

Steven Levy

"Television Reloaded"
Published in Newsweek, *May 30, 2005*

"The ethos of New TV can be captured in a single sweeping mantra: anything you want to see, any time, on any device."

M any experts claim that the turn of the twenty-first century marked the beginning of a revolution in American television. Since that time, a series of technological breakthroughs has changed some of the most fundamental aspects of the TV viewing experience. People increasingly can choose not only what TV programs to watch, but also when, where, and on what type of device to watch them.

One of the most important technological developments of the early twenty-first century is the switch to digital transmission of television signals, which was scheduled to be completed by 2009. In digital transmission, information is stored as a binary code consisting of long strings of the digits zero and one. These numbers indicate whether tiny electronic circuits should be switched on or off. Digital transmission of TV signals offers a number of advantages over analog transmission (the original system, which involved sending TV signals through the air as waves of electromagnetic energy). For instance, binary code can be understood by computers and all other types of digital devices, making television and computer technology compatible for the first time. Another advantage to digital transmission is that signals can be simplified and compressed by computers so that a great deal more data can be sent in the same amount of channel space. For television signals, this means that digital technology can provide viewers with movie-quality picture and sound, as well as a variety of interactive features.

One of the first technologies to take advantage of the compatibility between digital TV and computers was the digital video recorder (DVR).

Steven Levy

A digital video recorder (DVR) remote control. The "on demand" feature gives the audience more control over programming by allowing viewers to select the programs they want and at the times they want. © MARIANNA DAY MASSEY/ZUMA/CORBIS.

This type of device records television programs onto a computer hard drive. Although videocassette recorders (VCRs) have long given viewers the option of taping TV programs to watch later, a DVR makes the process much simpler. The growing popularity of DVR technology could have a major impact on the television industry in the future. For instance, DVRs allow viewers to watch programs according to their own schedules, rather than following the broadcast schedules devised by the television networks. The technology also makes it easy for viewers to skip all the commercials in TV programs, which poses a threat to the future of advertising on television.

The change to digital transmission of TV signals also makes high-definition television (HDTV) possible in the United States. In order to be scanned by a TV camera and reproduced on a TV screen, a visual image is divided into horizontal lines. The original American technical standard, which was established by the Federal Communications Commission (FCC) in 1941, dictated that TV screens would have a resolution of 525 lines. Increasing the resolution provides for clearer, sharper, brighter images on the screen. The FCC established a new technical standard for HDTV in 1994. This standard said that HDTV in the United States would have a resolution of up to 1,080 lines, making it more than twice as good as standard-definition images. In addition to sharp picture detail in a widescreen format, HDTV also provides for Dolby digital surround sound, like that found in movie theaters.

Another development in TV technology allowed for more interaction between the sender and receiver of TV signals. Modern interactive TV gives the audience more control over programming. Viewers can select, respond to, and even change the content of some programs. The main application of digital interactive TV technology in the early 2000s was video-on-demand (VOD) services, which allow customers to select new-release movies and real-time games from a menu. Interactive technology was anticipated to have the potential to redefine the relationship between television broadcasters and viewers.

TV promises to become more fully interactive when signals are delivered over the Internet through a new service called Internet Protocol Television (IPTV). Internet Protocol (IP) is a set of rules that guide how computers around the world communicate with each other over the vast network known as the Internet. In the 2000s, faster Internet connections and improved digital compression technology made it possible to adapt IP to carry TV signals. IPTV services offer a number of potential advantages over traditional broadcast, cable, and satellite delivery methods. For example, the Internet has a virtually unlimited capacity to host billions of Web pages, so it may also be able to deliver thousands or even millions of TV channels. In addition, people using IPTV would also have access to the Internet and all of its resources. This access would allow them to interact with TV programming in many new ways or perhaps to watch television programs and receive e-mail or use other Internet functions at the same time. Finally, IPTV could make producing a TV show as cheap and easy as creating a Web site, allowing viewers to create their own TV content and make it available online.

All of these advances in technology promised to help American viewers gain more control over how and when they watch television. Meanwhile, the introduction of portable video devices and TV programming for mobile phones made it possible for people to watch their favorite shows virtually anywhere.

In "Television Reloaded," the 2005 *Newsweek* article reprinted below, technology writer Steven Levy outlines some of the major trends affecting American television in the twenty-first century. Levy was born in Philadelphia and earned a bachelor's degree from Temple University and a

This screen shows Internet services available through a TiVo digital video recorder, allowing customers access to many options right from their TVs. © STEVE MARCUS/REUTERS/CORBIS.

master's degree from Pennsylvania State University. He is considered to be one of the pioneers of technology journalism, having written on the subject for more than twenty years. The author of five books, Levy joined the staff of *Newsweek* in 1995. His article "Television Reloaded" discusses the potential for various new technologies to change the entire broadcast industry. In the end, though, Levy questions whether all the changes will really improve the TV viewing experience for average Americans.

Things to remember while reading "Television Reloaded":

- In his article, Steven Levy makes reference to a famous speech by **Newton N. Minow** (1926–; see Chapter 7). Minow served as the chairman of the Federal Communications Commission (FCC)— the U.S. government agency in charge of regulating television and other electronic communication technologies—under President John F. Kennedy (1917–1963; served 1961–63). In a controversial 1961 address to the National Association of Broadcasters called "Television and the Public Interest," Minow criticized the content of TV programming as a "vast wasteland." He also argued that the broadcast networks had a responsibility to serve the public interest by providing educational and informational programming.

- In "Television Reloaded," Levy also provides some information about how people watched television in the early years of broadcasting. In the late 1940s and early 1950s, black-and-white television sets were a new invention, and color sets were not yet available. There were three major broadcast networks in the United States, which only aired programs for a few hours each evening. People who owned TV sets often invited family members, friends, and neighbors over to share the unusual experience of watching television. Levy compares this past era to today, when most American families own more than one TV set and viewers can choose from hundreds of specialized channels that air programs twenty-four hours per day.

• • •

"Television Reloaded"

Forty-four years ago, when Newton Minow famously described television as a vast wasteland [in a speech before the National Association of Broadcasters], he might have hit the bull's-eye on the wasteland part. But he didn't know from vast. TV back then—a few black-and-white channels with a **test pattern** after midnight—was a sleepy **three-light town** where everybody hung out at the same dull places because there wasn't much else going on. As **monochrome** moved to color, and we got pay TV, more channels, remote controls, VCRs and **cussin'** on HBO, television sprawled much wider. But compared with what's coming, our 2005 experience is only half vast.

Tomorrow's television? Now we're talking vast. Start with the screens—wide, flat, high-definition monsters that **delineate** tire treads on NASCAR rigs and zits on an anchorperson's chin—and move to the programming choices, which will expand from a lousy 200 or so channels to tens of thousands of 'em, if you figure in **video-on-demand (VOD)**. It'll be a cosmic video jukebox where you can fire up old episodes of *Cop Rock,* the fifth game of the 1993 World Series, a live high-school lacrosse game, a ranting video blogger and your own HD [high-definition]

Test pattern: A fixed image broadcast by early television stations during the hours that they did not offer programming.

Three-light town: A small town, with only three traffic lights.

Monochrome: Black and white.

Cussin': Swearing.

Delineate: Show in detail.

Video on demand (VOD): A technology that allows cable and satellite subscribers to watch programs when they want for a fee.

Cop Rock: A short-lived musical police series.

home-movie production of Junior's first karate tournament. While it's playing, you can engage in running voice commentary with your friends, while in a separate part of the screen you're slamming orcs in World of Warcraft [a video game]. Then you can pay your bill on screen. And if you ever manage to leave your home theater, you can monitor the whole **shebang** in your car, at a laptop at Starbucks [a chain of coffee houses] or via the laundry-ticket-size screen on your cell phone. The **ethos** of New TV can be captured in a single sweeping **mantra**: anything you want to see, any time, on any device. "We are at a watershed moment in home entertainment," says Brian Roberts, CEO [chief executive officer] of the cable giant Comcast.

To paraphrase sci-fi author William Gibson, the TV future is already here; it's just not evenly distributed yet. **Early adopters** have jumped on the new stuff because they offer two qualities traditionally lacking in the fading era of broadcast television: **personalization** and empowerment. All of which is worse news than a crummy **Nielsen rating** for the major networks, whose market share has already plummeted in the past decade.

Start with the **hardware**. Ever notice that no one uses the term "TV set" anymore? That's because people can watch on anything from a traditional box in the den to their computer, to a screen on the seat back of a JetBlue [a commercial airline] plane. But when it comes to the living room, the standard is a big-screen monitor that delivers high-definition quality. After years of hype and wrangling about standards, prices are down and a quarter of all TVs sold are now high def. Once you get one, you're hooked. "You find yourself **mesmerized**," says Mark Cuban, an entrepreneur who used his dot-com [Internet] earnings to buy the Dallas Mavericks [professional basketball team]—and now has started HDNet, a cable-and-satellite offering that hosts about 20 hours of original high-def programming a week. "You'll always give the benefit of the doubt to something in HD," he says. That's good for Cuban, who snags viewers with homegrown productions like *Bikini Destinations*. Meanwhile, HD is a must-have for network prime-time dramas, and just last week ABC announced that *Good Morning America* would go HD.

Another transition well underway is time-shifting, the ability to rearrange the schedule to watch programs at your convenience, not the networks'. Though videocassette recorders [VCRs] have enabled this for decades, those devices were always too hard to use and too dumb to really shape our habits. But a digital video recorder (DVR) can easily grab your favorite shows—even if you don't know they're on—and allows you to freeze-frame fast action and jump commercials. Former **FCC** head Michael Powell called it "God's machine." As DVRs are offered in cable and satellite set-top boxes, more people are finally enjoying the benefits.

Shebang: Thing.

Ethos: Character or nature.

Mantra: Saying or chant.

Early adopters: People who are first to try out a new technology.

Personalization: Customized to fit individual tastes.

Nielsen rating: A measure of the number of viewers who watched a TV program, conducted by the A. C. Nielsen company.

Hardware: Physical equipment.

Mesmerized: Spellbound; unable to look away.

FCC: Federal Communications Commission, the U.S. government agency charged with regulating television.

Video-on-demand provides another way to bypass what programmers offer at a given moment—and millions are already experimenting with it, commonly choosing old episodes of *Curb Your Enthusiasm* to the usual prime-time fare. VOD libraries will inevitably expand to the equivalent of the mammoth music boxes of iTunes and Rhapsody [Internet music stores]. And if you ever get tired of old movies, you'll have a chance to watch flicks at home while they're still in theaters. "All the studios say it's a matter of not if but when . . . new movie releases will quickly air on cable TV," says Comcast's Roberts.

Some people believe that between the recorders and VOD, people will follow schedules only for real-time events like sports and election night. Fox TV president Peter Ligouri says, "People want to watch shows like *American Idol* live, in the moment." But everything else can wait. "Look behind any programmer's desk and you'll see a chart with the prime-time schedule—in 20 years that model will be as **obsolete** as the **nickelodeon**," says Steve Perlman, CEO of Rearden, Inc., and founder of Web-TV.

Obsolete: Out of date; a thing of the past.

Nickelodeon: A type of early movie theater that no longer exists.

While time-shifting changes the when of television, "space-shifting" tinkers with the where. Now that you've stored your show on a TiVo [a popular brand of digital video recorder], it's only logical to take it with you on your laptop, hand-held viewer or PSP [Sony PlayStation Portable] game player. A company called Sling Media sells a device that allows you to watch the program playing in your living room on your computer, anywhere in the world. Other schemes are designed to beam programming directly to gadgets not normally regarded as TV devices. MobiTV, a service that sends programs to cell phones (like CNN and Discovery Channel), has 300,000 subscribers. It may call to mind the characters in *Zoolander* [a futuristic movie] squinting into their microscopic mobiles, but Idetic CEO Phillip Alvelda reminds us that people once **scoffed** at mobile phones. "The truth is, mobile devices have a lot of advantages over television," he says. "For one thing, it's personal." And while you might not want to watch a viewing of *Lawrence of Arabia* [an epic movie] on your Razr [a brand of cellular phone], new programming ("Mobisodes") will fit the size and time constraints of **commuter-potato** viewing.

Scoffed: Mocked; viewed with contempt.

Commuter-potato: A takeoff on the term "couch potato" that describes people relaxing on public transportation while traveling to work.

All these elements come together in what may be the most significant development of all—the movement of the television **platform** to the Internet. IPTV [Internet Protocol Television] hopes to merge the lay-back culture of the living room with the bustling activity of the lean-forward Net. "This is the future," gushes Microsoft chairman Bill Gates, who has a $400 million deal with telecom [telecommunications industry] giant SBC to implement it.

Platform: Basic plan or design.

Broadband: High-speed communications technology that operates on a wide range of frequencies.

"Moving from broadcast TV to **broadband** TV changes the whole industry," says Gates's IPTV **czar** Moshe Lichtman. While cable and satellite companies have limited channel capacity, the Net—which you'll recall, can host

Czar: Head expert.

Television is no longer confined to the living room. Viewing programs on a computer, laptop, or cell phone is growing in popularity. © KIM KULISH/CORBIS.

billions of Web pages without a sweat—has room for everything. You can stack as many shows on the screen as your eyes can handle. When you watch baseball, you can monitor several games at once, or choose to view the game from several different angles at the same time. A future presentation of the Masters [professional golf] Tournament might let you follow any golfer for every minute of his round.

Since the Internet is open to any digital content, your television will merge with other activities. Someone on the phone? You'll get caller-ID information on the TV screen. If you don't feel like fast-forwarding past the commercials, check your credit-card bills. And you know those news-channel "tickers" that run on the bottom of the screen with headlines, weather reports and updates on [pop singer] Britney Spears's wedding status? "Ninety percent of that stuff you don't care about," says Gates. "We'll let you have a custom ticker [with stock quotes, scores and other information that you pick]."

"Once you put this stuff up [on the Internet] nobody knows what will happen," says SBC's Randall Stephenson. What some people think might happen may not please media **middlemen** like . . . SBC. While IPTV originally requires a reliable high-**bandwidth** platform to ensure top-quality reception, fast connections will eventually become commonplace. In that case it might be feasible for programmers to reach the mass audience without going through a **gatekeeper**, be it a telecom, cable provider or satellite service. Video would be served directly, like everything else on the Web. "Most flat-panel TV sets will have Internet connections in their future," says Steve Shannon, founder of Akimbo, a Web video service that has content deals with more than 100 partners, including CNN, Turner Classic Movies and the BBC [British Broadcasting Corporation].

Others focus on the prospect of outsiders gaining access to your TV set, as **bloggers** have invaded media on the Web. "Already there is more data downloaded for video over the Internet than there is for music," says Mike Ramsay, cofounder of TiVo. "What happens when a 14-year-old creates a BitTorrent browser [a free computer software program that increases the speed of Internet downloads] that's easy to use and plugs right into your TV? You go from 500 channels to 50 million channels." We soon may find out, as a number of **open-source**-inspired Internet efforts hope to open the floodgates. "We have tools to let anyone make high-quality videos to reach millions of people," says Tiffiny Cheng of the Participatory Culture Foundation in Worcester, Mass[achusetts]. "We'll give a channel to anyone who wants a channel."

Given that future programming will be largely on demand, a "channel" could simply be a periodic video blog [or] a set of fly-fishing videos. . . . "The cost of establishing a traditional programming vehicle and securing distribution is incredibly high," says Jeremy Allaire, founder of online distributor Brightcove. In the era of Internet television, it will be as simple and cost-effective to create a **microchannel** as it is to create a Web site.

How would you figure out what to watch? "By the time you scroll through the listings, something else would already be on," says Bradley Horowitz, head of video-search at Yahoo [an Internet search company]. His suggestion? A personalized home-video page that stores your favorite channels and seeks out stuff you'd like. "Instead of a list of shows, you'd get 'Here's what's hot,' or 'Here's what psychologists are watching'."

Does this mean that traditional programming like *Desperate Housewives* and *The Daily Show* will get overwhelmed? Not necessarily. If two **obscure animators** at Web site JibJab could get millions of viewers for their Internet-based [George W.] Bush/[John] Kerry [2004 presidential election] campaign video, would a 2015 *Sopranos Reunion* have any difficulty reaching a mass audience? "There is a consistent hunger for good stories and good

Middlemen: People or companies that arrange deals between two other parties.

Bandwidth: The space within the radio spectrum needed to carry an electronic communication signal.

Gatekeeper: Company that controls access.

Bloggers: Short for Web loggers, or people who maintain personal sites on the Internet.

Open source: A type of computer programming that makes code available for outsiders to see and adapt for their own purposes.

Microchannel: Small channel to send video over the Internet.

Obscure: Unknown; not famous.

Animators: People who create cartoons.

David E. Kelley: Successful television writer and producer responsible for such hit programs as *L.A. Law, Ally McBeal,* and *Boston Legal.*

characters," says HBO's Carolyn Strauss. David Hill, a DirecTV [satellite service] exec[utive], contends that no matter how open the distribution is, the public will flock to tiny islands of quality, even if quality is defined by what's always been on TV. "People who say that everyone can be a **David E. Kelley** have no clue of this business," he says. The result may be that when all the time-shifting and space-shifting is accounted for, most people will watch the same stuff by the same creators.

In fact, even with today's relative abundance, most people stick to only a few channels. According to Nielsen Media Research, households that receive about 60 channels usually watch only 15. Households whose systems can receive 96 channels (around the national average) actually watch . . . 15.

What's more, a recent study conducted at the [University of Pennsylvania's] Annenberg School for Communications showed that when people were offered more programming choices, they stuck to fewer selections—and, alarmingly, watched fewer news shows.

This doesn't surprise Barry Schwartz, a Swarthmore [College] professor and author of "The Paradox of Choice." He fears that people may stick to a small group of selections that don't challenge any of their assumptions. "I worry about 250 million separate islands," he says. It's a long way from the first era of television, when there were so few choices that almost everything you viewed was a mass-shared experience. Schwartz does concede that when you have millions of options to choose from, you're more likely to find ones that really appeal to you. But even then, you won't necessarily be more satisfied. "Whatever you watch," he says, "you'll know that there's something else on that's good, and regret you're not watching it."

Nostalgic: A feeling of longing for the past.

Can it be that in the vast world of television's tomorrow, we'll be **nostalgic** for the wasteland?

• • •

What happened next . . .

Levy and many other technology experts claim that "choice" will be the watchword for the future of television. They predict that the number of programming options available to viewers will increase dramatically, until people can choose from among thousands or even millions of TV channels. They also claim that American viewers will soon be able to choose not only what programs to watch, but when and where to watch them. While having a broad range of programs and viewing options to choose from might allow viewers to find more shows that fit their individual interests, the expansion of choice also has some potential drawbacks.

Some critics believe that increasing channel options will encourage Americans to spend even more time watching television. They claim that an increase in TV viewing will reduce the amount of time people spend interacting with each other. They worry that this will cause social isolation, especially when every member of a family is watching a different TV program on a different sort of receiving device. Some experts claim that making TV programs available on all sorts of portable viewing devices will encourage people to watch television instead of pursuing healthier lifestyle alternatives, such as reading books, playing outdoors, or engaging in family activities. Finally, some critics argue that when there are TV programs targeted toward every imaginable interest, viewers will exclusively watch shows that confirm what they already think and believe, rather than expanding their horizons and learning new things.

Of course, no one really knows what the future will hold. The extensive changes taking place in television technology have the potential to bring many exciting changes to the industry. Whether or not the changes will lead to significant improvements in the viewing experience remains to be seen.

Did you know...

- Technology writer Steven Levy is also the author of *The Unicorn's Secret,* a nonfiction book published by Prentice-Hall in 1988. This book explored a sensational real-life murder case that had taken place in Levy's hometown of Philadelphia, Pennsylvania. A prominent figure in the counterculture movement of the 1960s, Ira Einhorn, was the prime suspect in the disappearance of his former girlfriend, Holly Maddux. In 1979, more than a year after she was reported missing, police found Maddux's decomposing body in a trunk in Einhorn's apartment and charged him with murder. Einhorn declared his innocence, claimed that he was being framed by his political enemies, and hired a big-name lawyer who got him released on bail before his trial. Then Einhorn fled the country, and his whereabouts remained unknown for the next sixteen years. He was finally captured in 1997 in France, where he had been living under a false name. But it took four more years of legal wrangling before Einhorn was sent back to the United States to stand trial. He was convicted of murder in 2002 and began serving a life sentence in prison. Levy's work on *The Unicorn's Secret* uncovered important new information in the case, and it was used as evidence in court to help convict Einhorn of the crime.

- Levy collects steel lunch boxes from the 1960s. Some of his favorites feature characters and scenes from early TV series like *The Man from U.N.C.L.E., The Flying Nun,* and *Laugh-In.* On his Web site, Levy noted that he is "always on the lookout for a well-priced pail with some camp panache [out-of-date style]."

Consider the following...

- Research shows that the average American household watches fifteen television channels regularly, regardless of how many additional channels are offered by their cable or satellite systems. What channels do the members of your household watch regularly? If your cable or satellite service allowed subscribers to order channels "a la carte" (one at a time, rather than together as a package), how many would your family pay a separate fee to keep?

- Despite the hundreds of channels available to American television viewers today, the same broadcast networks that dominated TV fifty years ago still attract the largest audiences. Is television really changing as much as Levy claims? Present arguments for both sides.

- What do you think television will be like in fifty years? Make a list of five predictions for the future.

For More Information

PERIODICALS

Balint, Kathryn. "For Television via Internet, the Future Is Now." *San Diego Union-Tribune,* July 13, 2005.

Gwinn, Eric, and Mike Hughlett. "TV-for-Phone Content Seen as Having Big Future." *Chicago Tribune,* October 5, 2005.

Levy, Steven. "Television Reloaded." *Newsweek,* May 30, 2005.

WEB SITES

Constantakis-Valdez, Patti. "Interactive Television." *Museum of Broadcast Communications.* http://www.museum.tv/archives/etv/I/htmlI/interactivet/interactivet. htm (accessed on July 31, 2006).

Federal Communications Commission. "FCC Consumer Facts: Digital Television," February 7, 2006. http://www.fcc.gov/cgb/consumerfacts/digitaltv.html (accessed on July 31, 2006).

Grant, August. "Digital Television." *Museum of Broadcast Communications.* http://www.museum.tv/archives/etv/D/htmlD/digitaltelev/digitaltelev.htm (accessed on July 31, 2006).

Rose, Frank. "The Fast-Forward, On-Demand, Network-Smashing Future of Television." *Wired.com.* http://www.wired.com/wired/archive/11.10/tv_pr.html (accessed on July 31, 2006).

Seel, Peter B. "High-Definition Television." *Museum of Broadcast Communications.* http://www.museum.tv/archives/etv/H/htmlH/high-definiti/high-definiti.htm (accessed on July 31, 2006).

Steven Levy Home Page. http://www.echonyc.com/∼steven (accessed on July 31, 2006).

14

Mitch Albom

"What If CNN Hadn't Happened?"
Published in the Detroit Free Press, *June 12, 2005*

> "There's value in being informed. But given the choice between not knowing something or claiming you know it because you saw a 20-second story on it, well, which is more dangerous?"

Cable television got its start in the United States in the late 1940s, when enterprising citizens began experimenting with alternative ways to transmit television signals so that TV broadcasts would reach small towns and rural areas. The early cable TV systems simply retransmitted existing broadcast network signals to communities that could not receive them over the airwaves. Unlike the extensive services cable TV companies provide in the 2000s, these systems offered just a few channels and did not create their own original programming.

Despite their limitations, however, cable television systems spread across the rural United States during the 1950s and 1960s. The growth of cable TV alarmed the "Big Three" broadcast television networks—ABC, CBS, and NBC—which had enjoyed a virtual lock on American TV audiences from the time television technology was first introduced. The networks argued that cable TV systems stole their programming by intercepting their over-the-air signals and then charging subscribers a fee for retransmitting them. The Big Three urged the Federal Communications Commission (FCC)—the U.S. government agency responsible for regulating television—to impose restrictions on cable operators.

Beginning in 1965, the FCC introduced a number of regulations designed to protect the interests of the broadcast networks by limiting the growth of cable TV. For instance, the FCC prohibited cable systems from entering urban markets, where they would compete directly with the broadcast networks. The rules also prevented cable systems from

Mitch Albom

Mitch Albom was born on May 23, 1958, in Trenton, New Jersey. He earned a bachelor's degree in sociology from Brandeis University and master's degrees in journalism and business administration from Columbia University. Before becoming a journalist, he fought in amateur boxing matches and worked as a singer and piano player in nightclubs. Albom eventually became a sports columnist for the *Detroit Free Press*. As of 2005, he had won more than 100 awards for his writing and been named the top sports columnist in the nation for ten consecutive years.

Albom has also served as the host of two radio talk shows in the Detroit area and appeared on television as a panelist on ESPN's *Sports Reporters* series. He is the author of eight books, including the national bestsellers *Tuesdays with Morrie* and *The Five People You Meet in Heaven*. In his spare time, he writes songs and does charity work.

providing current programming, including movies that were less than ten years old or sporting events that had occurred within the past five years.

This situation began to change during the 1970s, when various community groups and educational institutions began complaining about the limitations the government had placed on cable TV. They argued that cable had the potential to bring new social, educational, and entertainment services to the American people. They claimed that the FCC regulations, in protecting the interests of the powerful broadcast networks, actually harmed the public interest by preventing cable from reaching its potential.

The FCC responded to public pressure and slowly began loosening its restrictions on cable TV. In 1972, the information company Time Inc. took advantage of the changing rules to launch a regional cable network called Home Box Office (HBO). HBO started out offering movies and special-event programming to markets on the East Coast of the United States on a pay-per-view basis. In 1975, HBO began distributing its signal nationwide using communications satellites orbiting Earth.

Around this time, HBO filed a lawsuit against the FCC in order to force the agency to give cable operators greater access to current programming. In 1977, the judge in the case ruled that the FCC was not justified in restricting cable TV in order to protect the broadcast networks. Following this initial ruling, a whole series of judicial decisions overturned other FCC restrictions on cable TV. Cable operators gained the right to air current movies and sporting events, for instance, and to offer services in the nation's top television markets.

Ted Turner revolutionizes cable TV

Ted Turner (1938–; *see* Chapter 12) was a pioneer in forming national cable TV networks and offering innovative cable programming. Turner was born on November 19, 1938, in Cincinnati, Ohio. He started his career by working in his father's billboard advertising business. After purchasing several radio stations in the late 1960s, Turner bought his first television station—WTCG in Atlanta—in 1970. Turner disliked Big Three network programming and thought that independent stations could make TV more interesting. He decided to offer old movies, cartoons, and sporting events as counterprogramming to the network offerings.

In 1976, Turner turned his independent station into a national cable network. Like HBO had done the year before, Turner arranged to deliver his signal to cable systems across the country via satellite. He changed his call letters to WTBS (for Turner Broadcasting System) and referred to it as a "Superstation." He soon convinced national advertisers to begin placing their commercials on his cable network.

On June 1, 1980, Turner launched a new cable channel called the Cable News Network (CNN). CNN became the first network to provide TV viewers with news and information twenty-four hours per day. Turner said that he wanted to provide the American people with a source of news that was independent of the powerful broadcast networks. When CNN came on the air, the broadcast networks criticized its low-budget production methods and called it the "Chicken Noodle Network." At first it appeared that CNN would be a short-lived experiment, as the network lost $20 million in its first year. But Turner's all-news format gradually attracted viewers and became profitable.

Journalist Mitch Albom.
AP IMAGES.

CNN covers breaking news events

Within a few years of its creation, CNN became famous for its coverage of breaking news events. In 1986, for instance, CNN was the only TV channel to provide live coverage of the launch of the space shuttle *Challenger*. After the first American astronaut walked on the Moon in 1969, the broadcast networks had stopped paying much attention to the U.S. space program. So when *Challenger* exploded 73 seconds after liftoff, killing all seven astronauts on board, CNN was the first to report it. The broadcast networks rushed their top anchors into the studios and interrupted regular programming to provide coverage of the accident. Nevertheless, the incident helped make CNN the first choice for many TV viewers when important news broke.

CNN really moved to the forefront of TV news coverage during the 1991 Persian Gulf War. This conflict began when the Middle Eastern nation of Iraq invaded its smaller neighbor, Kuwait. When Iraqi leader Saddam Hussein (1937–) refused international requests to remove his troops from Kuwait, the United States and a coalition of other countries sent military forces to the Persian Gulf region. The coalition spent several weeks bombing strategic targets in Iraq, then launched a ground attack that forced the Iraqi troops to leave Kuwait.

On the night the coalition bombing raids began, CNN had three anchors stationed in the Iraqi capital of Baghdad. These men—Peter Arnett (1934–), Bernard Shaw (1940–), and John Holliman (1948–1998)—covered the attacks live from the balcony of their downtown hotel room. Their daring footage attracted 11 million viewers—or about 20 times the normal ratings for CNN. When Saddam Hussein ordered all foreign journalists to leave Iraq, Arnett was the only one allowed to remain. He continued reporting for CNN from within Iraq throughout the war. CNN's coverage of the Persian Gulf War, which was broadcast via satellite, helped the cable network become a prime news source for TV viewers around the world. Within five years, CNN was more profitable than the three major networks' news divisions combined.

CNN's impact on TV news

CNN launched a revolution in up-to-the-minute television news coverage. By the 1990s, CNN's success had led to the creation of numerous competing cable news channels. Microsoft and NBC teamed up to form MSNBC, for instance, while the Fox broadcast network launched the Fox News Channel. These cable news channels tried a variety of approaches to draw viewers' attention away from CNN and local and network news programming. For example, they introduced news programs with loud, brash, opinionated hosts who seemed to enjoy challenging and arguing with their guests. CNN remained at the forefront of breaking news events, though, and it was the first network to cover the terrorist attacks on New York City on September 11, 2001.

CNN has helped make news more plentiful and up to date than ever, and many TV viewers enjoy having access to news and information

A satellite dish brings television to this remote village in the African nation of Niger. JOHN CHIASSON/LIAISON/GETTY IMAGES.

twenty-four hours per day. At the same time, though, many critics claim that CNN's success has led to an overall decline in the quality of information that TV news provides to the American people. In order to attract and hold viewers' attention, TV news tends to focus on stories that can be presented in short segments and feature a dramatic visual element—like natural disasters and violent crime. Critics argue that this focus often prevents TV news from covering stories that may be more complex and less exciting, but also hold greater importance to society. They also complain that intense competition has forced TV news to become more like tabloid magazines, full of celebrity gossip and sex scandals.

CNN celebrated its twenty-fifth anniversary on June 1, 2005. *Detroit Free Press* columnist, radio host, television commentator, and best-selling author Mitch Albom chose this occasion to share his thoughts about CNN's impact on American society. In his article "What If

CNN Hadn't Happened," which is reprinted below, Albom argues that the tremendous influence of CNN around the world is not necessarily a good thing. He claims that twenty-four-hour news overwhelms people with input that makes them feel informed, but does not actually increase their level of knowledge. Albom concludes that people need to venture into the world and have real experiences in order to be truly informed.

Things to remember while reading "What If CNN Hadn't Happened?":

- In his column, Albom mentions a number of stories that received widespread television coverage in the 1990s and 2000s, including the murder trial of actor Robert Blake, the broken engagement of celebrities Ben Affleck and Jennifer Lopez, and the disappearance of political intern Chandra Levy in Washington D.C. He points out that CNN and other TV news outlets gave these stories nearly nonstop attention for months, despite the fact that they had questionable news value.

- Albom also makes reference to political divisions in the United States, using terms like "red state vs. blue state" and "liberal vs. conservative." In his view, debate-oriented cable news programs like CNN's *Crossfire,* MSNBC's *Hardball,* and Fox News' *Hannity and Colmes* have contributed to forging and deepening these political divisions.

• • •

"What If CNN Hadn't Happened?"

CNN was born 25 years ago this month. It was a simple yet awesome invention, the brainchild of Ted Turner, who saw a world of satellites and cable and got the idea for a 24-hour news channel. Turner is a man who often asks "Why not?" rather than "Why?"

Therein lies our difference.

Twenty-five years later, I find myself asking "Why?" all the time about CNN. Not just CNN, of course, but all it has **spawned.** You could argue that without CNN there [would be no other cable news outlets such as] Fox News, no MSNBC, no Court TV, no E! Entertainment, no **Bill O'Reilly,** no *Hardball,* no Hannity or Colmes, no updates every five minutes on Michael Jackson in his pajamas.

Imagine a world without all that.

Would our lives really be lessened?

Spawned: Produced or generated.

Bill O'Reilly ... Colmes: Albom is referring to several cable programs featuring political news and debate.

Genie: A powerful spirit that lives in a bottle and grants wishes for its master.

Branded networks: TV channels related to CNN, including CNN Headline News and CNN International.

Don't forget Ben and Jen

The problem with the magic of 24-hour news wasn't the **genie**, it was the bottle. The bottle burst. CNN began with less than 1 percent of U.S. homes as potential audience; that figure today, if you throw in all the **branded networks** around the world, has been estimated at 1.5 billion—nearly one-fourth the world's population.

Think about that. From Tasmania to Timbuktu. I read once about a **nomad** in the Middle East who lived in a tent but had a satellite dish and CNN on the screen.

What's wrong with this? It shrinks the world to a sheep herd of images. A single piece of footage, no more than 10 seconds long, now can **deify** or destroy a person across the planet.

We don't know facts; we know images. Among CNN's recently cited 25 biggest stories were the **space shuttle** *Columbia,* **Tiananmen Square** and **Monica Lewinsky**. Each one conjures up a visual: an exploding space-craft, a violent protest, a raven-haired intern hugging a president. Most of us don't know all the details. But we feel as if we do.

And we can't help feeling that way about the stuff CNN doesn't con-gratulate itself on: [highly publicized tabloid news stories such as] the **Robert Blake** trial, **Ben and Jennifer**, the **runaway bride**. We've been hypnotized by those overblown events, too. At times, we can't help it. Just try going to an airport these days and NOT seeing cable news. It's blasting everywhere, in hotel lobbies, in bars, in restaurants.

It's an **intravenous** drip. Input, input, input. **Mainlined** into your veins and brains.

Red State vs. Blue State

I'm not sure this is a good thing. The world is a majestic place for a reason. It requires **perspective**. It requires *effort.* It requires travel, face-to-face con-tact, smelling strange foods, walking in strange sand. A box will not deliver that, no matter how much **high-definition** it contains.

Sure, there's value in being informed. But given the choice between not knowing something or claiming you know it because you saw a 20-second story on it, well, which is more dangerous? We all feel smarter with cable news. But we also feel entitled to scream opinions about foreign govern-ments or some abusive parent in Florida. Are we better for that?

Are we better for the competition cable news has fostered, creating a **liberal vs. conservative hell storm**, a fight for **"gotcha" interviews** and end-less celebrity **fawning**? Are we better for all the repetition? I worked for a cable news network a few years ago. I remember being asked to talk about **Chandra Levy** every 10 minutes. As I said earlier: Why?

Nomad: Person who wanders about instead of settling in one place.

Deify: Give the status of a god.

Space shuttle *Columbia*: A U.S. space vehicle that broke apart as it re-entered Earth's atmosphere in 2003, killing all seven astronauts on board.

Tiananmen Square: A place in Beijing, China, where student protesters were killed or arrested by government troops in 1989.

Monica Lewinsky: (1973–) White House intern who had an affair with President Bill Clinton.

Robert Blake: (1933–) Famous actor who was accused of killing his wife in 2001.

Ben and Jennifer: Actors Ben Affleck and Jennifer Lopez, who had a romantic relationship in 2002–03.

Runaway bride: A woman who disappeared before her wedding and became the subject of a nationwide search.

Intravenous: (IV) Injected directly into a vein.

Mainlined: Slang term for injecting a narcotic drug.

Red State vs. Blue State: Political divisions in the United States. The term is based on the maps used in TV election coverage, which use colors to indicate whether the residents of individual states voted primarily for Republicans (red) or Democrats (blue).

Perspective: An understanding of the relative importance of things.

High-definition: A television technology that provides sharp, detailed picture quality.

Liberal vs. conservative hell storm: Vicious disagreements between people who hold opposing political viewpoints.

"Gotcha" interviews: Interviews with the biggest newsmaker or celebrity of the moment.

Fawning: Flattering attention.

Chandra Levy: (1977–2001) A political intern who had an affair with a U.S. representative, disappeared in 2001, and was found murdered in 2002.

Maybe I'm just getting older. But I'm not sure everybody knowing two minutes of everything is a goal to which humans should aspire. There's a value to smallness, to villages that are not global. There's also a value to life's mystery. To saying "I wonder what's happening across the planet" without having a machine you think can tell you.

There's no going back. The genie has run wild. I congratulate CNN on its 25th birthday but confess there are times I wish it hadn't been born.

• • •

What happened next...

Since it originated the twenty-four-hour news format in 1980, CNN has faced ever-increasing competition from other cable news outlets. In the early 2000s, the Fox News Channel began to challenge CNN for the top position. After the terrorist attacks of September 11, 2001, many critics claimed that Fox News became openly biased in its presentation of the news. For instance, the network placed an American flag logo on the screen, and Fox News anchors often expressed outright support for President Bush and his war on terrorism. Some American viewers found Fox's conservative slant on the news to be reassuring. As a result, Fox News enjoyed a 43 percent increase in viewers over the next few months. By 2003, Fox News led CNN in the ratings by a margin of 2-1.

The success of Fox News has encouraged other cable news channels to cater to the views of a specific audience with more opinionated, and less objective, news coverage. This trend toward biased TV news reporting could further complicate some of the issues Albom mentions in his column. For instance, some critics claim that it has increased the political divisions in the United States and made it more difficult to resolve important problems in American society.

Did you know...

- Thanks to CNN, cable became Americans' top choice for information about breaking news events. By the time of the terrorist attacks of September 11, 2001, surveys showed that 45 percent of viewers went to cable news first for the latest information, while 22 percent turned to the Big Three broadcast networks and 20 percent to local newscasts.

- CNN is such a respected source of up-to-the-minute information about breaking news events that world leaders have reportedly tuned in to get details about election results, political protests, natural disasters, and other situations taking place in their own countries. Some analysts claim that CNN's coverage of international news events has also influenced the U.S. government's foreign policy decisions. For instance, after CNN provided extensive coverage of a 1993 battle on the streets of Mogadishu, Somalia, that left eighteen American soldiers dead and eighty-four wounded, President Bill Clinton quickly withdrew U.S. troops from the country. Analysts even coined a new term, "The CNN Effect," to describe instances where the possibility of instantaneous news coverage influenced government decisions.

Consider the following...

- In his article, Albom challenges readers to imagine a world without access to twenty-four-hour news coverage. He then asks, "Would our lives really be lessened?" How would you answer this question?

- Albom also argues that developing a true understanding of the world requires "travel, face-to-face contact, smelling strange foods, walking in strange sand." Think about someplace you traveled where you did things that were outside your ordinary experience. What did you learn? Do you think you could have learned the same things by watching a news story on television?

- Today, more and more people rely on the Internet for information about news events. What are the advantages and disadvantages of online news sources, as compared to television news? Do you think the Internet will ever replace TV as Americans' first choice for news and information?

For More Information

BOOKS

Auletta, Ken. *Media Man: Ted Turner's Improbable Empire.* New York: W. W. Norton, 2004.

Bliss, Edward J., Jr. *Now the News: The Story of Broadcast Journalism.* New York: Columbia University Press, 1991.

Collins, Scott. *Crazy Like a Fox: The Inside Story of How Fox News Beat CNN.* New York: Portfolio, 2004.

Whittemore, Hank. *CNN: The Inside Story.* Boston: Little, Brown, 1990.

PERIODICALS

Albom, Mitch. "What If CNN Hadn't Happened?" *Detroit Free Press,* June 12, 2005.

"Cable Television's Long March." *The Economist,* November 16, 1996.

Foote, Joe S. "Television News: Past, Present, and Future." *Mass Communications Review,* Winter-Spring 1992.

Frank, Reuven. "The Shifting Shapes of TV News." *New Leader,* March 2001.

Small, William. "Television Journalism." *Television Quarterly* (special issue), Winter 1990.

WEB SITES

Kierstead, Phillip. "Network News." *Museum of Broadcast Communications.* http://www.museum.tv/archives/etv/N/htmlN/newsnetwork/newsnetwork.htm (accessed on July 31, 2006).

"Mitch Albom Bio." *Albom.com.* http://www.albom.com/about_mitch.htm (accessed on July 31, 2006).

Al Gore

Excerpt from a speech delivered at the We Media Conference, October 5, 2005

Reprinted from the Associated Press
Available online at The Media Center at the American Press Institute,
www.mediacenter.org/wemedia05/the_program

"Television programming is actually more accessible to more people than any source of information has ever been in all of history. But...it is accessible in only one direction; there is no true inter-activity, and certainly no conversation."

When the thirteen American colonies declared independence from England in 1776, their leaders were tired of taking orders from a king. In founding a new nation, they established a democracy in order to give common people a voice in government. Democracy is based on the idea that political power should rest in the hands of the people. Since it would be difficult to ask everyone's opinion on every important issue, though, citizens in a democracy typically vote to elect leaders to represent them in government. These representatives help ensure that the government hears the opinions and serves the interests of the people.

The free exchange of information and views between citizens and their elected officials is key to the functioning of a democracy. In the early years of television, many people believed that the new medium would provide valuable support for the American system of government. Supporters felt that television would be an important source of news and information for the people of the United States. They predicted that it would help citizens understand the inner workings of government, evaluate important issues, and elect the best candidates to represent their interests.

As television grew rapidly during the 1950s, it often fulfilled its potential as a tool for democracy. Hard-hitting news and public affairs programs such as *See It Now,* which aired on CBS from 1951 to 1958, investigated serious issues affecting American society. Its host, the legendary broadcast journalist *Edward R. Murrow* (1908–1965; see Chapter 5), constantly pushed to use the power of television to expose problems and fight against injustice.

See It Now is probably best known for a 1954 program about Joseph McCarthy (1908–1957), a U.S. senator from Wisconsin who had ruined the careers of many American politicians and entertainers by falsely accusing them of being Communists. McCarthy used the tensions of the Cold War (1945–91; a period of intense military and political rivalry that pitted the United States and its democratic system of government against the Soviet Union and its Communist system of government) to hurt his enemies and advance his own career. Murrow's show helped turn public opinion against McCarthy. Following televised hearings before Congress, the senator fell from power.

In 1960, a series of debates between two presidential candidates were broadcast on television for the first time. An estimated 77 million viewers— or more than 60 percent of the adult population of the United States at that time—tuned in to watch Democratic senator John F. Kennedy (1917–1963) face off against Republican vice president Richard M. Nixon (1913–1994). The debates helped Kennedy convince the American people that he had the experience and maturity to be president, and he ended up winning the election a few months later.

Network coverage of news and politics decreases

Over time, however, television gradually reduced the amount of air time that it devoted to news, politics, and public affairs. A 2002 study reported in *Electronic Media,* for instance, showed that fewer than half of the local newscasts in major cities carried any stories about the upcoming Congressional elections. The stories that did appear averaged 80 seconds in length, and only 20 percent of them included any quotations from political candidates.

Coverage of politics also declined at the national broadcast networks. By the time the Democratic and Republican parties held their presidential nominating conventions in 2004, the networks provided only about three hours of coverage for each four-day event. Critics claimed that television was no longer meeting its responsibility to inform the American people and support the democratic process. They said that the networks were more concerned about attracting large audiences and earning money. "That the networks see fit to turn their backs on this process is disturbing," stated an editorial in *Television Week*. "Their scaling back of convention coverage in recent years is obviously motivated by the bottom line, another step in the ongoing abandonment of any commitment to public service."

At the same time as the national networks and local stations reduced their coverage of news and politics, however, a number of new cable TV channels emerged to fill the gap. Some of these channels provided viewers with nearly constant footage of their government in action. For instance, the cable network C-SPAN showed everything that happened in the U.S. Congress, from speeches and debates to votes on important legislation. Similar channels were created in more than twenty-five states to cover the inner workings of state legislatures and local governments. Supporters claimed that these channels gave viewers unprecedented access to their elected leaders and were the next best thing to attending sessions of Congress in person. But critics argued that such channels only provided information in one direction—from elected leaders to the people—and did nothing to promote citizen participation in the democratic process.

Other critics complained that the rise of political cable channels made it easier for the national broadcast networks to ignore politics. They claimed that the lack of prime-time coverage of important political events like press conferences, debates, and conventions led voters to believe that the democratic process was less important than entertainment programs. They blamed such attitudes for the steady decline in the number of eligible voters who participated in national elections over time. In 1960, the year of the first televised presidential debates, 63 percent of the voting-age population of the United States cast ballots in the election. Voter turnout declined gradually over the next forty years to reach 51 percent in 2000, according to Federal Election Commission statistics quoted on the *Museum of Broadcast Communications* Web site.

Critics also argued that the lack of mainstream media attention given to politics forced candidates for public office to buy advertising time on television to make their case to voters. Instead of focusing on the qualifications of the candidate, many of these campaign commercials contained negative attacks on a political opponent's views, voting record, or personal life. Critics claimed that these negative campaign advertisements eventually became voters' main source of information about candidates and elections. When voters received mostly negative information, they tended to become disillusioned with the political process and stop paying attention. The Federal Election Commission statistics showed that the four presidential debates before the 1960 elections earned a 59.35 average rating (a measure of the percentage of American households that had their television sets tuned to the program). In contrast, the three presidential debates preceding the 2000 elections earned only a 28.13 average rating.

Al Gore expresses concerns about democracy

One of the main critics of television's impact on the democratic process was former vice president Al Gore. Albert Gore Jr. was born in 1948 in Washington, D.C. The son of a U.S. senator, he spent his childhood going back and forth between Washington and his home state of Tennessee. Gore earned a bachelor's degree from Harvard University in 1969. He then joined the U.S. Army and served as a military journalist during the Vietnam War. When his military service ended in 1971, Gore took a job as a reporter for the *Tennessean,* a newspaper based in Nashville.

In 1976, Gore was elected to the U.S. House of Representatives, and he earned re-election three times. In 1984, he launched a successful campaign to represent Tennessee in the U.S. Senate. One of his major accomplishments during his years in Congress was helping to secure government funding for the Internet. During the late 1980s, Gore also wrote a bestselling book about environmental issues called *Earth in the Balance: Ecology and the Human Spirit.* After an unsuccessful bid for the Democratic Party's presidential nomination in 1992, Gore agreed to become the vice presidential running mate for nominee Bill Clinton. Clinton won the both the 1992 and 1996 elections, and Gore served as vice president for Clinton's two terms in office.

In 2000, Gore ran for president against Republican Party candidate George W. Bush (1946–). The quality of television news coverage became a major issue during the election. On the night that Americans cast their votes, the TV networks used data collected at the polls to predict the results in various states. As the vote tallies came in, it became clear that the election would be very close. Ten minutes before the polls closed in Florida, the major broadcast networks announced Gore as the winner in the state. A short time later, however, the networks decided that the results were too close to call and placed Florida back into the undecided

Al Gore speaking at the We Media Conference in 2005. AP IMAGES.

column. Before the evening ended, the networks had changed their minds once again and predicted Bush as the winner in Florida.

The results in other states eventually made it clear that Florida controlled the outcome of the election. The ballots in Florida were recounted by hand, and even then the results were challenged in court. The 2000 election was ultimately decided by the U.S. Supreme Court, which halted all recounts in December and declared Bush the next president of the United States. Afterward, TV news came under harsh criticism for its election-night coverage. Critics said that the networks behaved in a reckless and irresponsible manner by predicting a winner in Florida before they had enough information to do so correctly. Some analysts claimed that the errors occurred because the networks had been forced to cut back on their political reporting staff in order to reduce costs. In any case, viewers disapproved of the way the networks handled the election results, and many lost faith in the accuracy of network news.

After the election, Gore returned to life as a private citizen. He became a lecturer at several universities and also served on the boards of directors for several major companies, including the Google Internet search company and Apple Computer. He eventually emerged as a vocal critic of the Bush administration and its handling of the U.S. economy, its record on environmental issues, and its decision to go to war with Iraq in 2003. Gore also spoke out publicly about the effects of the news media on the political process and American democracy.

In a speech presented at the We Media Conference in October 2005, which is excerpted below, Gore claims that democracy faces a significant threat because television has not done a good job of keeping the American people informed. He says that the broadcast networks have blurred the line between news and entertainment, often focusing on celebrity scandals and gossip instead of politics, in order to create programs that receive high ratings and earn big profits.

Gore argues that the dominance of television as a communications medium has made it impossible for individuals to participate in the American democracy. He says that television has destroyed the marketplace of ideas—or the free exchange of views and opinions between citizens and their elected representatives—that provides the foundation of the democratic process. He mentions that most of the government regulations intended to ensure that television served the public interest have gradually disappeared. He also provides several examples of individuals and groups who tried to purchase television air time to present their views on important issues, only to be denied the opportunity by the large media corporations that control American television.

Things to remember while reading the excerpt of Al Gore's We Media Conference speech:

- In his speech, Gore mentions the results of a 2005 survey that found between one-third and one-half of Americans believed that Saddam Hussein was responsible for the terrorist attacks against the United States of September 11, 2001. When President George W. Bush was preparing to launch a U.S. military invasion of the Middle Eastern nation of Iraq in 2003, he said that the attack was necessary to prevent Iraqi dictator Saddam Hussein from providing weapons of mass destruction to terrorist groups. The Bush administration claimed that it had evidence that Iraq possessed chemical and biological weapons. It also suggested that a link existed between Saddam Hussein and Al Qaeda, the terrorist group responsible for the September 11 attacks. After the invasion of Iraq took place, however, both of these statements were proved to be untrue. Gore argues that the news media did a poor job of informing the American people of this fact.

- Gore also asks why the American people are not more concerned about the abuse of prisoners. He is referring to a series of incidents that occurred at U.S. military prisons in Iraq, when American soldiers tortured Iraqi prisoners who were suspected of having ties to terrorist groups. Gore feels that there should have been more media coverage and public discussion of these incidents.

- Gore notes that in the 1960s, people who felt frustrated at their inability to participate in political discussions through the media could instead participate in demonstrations. During this era, millions of Americans took part in protests against U.S. involvement in the Vietnam War (1954–75). They also marched in support of equal rights and opportunities for women and minorities in American society.

- Gore also mentions *Network,* an award-winning 1976 movie about the inner workings of a fictional television network called Union Broadcasting System (UBS). UBS executives decide to fire a long-time news anchor, Howard Beale (played by Peter Finch), because the ratings for his program are declining. When they inform Beale that he will be replaced in two weeks, he goes crazy on the air and threatens to commit suicide during his final broadcast. As it turns out, though, Beale's unstable behavior attracts huge ratings, so the network decides to keep him on the job. *Network* commented on the priorities and decision-making processes of television news programs in a darkly funny way. Gore suggests that some of the situations that seemed absurd in the movie eventually became reality in the TV news business.

• • •

Excerpt of Al Gore's We Media Conference Speech

I came here today because I believe that American **democracy** is in grave danger. It is no longer possible to ignore the strangeness of our public **discourse**. I know that I am not the only one who feels that something has gone basically and badly wrong in the way America's fabled **"marketplace of ideas"** now functions.

Democracy: A system of government in which citizens make decisions, usually through elected representatives.

Discourse: Conversation or discussion.

Marketplace of ideas: The free expression of opinions on all sides of important issues.

Alternate universe: Strange and unfamiliar place.

Aberration: Unusual occurrence.

Saddam Hussein: (1937–) Former president of the Middle Eastern nation of Iraq who was removed from power by U.S. forces in 2003.

September 11, 2001: Date when members of the Al Qaeda terrorist group crashed commercial airplanes into the World Trade Center in New York City and the Pentagon building in Washington, D.C., killing nearly 3,000 people.

O. J. trial: The 1995 court case in which former professional football player O.J. Simpson (1947–) was found not guilty of murdering his ex-wife and her male friend.

Serial: Occurring one after another, in a series.

Economic stress: Worries about money.

Apathetic: Uncaring; indifferent.

Lethargic: Slow-moving and lazy.

Hurricane Katrina: A severe storm that devastated the city of New Orleans, Louisiana, and other parts of the U.S. Gulf Coast in 2005.

Founders: The Founding Fathers of the United States, who led the movement to declare independence from Great Britain in 1776.

How many of you, I wonder, have heard a friend or a family member in the last few years remark that it's almost as if America has entered "an **alternate universe**"?

I thought maybe it was an **aberration** when three-quarters of Americans said they believed that **Saddam Hussein** was responsible for attacking us on **September 11, 2001**. But more than four years later, between a third and a half still believe Saddam was personally responsible for planning and supporting the attack.

At first I thought the exhaustive, non-stop coverage of the **O. J. trial** was just an unfortunate excess that marked an unwelcome departure from the normal good sense and judgment of our television news media. But now we know that it was merely an early example of a new pattern of **serial** obsessions that periodically take over the airwaves for weeks at a time.

Are we still routinely torturing helpless prisoners, and if so, does it feel right that we as American citizens are not outraged by the practice? And does it feel right to have no ongoing discussion of whether or not this abhorrent, medieval behavior is being carried out in the name of the American people? If the gap [in income levels] between rich and poor is widening steadily and **economic stress** is mounting for low-income families, why do we seem increasingly **apathetic** and **lethargic** in our role as citizens? . . .

In the aftermath of **Hurricane Katrina**, there was—at least for a short time—a quality of vividness and clarity of focus in our public discourse that reminded some Americans—including some journalists—that vividness and clarity used to be more common in the way we talk with one another about the problems and choices that we face. But then, like a passing summer storm, the moment faded.

In fact, there was a time when America's public discourse was consistently much more vivid, focused and clear. Our **Founders**, probably the most **literate** generation in all of history, used words with astonishing precision and believed in the **Rule of Reason**.

Their faith in the **viability** of Representative Democracy rested on their trust in the wisdom of a well-informed citizenry. But they placed particular emphasis on insuring that the public could be well-informed. And they took great care to protect the openness of the marketplace of ideas in order to ensure the free-flow of knowledge. . . .

Though they feared that a government might try to **censor** the printing press—as **King George** had done—they could not imagine that America's public discourse would ever consist mainly of something other than words in print.

And yet, as we meet here this morning, more than 40 years have passed since the majority of Americans received their news and information from the printed word. Newspapers are **hemorrhaging** readers and, for the most part, resisting the temptation to inflate their **circulation** numbers. Reading itself is in sharp decline, not only in our country but in most of the world. The **Republic of Letters** has been invaded and occupied by television.

Radio, the Internet, movies, telephones, and other media all now vie for our attention—but it is television that still completely dominates the flow of information in modern America. In fact, according to an authoritative global study, Americans now watch television an average of four hours and 28 minutes every day—90 minutes more than the world average.

When you assume eight hours of work a day, six to eight hours of sleep and a couple of hours to bathe, dress, eat and commute, that is almost three-quarters of all the **discretionary** time that the average American has. And for younger Americans, the average is even higher. . . .

Television first overtook newsprint to become the dominant source of information in America in 1963. But for the next two decades, the television networks mimicked the nation's leading newspapers by faithfully following the **standards** of the journalism profession. Indeed, men like **Edward R. Murrow** led the profession in raising the bar.

But all the while, television's share of the total audience for news and information continued to grow—and its lead over newsprint continued to expand. And then one day, a smart young political consultant turned to an older elected official and **succinctly** described a new reality in America's public discourse: "If it's not on television, it doesn't exist."

But some extremely important elements of American Democracy have been pushed to the sidelines. And the most prominent **casualty** has been the "marketplace of ideas" that was so beloved and so carefully protected by our Founders. It effectively no longer exists.

It is not that we no longer share ideas with one another about public matters; of course we do. But the "Public **Forum**" in which our Founders searched for general agreement and applied the Rule of Reason has been grossly distorted and "restructured" beyond all recognition.

And here is my point: it is the destruction of that marketplace of ideas that accounts for the "strangeness" that now continually haunts our efforts to reason together about the choices we must make as a nation. . . .

Consider the rules by which our present "public forum" now operates, and how different they are from the forum our Founders knew. Instead of the easy and free access individuals had to participate in the national conversation by means of the printed word, the world of television makes it virtually impossible for individuals to take part in what passes for a national conversation today.

Literate: Skilled in reading and writing.

Rule of Reason: Governing through logic and good judgment.

Viability: Lasting power.

Censor: Control.

King George III: (1738–1820) Ruler of England whose policies led the American colonies to seek independence in the Revolutionary War (1776–1781).

Hemorrhaging: Bleeding a lot; losing quickly.

Circulation: Copies sold.

Republic of Letters: Literate and well-informed America.

Discretionary: Free or leisure.

Standards: Basic rules or guidelines.

Edward R. Murrow: (1908–1965) Respected CBS News reporter.

Succinctly: Briefly; getting straight to the point.

Casualty: Victim.

Forum: Meeting place for the exchange of ideas.

Interactivity: Communication; back-and-forth contact.

Monopoly: Situation in which one company controls an entire business or industry.

Spectrum: Range of frequencies able to carry communication signals.

Capital: Financial or monetary.

Plaintively: Dramatically.

Predecessor: Something that came before.

Apprehension: Concern or worry.

Public Interest Standard: A phrase included in the Communications Act of 1934 that said broadcasters using the public airwaves had a responsibility to serve the "public interest, convenience, and necessity."

Equal Time Provision: An FCC regulation that required TV stations to make equal amounts of air time available to all qualified candidates for political office.

Fairness Doctrine: An FCC policy that required broad-casters to present opposing viewpoints about controversial issues of public importance.

Repealed: Canceled or no longer enforced.

Rush Limbaugh: (1931–) Conservative radio talk show host.

Hate-mongers: People who spread hatred.

Farce: Comedy; something too absurd to be true.

Prophecy: Accurate prediction of later events.

Morphed: Changed or transformed.

Conglomerates: Large corporations with a wide range of business interests.

Inexpensive metal printing presses were almost everywhere in America. They were easily accessible and operated by printers eager to typeset essays, pamphlets, books or flyers.

Television stations and networks, by contrast, are almost completely inaccessible to individual citizens and almost always uninterested in ideas contributed by individual citizens.

Ironically, television programming is actually more accessible to more people than any source of information has ever been in all of history. But here is the crucial distinction: it is accessible in only one direction; there is no true **interactivity**, and certainly no conversation.

The number of [television] cables connecting to homes is limited in each community and usually forms a natural **monopoly**. The broadcast and satel-lite **spectrum** is likewise a scarce and limited resource controlled by a few. The production of programming has been centralized and has usually required a massive **capital** investment. So for these and other reasons, an ever-smaller number of large corporations control virtually all of the televi-sion programming in America.

Soon after television established its dominance over print, young people who realized they were being shut out of the dialogue of democracy came up with a new form of expression in an effort to join the national conversa-tion: the "demonstration." This new form of expression, which began in the 1960s, was essentially a poor quality theatrical production designed to cap-ture the attention of the television cameras long enough to hold up a sign with a few printed words to convey, however **plaintively**, a message to the American people. Even this outlet is now rarely an avenue for expression on national television. . . .

It did not come as a surprise that the concentration of control over this powerful one-way medium carries with it the potential for damaging the operations of our democracy. As early as the 1920s, when the **predecessor** of television, radio, first debuted in the United States, there was immediate **apprehension** about its potential impact on democracy. One early American student of the medium wrote that if control of radio were concentrated in the hands of a few, "no nation can be free."

As a result of these fears, safeguards were enacted in the U.S.—including the **Public Interest Standard**, the **Equal Time Provision**, and the **Fairness Doctrine**—though a half century later, in 1987, they were effectively **repealed**. And then immediately afterwards, **Rush Limbaugh** and other **hate-mongers** began to fill the airwaves.

And radio is not the only place where big changes have taken place. Television news has undergone a series of dramatic changes. The movie *Network*, which won the Best Picture Oscar in 1976, was presented as a **farce** but was actually a **prophecy**. The journalism profession **morphed** into the news business, which became the media industry and is now completely owned by **conglomerates**.

The news divisions—which used to be seen as serving a public interest and were **subsidized** by the rest of the network—are now seen as profit centers designed to generate **revenue** and, more importantly, to advance the larger **agenda** of the corporation of which they are a small part. They have fewer reporters, fewer stories, smaller budgets, less travel, fewer **bureaus**, less independent judgment, more vulnerability to influence by management, and more dependence on government sources and **canned** public relations hand-outs. This tragedy is compounded by the ironic fact that this generation of journalists is the best trained and most highly skilled in the history of their profession. But they are usually not allowed to do the job they have been trained to do. . . .

Among the other factors damaging our public discourse in the media, the imposition by management of entertainment values on the journalism profession has resulted in scandals, **fabricated** sources, fictional events and the **tabloidization** of mainstream news. As recently stated by **Dan Rather**— who was, of course, forced out of his anchor job after angering the White House—television news has been "dumbed down and **tarted up**."

The coverage of political campaigns focuses on the "**horse race**" and little else. And the well-known **axiom** that guides most local television news is "**if it bleeds, it leads**." (To which some disheartened journalists add, "**If it thinks, it stinks**.")

In fact, one of the few things that **Red state and Blue state** America agree on is that they don't trust the news media anymore.

Clearly, the purpose of television news is no longer to inform the American people or serve the public interest. It is to "glue eyeballs to the screen" in order to build ratings and sell advertising. If you have any doubt, just look at what's on: The **Robert Blake** trial. The **Laci Peterson** tragedy. The **Michael Jackson** trial. The **Runaway Bride**. The **search in Aruba**. The latest twist in various celebrity couplings, and on and on and on.

And more importantly, notice what is not on: the **global climate crisis**, the nation's **fiscal catastrophe**, the hollowing out of America's industrial base, and a long list of other serious public questions that need to be addressed by the American people.

One morning not long ago, I flipped on one of the news programs in hopes of seeing information about an important world event that had happened earlier that day. But the lead story was about a young man who had been hiccupping for three years. And I must say, it was interesting; he had trouble getting dates. But what I didn't see was news.

Subsidized: Supported financially.

Revenue: Money or earnings.

Agenda: Plan or schedule for working toward goals.

Bureaus: Offices in major news cities around the world.

Canned: Organized or packaged in advance; predictable.

Fabricated: Fictional or made-up.

Tabloidization: Placing an emphasis on celebrities and popular culture rather than important news and issues, similar to tabloid magazines.

Dan Rather: (1931–) Longtime anchor of the CBS Evening News who retired in 2005, possibly due to his role in broadcasting a 2004 story questioning President George W. Bush's service in the Texas Air National Guard during the Vietnam War.

Tarted up: Made sensational or sleazy.

Horse race: Competition to lead in statistical polls of voters.

Axiom: Widely accepted truth.

If it bleeds, it leads: Stories that are violent or sensational receive the most prominent coverage.

If it thinks, it stinks: Stories that are complex and require viewers to pay attention receive the least coverage.

Red state and Blue state:
A reference to political
divisions in the United
States. The term is based on
the maps used in TV election
coverage, which use colors
to indicate whether the
residents of individual states
voted primarily for
Republicans (red) or
Democrats (blue).

Robert Blake: (1933–) Actor
who starred in the 1970s TV
cop show *Baretta* and was
accused of killing his wife
Bonnie Lee Bakely in 2001.

Laci Peterson: A pregnant
woman who disappeared in
California in 2002 and was
found murdered; her
husband was eventually
found guilty of the crime.

Michael Jackson: (1958–)
Pop singer who was accused
of molesting children.

Runaway Bride: A woman
who disappeared before her
wedding and became the
subject of a nationwide
search.

Search in Aruba: The search
for Natalee Holloway, an
Alabama teenager who
disappeared while visiting the
Caribbean island in 2005.

Global climate crisis: A
gradual warming of the
Earth that many scientists
blame for severe weather
patterns and other
problems.

Fiscal catastrophe: Financial
problems that occur when
the government spends
more money than it takes in
from taxes.

This was the point made by **Jon Stewart**, the brilliant host of *The Daily Show*, when he visited CNN's *Crossfire*: there should be a distinction between news and entertainment.

And it really matters because the **subjugation** of news by entertainment seriously harms our democracy: it leads to dysfunctional journalism that fails to inform the people. And when the people are not informed, they cannot hold government accountable when it is incompetent, corrupt, or both.

One of the only avenues left for the expression of public or political ideas on television is through the purchase of advertising, usually in 30-second chunks. These short commercials are now the principal form of communication between candidates and voters. As a result, our elected officials now spend all of their time raising money to purchase these ads.

That is why the House and Senate campaign committees now search for candidates who are multi-millionaires and can buy the ads with their own personal resources. As one consequence, the halls of Congress are now filling up with the wealthy.

Campaign finance reform, however well it is drafted, often misses the main point: so long as the only means of engaging in political dialogue is through purchasing expensive television advertising, money will continue by one means or another to dominate American politics. And ideas will no longer **mediate** between wealth and power.

And what if an individual citizen, or a group of citizens wants to enter the public debate by expressing their views on television? Since they cannot simply join the conversation, some of them have resorted to raising money in order to buy 30 seconds in which to express their opinion. But they are not even allowed to do that.

MoveOn.org tried to buy ads last year to express opposition to [President George W.] Bush's Medicare proposal which was then being debated by Congress. They were told "**issue advocacy**" was not permissible. Then, one of the networks that had refused the MoveOn ad began running advertisements by the White House in favor of the President's Medicare proposal. So MoveOn complained and the White House ad was temporarily removed. By temporary, I mean it was removed until the White House complained and the network immediately put the ad back on, yet still refused to present the MoveOn ad.

The advertising of products, of course, is the real purpose of television. And it is difficult to overstate the extent to which modern **pervasive** electronic advertising has reshaped our society. In the 1950s, **John Kenneth Galbraith** first described the way in which advertising has altered the classical relationship by which supply and demand are balanced over time by the **invisible hand** of the marketplace. According to Galbraith, modern advertising campaigns were beginning to create high levels of demand for products that consumers never knew they wanted, much less needed.

Jon Stewart, right, hosts The Daily Show, *a comedic program that pokes fun at so-called serious news programs.* FRANK MICELOTTA/GETTY IMAGES.

The same phenomenon Galbraith noticed in the commercial marketplace is now the dominant fact of life in what used to be America's marketplace for ideas. The **inherent** value or validity of political propositions put forward by candidates for office is now largely **irrelevant** compared to the advertising campaigns that shape the perceptions of voters.

Our democracy has been **hollowed out**. The opinions of the voters are, in effect, purchased, just as demand for new products is artificially created. . . .

It is true that **video streaming** is becoming more common over the Internet, and true as well that cheap storage of streamed video is making it possible for many young television viewers to engage in what the industry calls "**time shifting**" and personalize their television watching habits. Moreover, as higher bandwidth connections continue to replace smaller information pipelines, the Internet's capacity for carrying television will continue

Jon Stewart: (1962–) Host of a popular late-night, satirical news program on the cable TV network Comedy Central. In a controversial guest appearance on CNN's debate-oriented news program *Crossfire,* Stewart argued with the hosts about the news value of the show.

Subjugation: Conquering and controlling.

Campaign finance reform:
Proposed laws to limit fund-raising and spending by candidates for political office.

Mediate: Balance between competing interests.

MoveOn.org: An Internet-based organization dedicated to helping individual citizens have a voice in politics.

Issue advocacy: Expressing an opinion about a social or political issue.

Pervasive: Always present; seen and heard everywhere.

John Kenneth Galbraith:
(1908–2006) Famous economist, author, and college professor.

Invisible hand: An economic theory that states a competitive market for goods and services regulates itself.

Inherent: Basic, underlying; essential.

Irrelevant: Not important.

Hollowed out: Made empty or lacking in inner substance.

Video streaming: Technology that allows the reception and display of video signals on a computer.

Time shifting: Recording television programs to watch at a time other than when they are originally broadcast.

to dramatically improve. But in spite of these developments, it is television delivered over cable and satellite that will continue for the remainder of this decade and probably the next to be the dominant medium of communication in America's democracy. And so long as that is the case, I truly believe that America's democracy is at grave risk.

• • •

What happened next...

After making his address at the We Media Conference, Gore continued to speak out about a variety of important issues. In 2005, he helped launch a new cable television network called Current. The channel's Web site proclaimed that it would help people learn about and understand the world by presenting information from an independent political viewpoint. In 2006, Gore published a book and appeared in a documentary (fact-based) film called *An Inconvenient Truth*. Based on a series of lectures he gave across the country, the book and movie present information about the causes and consequences of global warming (a gradual increase in average temperatures on Earth).

Did you know...

- In 2006, Al Gore hosted the popular late-night comedy-variety program *Saturday Night Live*. As the show opened, Gore was shown sitting behind a desk at the White House. He then delivered a humorous speech to the American people, describing the situation in the United States as it might have been if he had become president in the 2000 elections.
- One of Gore's roommates at Harvard University was actor Tommy Lee Jones, star of such films as *The Fugitive, Thelma and Louise,* and *Men in Black*.

Consider the following...

- Each member of the class should watch the news on television (whether a national network newscast, a local newscast, or an all-news cable channel) for several nights. Keep track of what stories receive the most attention and the order in which the stories are presented. Upon comparing results, what patterns do students notice? How much of the TV news coverage was devoted to politics?

- Do you think that watching television is a good way for Americans to become politically informed? Why or why not?

- Imagine that you feel very strongly about a political issue and want to express your opinion publicly. Make a list of some of the things you might do to bring attention to your cause. How many people could you hope to reach using each option on your list? Is any other medium of communication as effective as television in influencing other people?

- Many people believe that television can be used as a tool to strengthen the American democracy. Can you also think of ways that television might serve to weaken American democracy?

For More Information

BOOKS

Hilliard, Robert L., and Michael C. Keith. *The Broadcast Century: A Biography of American Broadcasting.* Boston: Focal Press, 1992.

McChesney, Robert W. *Rich Media, Poor Democracy: Communications Politics in Dubious Times.* Urbana and Chicago: University of Illinois Press, 1999.

PERIODICALS

"Democracy on TV: Don't Blink." *Electronic Media,* October 21, 2002.

"Editorial: Networks Cavalier about Democracy." *Television Week,* August 2, 2004.

Gitlin, Todd. "How TV Killed Democracy on November 7." *Los Angeles Times,* February 14, 2001.

Jackson, Sarah. "Prime Time Democracy: A Growing Number of Public Affairs Networks Demystify Democracy." *State Legislatures,* January 2006.

O'Brien, Meredith. "How Did We Get It So Wrong?" *Quill,* January 2001.

WEB SITES

Campbell, Angus. "Has Television Reshaped Politics?" *Museum of Broadcast Communications.* http://www.museum.tv/debateweb/html/equalizer (accessed on July 27, 2006).

"Gore, Albert Arnold, Jr." *Biographical Directory of the United States Congress.* http://bioguide.congress.gov/scripts/biodisplay.pl?index=G000321 (accessed on July 27, 2006).

Kierstead, Phillip. "Network News." *Museum of Broadcast Communications.* http://www.museum.tv/archives/etv/N/htmlN/newsnetwork/newsnetwork.htm (accessed on July 27, 2006).

"The Life of Al Gore." *Washington Post.* http://www.washingtonpost.com/wp-srv/politics/campaigns/wh2000/stories/goremain100399.htm (accessed on July 27, 2006).

The Media Center at the American Press Institute. http://www.mediacenter.org/wemedia05/the_program (accessed on July 27, 2006).

Where to Learn More

Books

Barnouw, Erik. *Tube of Plenty: The Evolution of American Television.* New York: Oxford University Press, 1975.

Calabro, Marian. *Zap! A Brief History of Television.* New York: Four Winds Press, 1992.

Castleman, Harry, and Walter Podrazik. *Watching TV: Four Decades of American Television.* New York: McGraw-Hill, 1982.

Fisher, David E., and Marshall Jon Fisher. *Tube: The Invention of Television.* Washington, DC: Counterpoint, 1992.

Garner, Joe. *Stay Tuned: Television's Unforgettable Moments.* Kansas City: Andrews McMeel Publishing, 2002.

Gitlin, Todd. *Inside Prime Time.* New York: Pantheon, 1983.

Hilliard, Robert L., and Michael C. Keith. *The Broadcast Century: A Biography of American Broadcasting.* Boston: Focal Press, 1992.

Lichter, S. Robert. *Prime Time: How TV Portrays American Culture.* Washington DC: Regnery Publishers, 1994.

MacDonald, J. Fred. *One Nation under Television: The Rise and Decline of Network TV.* New York: Pantheon, 1990.

McNeil, Alex. *Total Television: The Comprehensive Guide to Programming from 1948 to the Present.* New York: Penguin Books, 1996.

Owen, Rob. *Gen X TV: "The Brady Bunch" to "Melrose Place."* New York: Syracuse University Press, 1997.

Sackett, Susan. *Prime-Time Hits: Television's Most Popular Network Programs, 1950 to the Present.* New York: Billboard Books, 1993.

Schwartz, Evan I. *The Last Lone Inventor: A Tale of Genius, Deceit, and the Birth of Television.* New York: HarperCollins, 2002.

Stark, Steven D. *Glued to the Set: The 60 Television Shows and Events That Made Us Who We Are Today.* New York: The Free Press, 1997.

Stashower, Daniel. *The Boy Genius and the Mogul: The Untold Story of Television.* New York: Broadway Books, 2002.

Web Sites

"Encyclopedia of Television." *Museum of Broadcast Communications.* http:// www.museum.tv/archives/etv (accessed on August 9, 2006).

"The FCC History Project," 2003. *Federal Communications Commission.* http:// www.fcc.gov/omd/history/tv (accessed on August 9, 2006).

Text Credits

The following is a list of the copyright holders who have granted permission to reproduce excerpts from primary source documents in *Television in American Society: Primary Sources*. Every effort has been made to trace copyright; if omissions have been made, please contact us.

Copyrighted excerpts were reproduced from the following periodicals:

Detroit Free Press, June 12, 2005. © McClatchy-Tribune Information Services. All rights reserved. Reprinted with permission.

Grey Advertising, June, 1947. Reproduced by permission.

Newsweek, May 30, 2005. Copyright © 2005 Newsweek, Inc. All rights reserved. Reprinted by permission.

TV Guide, November 14, 1959. Reproduced by permission.

Washington Monthly, July 1, 2004. Copyright © 2004 by Washington Monthly Publishing, LLC, 733 15th St. NW, Suite 520, Washington DC 20005. (202) 393-5155. Website: www.washingtonmonthly.com. Reproduced by permission.

Copyrighted excerpts were reproduced from the following books:

Allen, Steve. From *Vulgarians at the Gate: Trash TV and Raunch Radio: Raising the Standards of Popular Culture.* Prometheus Books, 2001. Copyright © 2001 by Meadowlane Enterprises, Inc. All rights reserved. Reprinted with permission.

Hewitt, Don. From *Tell Me A Story: Fifty Years and 60 Minutes in Television.* Perseus Books, 2001. Copyright © 2001 by Don Hewitt. Reprinted by permission of Public Affairs, a member of Perseus Books, L. L. C.

Copyrighted excerpts were reproduced from the following Web sites or other sources:

From a transcript of "Paramount Eyes and Ears of the World," Popular Science Newsreel, 1937. Reproduced by permission.

Gore, Al. From a speech on October 5, 2005. Associated Press, October 6, 2005. Reproduced by permission.

Minow, Newton N. From his speech "Television and the Public Interest," Washington, D. C., May 9, 1961. Reproduced by permission of the author.

Murrow, Edward R. From his speech "Convention of the Radio and Television News Directors Association," Chicago, IL, October 15, 1958. Reproduced by permission of the Literary Estate of the author.

Sarnoff, David. From a press statement, November 6, 1936. *The Restelli Collection at HistoryTV.net*. Reprinted with permission.

Zworykin, Vladimir. From an oral history conducted in 1975 by Mark Heyer and Al Pinsky. IEEE History Center, July 4, 1975. Copyright © 2006 IEEE. All rights reserved. Reproduced by permission.

Index

Bold type indicates main entries and their page numbers. Illustrations are marked by (ill.).